THE TR
BOND E

THE TREASURY BOND BASIS

An In-Depth Analysis for Hedgers, Speculators, and Arbitrageurs

Third Edition

GALEN D. BURGHARDT

TERRENCE M. BELTON

MORTON LANE

JOHN PAPA

McGraw-Hill

New York Chicago San Francisco Lisbon London Madrid
Mexico City Milan New Delhi San Juan Seoul
Singapore Sydney Toronto

Appendix to Chapter 5 was originally published January 28, 1998, as a Carr Futures (now Calyon Financial) research note.

Chapter 7 is a reprint of a *Journal of Portfolio Management* article. ©1993 by *The Journal of Portfolio Management*, Spring 1993. Reprinted with permission.

Appendixes C and E are excerpted from JPMorgan Government Bond Outlines, October 2001. Reprinted with permission of JPMorgan.

Appendixes D, F, and G are excerpted from JPMorgan Government Bond Outlines, April 2005. Reprinted with permission of JPMorgan.

To Birch and Mary

CONTENTS

Chapter 7

Volatility Arbitrage in the Treasury Bond Basis   157

Chapter 8

Nine Eras of the Bond Basis   173

LIST OF EXHIBITS

PREFACE TO THE
THIRD EDITION

In 2000, when the Chicago Board of Trade adopted a 6% coupon for calculating conversion factors, Terry and I resolved to update *The Treasury Bond Basis*. It has been our good fortune that the theory and insights were sound and that readers were able to make much of the leap from 8% to 6% conversion factors without our help.

Even so, we are pleased with this version. It has given us a chance to improve our discussions of several aspects of basis valuation, hedging, trading, and the uses of Treasury futures for portfolio managers. Also, we have greatly expanded our chapter on non-dollar government bond futures and have included several new appendixes that provide useful information on bond markets in Germany, Japan, and the United Kingdom.

Several notable changes and innovations have taken place since we released the Revised Edition. For one, the most actively traded Treasury futures contracts are now the 10-year and 5-year contracts. The shift has been so pronounced that this book would be more aptly named *The Treasury Note Basis*. For another, the emergence of the credit default swap market has greatly enriched the usefulness of Treasury futures for creating synthetic assets. It is now possible, by combining Treasury futures with high-yielding term cash instruments and credit default swaps, to create synthetic corporate bonds with very desirable return characteristics.

Both Terry and I have a number of debts that we would like to acknowledge. Terry would like to thank Hussein Malik, Holly Huffman, and Josh Brodie, who were a great help in editing manuscripts and helping us bring this project to completion. In addition, we would like to acknowledge the support of JPMorgan. Excerpts from their *Government Bond Outlines* publication are included in Appendixes C to G. Moreover, much of the empirical work in this edition makes use of JPMorgan's extensive historical data on bond bases, which are available to their clients on their Web site via *DataQuery*.

I would like to thank Bill Hoskins, who greatly increased my understanding of interest rate markets and heightened my appreciation for the importance of using forward prices for just about everything. Also, he and Niels Johnson provided the groundwork for modeling the basis that we use now at Calyon Financial.

We both would like to thank the MBA students at the University of Chicago's Graduate School of Business who have taken our respective courses on futures, swaps, and options over the past 10 years and who have provided valuable comments on earlier drafts and manuscripts. And lastly, we would like to thank, once again, Morton Lane and John Papa for their contributions to the original edition of this book.

Galen Burghardt
Eastsound, Washington

PREFACE TO THE
SECOND EDITION

Since the original edition of *The Treasury Bond Basis* was released in 1989, a number of important things have happened, some of them almost on the heels of the book's release and others over the years since then.

The first was that bond futures became fairly priced on almost the same day that the original edition was released. This development was acutely embarrassing because the last chapter of the original edition was devoted chiefly to the ease with which portfolio managers could improve portfolio yields by combining money market investments with cheap Treasury bond futures to create synthetic Treasury bonds. The end to cheap bond futures brought an abrupt end to what we have since come to call the "golden age of yield enhancement" with bond futures.

The second was Terry Belton's arrival on the scene at Discount Corporation of New York Futures, where he worked with me in the research group. Until then, our understanding of the strategic delivery options embedded in bond and note futures was clear but rudimentary. Terry, who had spearheaded the effort to price mortgage-backed securities for the Federal Home Loan Mortgage Corporation, brought with him the skills needed to put reliable values on the delivery options. On the basis of his work, we can now determine the option-adjusted fair values for bond and note futures prices and option-adjusted hedge ratios for bonds and notes. Also, we pioneered the technology for arbitraging the price paid for yield volatility in the bond options market against the price paid for yield volatility in the bond basis market.

The third has been a steady growth in the breadth of the government bond futures market. In the United States, for example, we have seen substantial growth in activity in Treasury note futures. The 10-year and 5-year Treasury note futures contracts are fixtures at the Chicago Board of Trade, and the two-year note contract is at least active enough to pay the rent. Outside of the United States, trading in futures on other countries' government bonds has grown by leaps and bounds. Today, almost half the world's bond futures trading takes place in futures on other countries' government bonds.

All of these developments are reflected in this new edition of *The Treasury Bond Basis*. Terry and I have included completely new discussions of the strategic delivery options and how they are priced. We show what option-adjusted hedge ratios are and why we think they are better than the standard rules of thumb. We have expanded our discussion of basis trading and have included a chapter on volatility arbitrage between the bond basis and bond options. We have updated our description of how the basis has behaved, included a new chapter on the non-dollar government bond futures contracts, and updated and expanded the chapter on applications for portfolio managers.

In addition, we have improved the book as a reference work. In particular, we have included tables showing the basic futures contract specifications (which somehow escaped the original edition) and appendixes on calculating conversion factors and carry. We have updated our delivery histories and have expanded our coverage to include deliveries on the five-year and two-year Treasury note contracts.

Although Morton and John were not able to participate in the rewriting of this book, some of their contributions to the original edition can be found here. The early part of the chapter on how the basis has behaved since 1977 owes its message largely to Morton's presence on the Treasury bond futures scene more or less since its inception. And it was Morton's interest in what was going on outside of the United States that first prompted us to expand our coverage to include the non-dollar government bond futures in our work. John's experience as a basis trader is still reflected in the material on practical considerations for basis traders as well as in some of the basis reports exhibited in Chapters 1 and 2.

Terry and I also owe a great deal to those who helped us pursue our work on pricing bond and note futures. Jeff Kleban, for one, was the main driving force behind our very first work on pricing embedded delivery options, which appeared initially in a memo discussing cheap straddles in the bond basis. And it was a customer of ours who allowed us to put his money where our mouth was when it came to trying out our highly engineered volatility arbitrage trades with real money in real markets.

Larry Anderson deserves much of the credit for creating the encouraging atmosphere that is required to complete a project like this. Everyone in this business is aware of the pressures to produce research pieces both early and often. A book doesn't fit this bill at all, but Larry has been a patient supporter of ours and has helped others see and appreciate the merit in our work.

Much of our empirical work on the history of the bond basis and on the behavior of yield spreads could not have been done without a carefully constructed data base keyed to the 2:00 p.m. Chicago close of the Treasury bond and note futures contracts. Several people have contributed to this effort over the years, including Steve Nosal (who stepped in for John Papa), Liz Flores, and Michael Hughes. Michael also has taken a lively interest in our work over the past several years and has offered many pointed and helpful comments and suggestions. Ed Landers deserves credit, too, for allowing Steve to take the time away from his other duties on our New York desk.

We also owe much to the people who helped us pull the book together in final form. In particular, we would like to thank Millicent John, Wendell Kapustiak, Susan Kirshner, Alison Kline, Pam Moulton, Cynthia Nelson, Bob Nightingale, Cynthia Riddle, John Schewe, and Brian Wells. Susan in particular devoted herself during the final weeks of preparation and proofing to making this book as nearly perfect as it could be. If there are any remaining errors, they are certainly no fault of hers.

Galen Burghardt
January 1994

PREFACE TO THE FIRST EDITION

Our aim when we began this book was to provide newcomers to the Treasury bond futures market with a primer on the price relationship between T-bonds and T-bond futures. To this end, Bob Griswold, as an intern in our research group, was given the task of putting together an introduction to the Treasury bond basis that would answer basic questions such as, "What is it?" and "What does it mean to buy or sell the basis?"

It soon became apparent, however, that a primer could not convey the richness of the Treasury bond futures contract and would ignore most of the contract's history. Bond futures have been trading for only 11 years, but we are already seeing a second generation of traders enter the market, many of whom could benefit from an accounting of how the contract came to behave as it does. Furthermore, as of this writing, we are approaching what may be the end of the longest economic expansion since the end of World War II. Economic turning points produce unusual interest rate settings, and in this case we might encounter a negatively sloped yield curve, but without the extreme volatility and turmoil that accompanied Volcker's great monetary experiment in the early 1980s. If so, the Treasury bond basis is likely to behave differently from the way it has previously. and anyone who trades the basis or uses bond futures to hedge should be prepared to understand why.

What began as a simple primer, then, has become this book, and its preparation owes a great deal to the contributions of several past and present employees of Discount Corporation of New York Futures. First, I would like to acknowledge Michael Berg, who was responsible for our Chicago Board of Trade operation in the early 1980s. He and I spent several weekends trying to solve the puzzle of the behavior of T-bond deliveries. It was during these sessions that we encountered the wild card trade. Our report to clients on that trade became the basis of Discount Corporation's "Blue Book," which was compiled with Vir Doshi's help and was used widely as a primer for analyzing cash/futures relationships in all financial futures contracts.

Michael's place at the Board of Trade was taken by Bob Palazola, who, with Dennis Malec, helped us understand the hedging implications of the contract's behavior. Ed Landers, Linda Reynolds, and Craig Zucker have also made their contributions.

More recently, David Emanuel evaluated the distinctions between the Treasury bond futures that were listed in Sydney, London, and Chicago. His work led to a finer appreciation of the value of the short's various delivery options, and much of that work is contained in the volume. It was Jeff Kleban who brought the switch option to our attention and who has helped us unravel the intricacies of that trade.

Galen Burghardt has pulled the various threads together in this book, using his analytic abilities to clarify my occasionally woolly thinking. Apart from that, he put his own stamp on the book with his extensions of the rules of thumb relating duration and yield to the cheapest to deliver. That work is reflected in our portrayal of shifting deliverables and, in a related field, in our understanding of options on bond futures.

All of this theorizing would have been far less valuable without the considerable practical experience of John Papa. John has executed basis trades on our clients' behalf for several years and is one of the most experienced basis traders in the business.

Finally, there were several people who helped to keep us honest and who provided many of the raw materials for this book. Michael Hughes, who monitors the basis daily for his clients, read several drafts and made many improvements. Further, without Michael and Liz Stump, we would not have a running record of cash market prices that correspond to the daily close of the futures market. Vir Doshi is responsible for most of the programs that allow us to analyze the basis and to anticipate likely shifts in the cheapest to deliver. John Gury put together a complete history of bond and note deliveries at the Chicago Board of Trade and contributed greatly to the graphics, especially in the chapter on the four eras of the bond basis. Cheryl Catlin put together most of the tables and several of the graphics. Geoffrey Luce, another intern in the research group, played a vital role. His careful and enthusiastic reading of the text, tables, and charts brought this project to a close much sooner and in much better shape than could have been done without him.

As I write these acknowledgments, I realize how much has been contributed by so many people over the years. We have not always been the first to take advantage of shifts in the way the bond basis behaves, but we have been vigorous in our pursuit of understanding why such shifts have taken place. This pursuit has allowed us to take advantage of opportunities well before they have disappeared altogether. The detective work has been both profitable and fun.

Morton Lane

THE TREASURY
BOND BASIS

Basic Concepts

"Basis" is a term common to all futures contracts. For example, the difference between the price of wheat today (its spot price) and its futures price is the wheat basis. Because the wheat futures market is competitive, the wheat basis tends to equilibrate the cost of financing and storing wheat until the future delivery date. To make it worth anyone's while to set aside wheat for future delivery, the futures price of wheat must be higher than the spot price of wheat. As a result, the wheat basis typically is negative.

Bonds can be set aside for future delivery as well. The chief differences between bonds and wheat are in the physical costs of storage and in what is often called convenience yield. U.S. Treasury bonds are nearly all held in electronic book entry form with the Federal Reserve; thus, the physical costs of storage for bonds are zero. Additionally, bonds throw off a yield in the form of actual or accrued coupon income that works to offset the cost of financing the bond until future delivery.

Moreover, if the yield curve is positively sloped so that long-term interest rates are higher than short-term interest rates, holding a bond position for future delivery actually produces a net income rather than a net outgo. For this reason and other reasons explored in this book, the futures price of a Treasury bond tends to be lower than the spot price; the bond basis tends to be positive.

There is one more striking similarity between wheat and bonds. Not all wheat is the same. There are slight differences in quality, and wheat from Kansas is not the same (because of transportation costs if nothing else) as wheat from Nebraska. Nevertheless, wheat futures contracts allow for the delivery of different grades of wheat in different locations. Also, it is the person who is short the futures contract who decides what to deliver and where. As a result, the wheat basis is geared to the grade of wheat and location that combine to make the cost of delivering wheat into the futures contract as low as it can be. That is, the wheat futures price is driven by the "cheapest to deliver."

So it is with bonds. The physical location of bonds is irrelevant, but the Treasury bond futures contract allows the delivery of any U.S. Treasury bond that has at least 15 years remaining to maturity. Currently, there are about two dozen such bonds, each with its own coupon and maturity. These coupon and maturity differences make up the different grades of bonds. Much of the challenge in understanding the bond basis is in understanding what makes a bond cheap to deliver. The rest of the challenge is in understanding when it is best to make delivery.

This chapter lays out the basic tools needed for an understanding of the bond basis. In particular, it addresses the following topics:

- Futures contract specifications
- Definition of the bond basis
- Conversion factors
- Futures invoice price
- Carry: the profit or loss of holding bonds
- Implied repo rate
- Buying and selling the basis
- Sources of profit in a basis trade
- RP versus reverse RP rates
- An idealized strategy for trading the bond basis

TREASURY BOND AND NOTE FUTURES CONTRACT SPECIFICATIONS

The Chicago Board of Trade lists futures contracts on Treasury bonds, 10-year Treasury notes, 5-year Treasury notes, and 2-year Treasury notes. In addition, the CBOT lists a futures contract on 10-year Agency securities that is similar in design to Treasury futures. The basic specifications for each of the Treasury futures contracts are shown in Exhibit 1.1.

Each contract has a "size," which defines the par amount of the bond or note that is deliverable into the contract. With the exception of the 2-year note contract, this is $100,000 par value. Because of the inherently lower volatility of the price of 2-year notes, the CBOT increased the size of that contract to $200,000.

Each contract has its own "contract grade," which in the case of Treasury bond and note contracts defines the range of maturities of the bonds or notes that are eligible for delivery.

A firm grasp on the concept of contract grade is perhaps the most important key to understanding how note and bond futures work. A widely held misconception about bond futures is that the bond futures contract is based on a 20-year, 6% coupon Treasury bond. In fact, bond and note futures are based on deliverable baskets of Treasury issues with widely different price and yield characteristics. For example, any U.S. Treasury bond with at least 15 years remaining to maturity on the first delivery day of the contract is eligible for delivery. Any original issue Treasury note with at least 6-1/2 years remaining to maturity is eligible for delivery into the 10-year note contract. The result is that the futures price not only does not behave like any one bond or note but behaves instead like a complex hybrid of the bonds or notes in the deliverable set depending on their respective likelihood of being delivered. We explain these relationships in detail in Chapters 2 and 3.

Futures exchanges regulate the minimum amount by which the futures price is allowed to change. This minimum price change is called a "tick." The tick size for the bond contract is 1/32nd of a point. Given a nominal face value of $100,000 for one contract, the value of this tick is $31.25, which is 1/32nd of $1,000. The allowable tick size for the 10-year and 5-year note contract is 1/2 of 1/32nd of a point and is worth $15.625. The 2-year contract's tick size is 1/4th of 1/32nd of a point, but because the nominal face value of the contract is $200,000, the value of the tick is also $15.625, the same as for 5-year and 10-year futures.

In most other important respects, the contracts are the same. They share the same trading hours, delivery months, and (except for the 2-year) have the same delivery days and expiration day.

Because the contracts are so much alike, we will focus mainly on the long-term Treasury bond contract when laying out the key conceptual underpinnings of these contracts. In later chapters, however, we will provide you with a comparison of the key differences between the contracts.

CHAPTER 1

EXHIBIT 1.1

Treasury Futures Contract Specifications

Term	Bond	10-Year note	5-Year note
Size	$100,000 par value	$100,000 par value	$100,000 par value
Contract grade	U.S. Treasury bonds with at least 15 years remaining to maturity	Original issue U.S. Treasury notes with at least 6-1/2 years remaining to maturity	Original issue U.S. Treasury notes with an original maturity of not more than 5 years, 3 months and a remaining maturity of not less than 4 years, 2 months
Price quotes	Points and 32nds of a point	Points and 32nds of a point*	Points and 32nds of a point*
Tick size and value Tick Value	1/32 of a point ($31.250)	1/2 of 1/32 of a point ($15.625)	1/2 of 1/32 of a point ($15.625)
Daily price limit	None	None	None
Trading hours (Chicago time)	7:20 a.m. - 2:00 p.m. (pit); 8:00 p.m. - 4:00 p.m. (a/c/e)	Same	Same
Delivery months	March, June, Sep, Dec	Same	Same
Last trading day	12:00 noon on the eighth-to-last business day of contract month	Same	Same
Last delivery day	Last business day of contract month	Same	Same

* The minimum price fluctuation is 1/2 of 1/32
§ The minimum price fluctuation is 1/4 of 1/32

DEFINITION OF THE BOND BASIS

A bond's basis is the difference between its cash price and the product of the futures price and the bond's conversion factor:

$$B = P - (F \times C)$$

where

B is the basis for the bond/futures combination

P is the spot or cash bond price per $100 face value of the bond

F is the futures price per $100 face value of the futures contract

C is the conversion factor for the bond

2-Year note	10-Year Agency (CBOT)
$200,000 par value	$100,000 par value
Original issue U.S. Treasury notes with an original maturity of not more than 5 years, 3 months and a remaining maturity of not less than 1 year, 9 months from the first day of the delivery month but not more than 2 years from the last day of the delivery month. The 2-year note issued after the last trading day of the contract is also deliverable into that month's contract	Noncallable Fannie Mae Benchmark notes or Freddie Mac Reference notes maturing at least 6-1/2 years but not more than 10-1/4 years from the first day of the delivery month. Total minimum outstanding principal amount of $3 billion
Points and 32nds of a point §	Points and 32nds of a point*
1/4 of 1/32 of a point ($15.625)	1/2 of 1/32 of a point ($15.625)
None	None
Same	Same
Same	Same
12:00 noon on the earlier of 1) the second business day prior to the issue day of the 2-year note auctioned in the contract month or 2) the last calendar day of the contract month	12:00 noon on the seventh business day preceding the last business day of the delivery month
Third business day following the last trading day	Last business day of contract month

Units

Bond and bond futures prices typically are quoted for $100 face value, and the prices themselves are stated in full points and 32nds of full points. In practice, the 32nds are broken down further into 64ths for bonds that are traded actively and in size, but the conventional quote is still in 32nds with the 64ths represented by a "+."

The 32nds are represented differently in different places. In the *Wall Street Journal,* for example, the 32nds are set off from the whole points by a hyphen. That is, 91 and 14/32nds would appear as 91-14. Occasionally, you will find the 32nds stated explicitly as 91-14/32nds. Also, because of programming and formatting problems, the dash may be replaced by a period, so that 91-14 appears as 91.14. In this book, the 32nds are stated for the sake of the clarity. Conversion factors are expressed in decimal form.

Important Point   In practice, all prices are converted first to decimal form when calculating the basis. The resulting basis, which is then in decimal form, is converted into 32nds simply by multiplying the decimal basis by 32.

Basis Comparison   Exhibit 1.2 shows the bases in 32nds of the bonds and notes that were eligible for delivery into the Chicago Board of Trade June 2001 bond and notes futures contracts on April 4, 2001.

CONVERSION FACTORS

With the wide range of bonds available for delivery, the Board of Trade uses *conversion factors* in the invoicing process to put these bonds on roughly equal footing. Exhibit 1.3 shows the conversion factors of all bonds that were eligible for delivery as of April 4, 2001, for contract months through June 2002.

The conversion factor is the approximate price, in decimals, at which the bond would trade if it yielded 6% to maturity (rounded to whole quarters). An exact formula for calculating conversion factors can be found in Appendix A.

Consider the 8-7/8% of 8/15/17. For the June 2001 contract, the conversion factor for this bond is 1.2931. On the first day of the delivery month, which was June 1, 2001, this bond had 16 years, 2 months, and 14 days left to maturity. The Chicago Board of Trade rounds this number down to the number of whole quarters remaining from the first day of the delivery month until expiration, truncating the odd days, leaving 16 years and 0 months. Thus, 129.31 is the decimal price of an 8-7/8% bond with 16 years to maturity that yields 6%.

Characteristics of Conversion Factors

- Conversion factors are unique to each bond *and* to each delivery month. Note in Exhibit 1.3 that conversion factors for bonds with coupons higher than 6% become smaller for each successive contract month to reflect the drift toward par of its price as it approaches maturity. Similarly, the conversion factors of bonds with coupons less than 6% drift upward for successive contract months.

- Conversion factors are constant throughout the delivery cycle.
- Conversion factors are used to calculate the invoice prices of bonds delivered into the CBOT T-bond futures contracts.
- If the coupon is greater than 6%, the conversion factor is greater than 1. If the coupon is less than 6%, the conversion factor is less than 1.
- Inexperienced hedgers sometimes use the conversion factor as a hedge ratio. As you will find in Chapter 5, however, this can lead to serious hedging errors.

Example: Basis Calculation   Consider the 7-1/2% of 11/15/16. The conversion factor for this bond for the June 2001 delivery cycle is 1.1484. On April 4, 2001, at 2 p.m. Chicago time, it was trading in the cash market at 120-20/32nds, while the futures price at that time was 103-30/32nds. Recall that the basis is defined as

Basis = Cash Price – (Futures Price × Conversion Factor)

To calculate the basis, first convert the cash and futures prices to decimal form. Then calculate the basis as

$$\text{Basis} = 120.6250 - (103.9375 \times 1.1484)$$
$$= 1.2632$$

which is the basis in decimal form. Convert the result back to 32nds to get 40.4, which you can find in column 6 of Exhibit 1.2.

FUTURES INVOICE PRICE

When a bond is delivered into the CBOT Treasury bond contract, the receiver of the bond pays the short an invoice price equal to the futures price times the conversion factor of the bond chosen by the short plus any accrued interest on the bond. That is

$$\text{Invoice Price} = (\text{Futures Price} \times \text{Conversion Factor})$$
$$+ \text{Accrued Interest}$$

where accrued interest is also expressed per $100 face value of the bond.

Suppose that the 7-1/2% of 11/15/16 are delivered on 6/29/01 at a futures price of 103-30/32nds. This bond's conversion

EXHIBIT 1.2

Deliverable Notes and Bonds; June 2001 Future

			June '01 Futures Price:	
Pricing Date	4/4/01		Bond	103-30
Trade Date	4/5/01		10-year	106-08
Settlement Date	4/6/01		5-year	105-22
L. Delivery Day	6/29/01		2-year	103-04+

Note/Bond*	Coupon	Maturity	Closing Price (32nds)	Conversion Factor	Basis	Yield	Dollar Value of a Basis Point	Modified Duration	Full Price	Carry (32nds)	BNOC (32nds)	Implied RP Rate	Term RP Rate
(1)	(2)	(3)	(4)	(5)	(6)	(7)	(8)	(9)	(10)	(11)	(12)	(13)	(14)
B**	5.375	2/15/31	98-08	0.9140	104.04	5.494	1440	14.55	98.9924	7.0	97.0	-8.68	4.45
B	6.25	5/15/30	109-14	1.0339	63.25	5.589	1531	13.69	111.8892	9.5	53.7	-2.10	4.43
B	6.125	8/15/29	107-02	1.0169	43.79	5.623	1484	13.75	107.9085	8.9	34.9	0.21	4.54
B	5.25	2/15/29	94-18	0.8996	33.93	5.639	1340	14.07	95.2876	6.7	27.2	0.71	4.54
B	5.25	11/15/28	94-15	0.8999	29.93	5.647	1333	13.81	96.5281	6.4	23.5	1.23	4.54
B	5.5	8/15/28	97-30	0.9336	28.85	5.648	1364	13.82	98.6972	7.4	21.5	1.63	4.54
B	6.125	11/15/27	106-14	1.0163	25.79	5.654	1433	13.16	108.8401	8.7	17.0	2.41	4.54
B	6.375	8/15/27	109-25	1.0491	23.69	5.656	1460	13.19	110.6618	9.8	13.9	2.86	4.54
B	6.625	2/15/27	113-03	1.0811	23.26	5.655	1480	12.98	114.0088	10.5	12.7	3.05	4.54
B	6.5	11/15/26	111-10+	1.0645	21.97	5.657	1456	12.78	113.8778	9.8	12.1	3.09	4.54
B	6.75	8/15/26	114-21+	1.0965	22.54	5.653	1482	12.82	115.6042	10.9	11.6	3.20	4.54
B	6	2/15/26	104-18	1.0000	20.00	5.655	1370	13.00	105.3912	8.8	11.2	3.12	4.54
B	6.875	8/15/25	116-01	1.1105	19.48	5.654	1466	12.53	116.9808	11.4	11.2	3.61	4.54
B	7.625	2/15/25	125-22+	1.2033	20.32	5.650	1542	12.17	126.7563	13.7	8.1	3.83	4.54
B	7.5	11/15/24	124-00	1.1866	21.37	5.646	1518	11.96	126.9420	12.9	6.7	3.63	4.54
B	6.25	8/15/23	107-18	1.0303	15.22	5.649	1328	12.25	108.4258	9.7	8.5	3.85	4.54
B	7.125	2/15/23	118-16	1.1349	17.32	5.641	1410	11.80	119.4841	12.4	4.9	3.99	4.54
B	7.625	11/15/22	124-20	1.1936	18.09	5.639	1455	11.40	127.6160	13.6	4.5	4.06	4.54

B	7.25	8/15/22	119-28	1.1481	17.42	5.637	1405	11.62	120.8764	12.9	4.6	4.03	4.54
B	8	11/15/21	128-23+	1.2325	20.20	5.626	1452	11.01	131.8725	14.9	5.3	3.99	4.54
B	8.125	8/15/21	130-04+	1.2456	21.63	5.620	1455	11.08	131.2629	15.8	5.8	3.95	4.54
B	8.125	5/15/21	129-30	1.2438	21.12	5.620	1443	10.84	133.1247	15.4	5.7	3.96	4.54
B	7.875	2/15/21	126-25+	1.2138	20.40	5.618	1407	11.00	127.8846	15.1	5.3	3.99	4.54
B	8.75	8/15/20	136-28	1.3093	25.27	5.604	1468	10.63	138.0836	18.2	7.1	3.85	4.54
B	8.75	5/15/20	136-22+	1.3069	27.75	5.597	1456	10.39	140.1354	17.7	10.1	3.56	4.54
B	8.5	2/15/20	133-18+	1.2771	26.87	5.595	1420	10.54	134.7522	17.4	9.4	3.60	4.54
B	8.125	8/15/19	128-28	1.2320	26.37	5.589	1361	10.47	129.9972	16.3	10.1	3.50	4.54
B	8.875	2/15/19	137-02+	1.3089	33.10	5.570	1402	10.14	138.3040	19.0	14.1	3.18	4.54
B	9	11/15/18	138-11	1.3195	38.34	5.557	1400	9.87	141.8741	19.0	19.4	2.68	4.54
B	9.125	5/15/18	139-07	1.3272	40.73	5.545	1382	9.68	142.7982	19.6	21.1	2.52	4.54
B	8.875	8/15/17	135-24+	1.2931	43.65	5.525	1320	9.64	136.9915	19.5	24.2	2.18	4.54
B	8.75	5/15/17	134-06+	1.2775	45.53	5.517	1296	9.42	137.6354	18.5	27.0	1.87	4.54
B	7.5	11/15/16	120-20	1.1484	40.42	5.512	1178	9.53	123.5670	14.0	26.4	1.63	4.54
N**	5	2/15/11	100-17	0.9284	60.44	4.931	776	7.67	101.2219	17.0	43.4	-3.08	2.66
N	5.75	8/15/10	105-12+	0.9828	30.98	5.020	764	7.19	106.1848	10.3	20.7	1.48	4.09
N	6.5	2/15/10	110-17+	1.0329	25.64	5.010	754	6.76	111.4447	11.2	14.5	2.72	4.46
N	6	8/15/09	106-28+	1.0000	20.50	4.981	705	6.55	107.7194	8.7	11.8	2.99	4.46
N	5.5	5/15/09	103-21	0.9693	21.38	4.946	676	6.39	105.8137	5.7	15.6	2.45	4.46
N	4.75	11/15/08	98-31	0.9273	14.18	4.913	625	6.20	100.8320	1.8	12.4	2.80	4.46
N	5.625	5/15/08	104-15+	0.9793	13.88	4.870	611	5.72	106.6909	5.2	8.7	3.50	4.61
N	5.5	2/15/08	103-27	0.9734	13.44	4.834	591	5.65	104.6034	6.0	7.4	3.51	4.46
F**	5.75	11/15/05	105-02+	0.9904	12.97	4.516	424	3.95	107.3336	13.7	-0.8	3.72	3.62
T**	5.375	6/30/03	102-17	0.9884	18.79	4.174	215	2.07	103.9567	5.3	13.5	2.83	4.49
T	5.5	5/31/03	102-21	0.9910	14.20	4.193	207	1.98	104.5752	6.1	8.1	3.49	4.49
T	5.75	4/30/03	103-03+	0.9956	13.52	4.162	200	1.89	105.6032	7.8	5.7	3.79	4.49
T	4.25	3/31/03	100-08+	0.9713	2.72	4.109	189	1.88	100.3353	-2.6	5.3	3.82	4.64
T	5.5	3/31/03	102-16+	0.9917	7.39	4.165	192	1.87	102.6058	6.3	1.1	4.35	4.49

* T denotes eligible for two-year notes, F five-year notes, N ten-year notes, and B bonds.
** Denotes on-the-run issue.
Source: JPMorgan

EXHIBIT 1.3

Conversion Factors for Deliverable Bonds

Coupon	Maturity	Contract Month				
		Jun-01	Sep-01	Dec-01	Mar-02	Jun-02
5.375	2/15/31	0.9140	0.9142	0.9146	0.9148	0.9152
6.25	5/15/30	1.0339	1.0339	1.0337	1.0337	1.0335
6.125	8/15/29	1.0169	1.0167	1.0167	1.0166	1.0166
5.25	2/15/29	0.8996	0.8999	0.9003	0.9006	0.9011
5.25	11/15/28	0.8999	0.9003	0.9006	0.9011	0.9014
5.5	8/15/28	0.9336	0.9337	0.9341	0.9342	0.9346
6.125	11/15/27	1.0163	1.0164	1.0162	1.0162	1.0160
6.375	8/15/27	1.0491	1.0487	1.0487	1.0483	1.0482
6.625	2/15/27	1.0811	1.0806	1.0804	1.0799	1.0797
6.5	11/15/26	1.0645	1.0643	1.0639	1.0638	1.0633
6.75	8/15/26	1.0965	1.0959	1.0956	1.0951	1.0948
6	2/15/26	1.0000	0.9999	1.0000	0.9999	1.0000
6.875	8/15/25	1.1105	1.1099	1.1095	1.1088	1.1084
7.625	2/15/25	1.2033	1.2022	1.2013	1.2001	1.1992
7.5	11/15/24	1.1866	1.1858	1.1847	1.1839	1.1828
6.25	8/15/23	1.0303	1.0300	1.0300	1.0297	1.0296
7.125	2/15/23	1.1349	1.1340	1.1333	1.1324	1.1317
7.625	11/15/22	1.1936	1.1926	1.1913	1.1902	1.1889
7.25	8/15/22	1.1481	1.1471	1.1463	1.1453	1.1445
8	11/15/21	1.2325	1.2311	1.2295	1.2281	1.2264
8.125	8/15/21	1.2456	1.2438	1.2423	1.2405	1.2390
8.125	5/15/21	1.2438	1.2423	1.2405	1.2390	1.2371
7.875	2/15/21	1.2138	1.2122	1.2109	1.2092	1.2078
8.75	8/15/20	1.3093	1.3069	1.3048	1.3024	1.3002
8.75	5/15/20	1.3069	1.3048	1.3024	1.3002	1.2977
8.5	2/15/20	1.2771	1.2749	1.2729	1.2706	1.2686
8.125	8/15/19	1.2320	1.2300	1.2283	1.2263	1.2245
8.875	2/15/19	1.3089	1.3062	1.3038	1.3010	1.2985
9	11/15/18	1.3195	1.3170	1.3141	1.3115	1.3085
9.125	5/15/18	1.3272	1.3245	1.3214	1.3186	1.3154
8.875	8/15/17	1.2931	1.2902	1.2875	1.2845	1.2818
8.75	5/15/17	1.2775	1.2750	1.2721	1.2695	1.2665
7.5	11/15/16	1.1484	1.1470	1.1453	1.1439	1.1422

factor is 1.1484 and accrued interest would be $0.91712. Accrued interest is calculated from the last coupon payment date, which would be 5/15/01, to 6/29/01. Thus, the invoice price would be

$$\text{Invoice Price} = (103.9375 \times 1.1484) + 0.91712$$
$$= 120.2789$$

The futures contract calls for delivery of $100,000 face value of bonds. For each futures contract, then, the total dollar amount of the invoice would be

$$\text{Invoice Amount} = \$1,000 \times 120.2789$$
$$= \$120,278.90$$

CARRY: PROFIT OR LOSS OF HOLDING BONDS

The price at which you would be willing to hold a bond for future delivery depends on what you will make or lose in net interest income while holding the bond.

Carry is the difference between the coupon income you make by holding the bond and what you pay to finance the bond. If carry is positive, as it will be if the yield curve is positively sloped, you can earn interest income holding a bond for future delivery. If carry is negative, as it will be if the yield curve is negatively sloped, you lose interest income.

Exhibit 1.2 shows total carry to last delivery day in column 11 for each deliverable bond using the term financing (RP or repo) rate shown in column 14. We show total carry to last delivery day because it happens to be the optimal delivery date given positive carry. We have more to say on the problem of optimal delivery in Chapter 2.

The following formula gives total carry to last delivery day in dollars for each $100 par value of the bonds.

$$\text{Carry} = \text{Coupon Income} - \text{Financing Cost}$$

where

$$\text{Coupon Income} = \left(\frac{C}{2}\right) \times \left(\frac{\text{Days}}{\text{DC}}\right)$$

where the dollar value of the coupon (C) is based on the coupon rate and the face value of the bond, and

$$\text{Financing Cost} = (P + \text{AI}) \times \left(\frac{\text{RP}}{100}\right) \times \left(\frac{\text{Days}}{360}\right)$$

is based on the total market value of the bond. The symbols used are these:

C is the dollar value of the annual coupon for $100 face value of the bonds. As such, it can be thought of as the coupon stated in full percentage points. C is divided by 2 to put it on a semiannual basis.

Days   is the actual number of days between settlement of the bond and delivery day. Treasury bonds settle one business day after trade date. In Exhibit 1.2, trade date is 4/5/01, settlement date is 4/6/01, and delivery day, which is assumed to be the last delivery day of the month, is 6/29/01.

DC   is the actual number of days between coupon payments and ranges between 181 and 186, so that coupon income works on a 365-day year

P is the market price per $100 face value of the bonds.

AI   is accrued interest per $100 face value of the bonds.

RP   is the repo or financing rate for the bond, which is stated in full percentage points and is divided by 100 to restate in percent. The correct RP rate that should be used for valuing futures is a term repo rate that corresponds to the number of days between settlement and delivery day.

360   is the assumed number of days in a year for RP calculations.

Example: Carry Calculation   Consider the 7-1/4% of 8/15/22 on April 5, 2001. This bond's price plus accrued interest was 120.8764, which can be found in column 10 of Exhibit 1.2. The RP rate was 4.54%, and the number of days between coupons, which for this bond are paid on February 15 and August 15, was 181. There are 84 days between settlement day (4/6/01) and last delivery day (6/29/01). Given these particulars, and for each $100 par value of the bond, we have

$$\text{Coupon Income} = \left(\frac{\$7.25}{2}\right) \times \left(\frac{84}{181}\right)$$

$$= \$1.68232$$

$$\text{Financing Cost} = \$120.8764 \times \left(\frac{4.54}{100}\right) \times \left(\frac{84}{360}\right)$$

$$= \$1.280484$$

so that carry is

$$\text{Carry} = \$1.68232 - \$1.280484$$
$$= \$0.401836$$

or 40 cents for each $100 face value of bonds. For $1 million face value of the 7-1/4%, total carry in dollars would be

$$\text{Total Carry} = \$.401836 \times 10,000$$
$$= \$4,018.36$$

Standard bond trading practice is to state carry in 32nds. The value of a 32nd for $1 million par value of a bond is $312.50. Thus, carry in 32nds is found simply by dividing carry in dollars by $312.50. For the carry calculation example, where total carry was $4,018.36, total carry in 32nds would be

$$\text{Carry in 32nds} = \frac{\$4,018.36}{\$312.50}$$
$$= 12.9/32\text{nds}$$

which you can find in column 11 of Exhibit 1.2.

In practice, the carry calculation shown previously is an approximation. The reason is that even if you have locked in a term financing rate in the RP market, most repurchase agreements require changes in collateral if bond prices change by more than a specified threshold. If bond prices fall by more than the threshold, the party financing the position may need to pledge additional collateral. This additional collateral may need to be borrowed, resulting in higher financing costs on the trade. Similarly, if bond prices rise, the party financing the position may have excess collateral that can be lent out, resulting in additional income on the transaction. Note that in a basis trade, where there is an offsetting position in bonds and futures, the net interest cost of managing collateral is likely to be small. This is because a decline in the value of the bond that is collateral for the repurchase agreement is likely to lead to an offsetting gain in the futures position. In this case, futures variation margin can be used to meet any additional collateral that is required on the repurchase agreement.

THEORETICAL BOND BASIS

If there were only one bond available for delivery, or if there were never any question about what the deliverable bond would be or when the bond would be delivered, the bond basis would be very easy to figure. To simplify matters still more, suppose the bond in question bears a 6% coupon, so that its conversion factor is 1.000. In such a simple setting, the futures price would be approximately

Futures Price = Bond Price – Total Carry to Delivery

Because the bond's conversion factor is 1.000, the bond's basis in this case is just the difference between the bond's price and the futures price. If we take this difference, we find that

$$
\begin{aligned}
\text{Basis} &= \text{Bond Price} - \text{Futures Price} \\
&= \text{Bond Price} - (\text{Bond Price} - \text{Total Carry}) \\
&= \text{Total Carry}
\end{aligned}
$$

Total carry, of course, has two parts. The first is daily carry, which depends both on the difference between the RP rate and the bond yield and on the price of the bond. The second is the total number of days to delivery. Taking the two together produces a relationship between a bond's basis and the time to delivery like that shown in Exhibit 1.4. Exhibit 1.4 illustrates three key points given the following simplifying assumptions:

EXHIBIT 1.4

Basis of Cheapest to Deliver with One Deliverable Bond

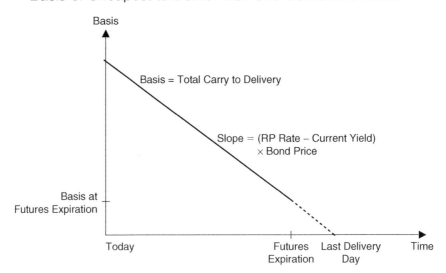

- The height of the curve is the total carry to delivery.
- The slope of the curve is equal to the negative daily carry.
- The basis converges to zero as time approaches delivery.

In Exhibit 1.4, the basis relationship is drawn for a setting in which carry is positive. Also note that the basis is represented by a solid line only until the last trading day is reached. After trading in the futures contract has expired, the futures price is fixed, while the bond's price is free to change. Both of these are important features of the bond basis market, and we discuss them further in Chapters 2 and 3.

IMPLIED REPO RATE

The implied repo rate is the theoretical return you would earn if you bought the cash bond, sold futures short against it, and then delivered the cash bond into the futures. If there is no coupon payment before delivery day, the formula for the implied repo rate is

$$IRR = \left(\frac{\text{Invoice Price} - \text{Purchase Price}}{\text{Purchase Price}} \right) \times \left(\frac{360}{n} \right)$$

which simplifies to

$$IRR = \left(\frac{\text{Invoice Price}}{\text{Purchase Price}} - 1 \right) \times \left(\frac{360}{n} \right)$$

where n is the number of days to delivery, and both the invoice and purchase price include accrued interest.

If a coupon payment is made before the delivery date, the implied repo rate is the funding rate that produces a forward price equal to the invoice price. This calculation assumes that intervening coupons are reinvested at the implied repo rate. If there is one intervening coupon, IRR is the solution to

$$IRR = \frac{\left(\left[\text{Invoice Price} + \left(\frac{C}{2} \right) \times \left(1 + IRR \times \left(\frac{n_2}{360} \right) \right) \right] - \text{Purchase Price} \right) \times \left(\frac{360}{n} \right)}{\text{Purchase Price}}$$

where $C/2$ is half the annual coupon, and n_2 is the number of days from the coupon date to delivery day. This simplifies to

$$\text{IRR} = \frac{\left(\text{Invoice Price} + \dfrac{C}{2} - \text{Purchase Price}\right) \times 360}{\left(\text{Purchase Price} \times n\right) - \left(\dfrac{C}{2} \times n_2\right)}$$

Consider the calculation of the implied repo rate on April 5, 2001, for the 7-1/4% of 8/15/22, assuming delivery on the last possible date for delivery into the June 2001 contract (that is, June 29). On April 5, the futures price settled at 103-30/32nds. The number of days from the settlement date of April 6 to the last delivery date of June 29 was 84.[1] The cash price of the 7-1/4% was quoted at 119-28/32nds, and accrued interest for each $100 face value of the bonds from the last coupon payment date on February 15 to the settlement date on April 6 was $1.0014. At delivery, accrued interest would be $2.683702.

To calculate the implied repo rate for $100,000 par value of the bond, you first need the purchase price or full price, which was

$$\begin{aligned}
\text{Purchase Price} &= \text{Quoted Price} + \text{Accrued Interest} \\
&= \$119.875 + \$1.0014 \\
&= \$120.8764
\end{aligned}$$

You can find this in column 10 of Exhibit 1.2.

Next you need the invoice price. Given delivery on June 29 and a futures price of 103-30/32nds, the invoice price would be

$$\begin{aligned}
\text{Invoice Price} &= (\text{Futures Price} \times \text{Conversion Factor}) \\
&\quad + \text{Accrued Interest} \\
&= (\$103.9375 \times 1.1481) + \$2.683702 \\
&= \$119.330644 + \$2.683702 \\
&= \$122.014346
\end{aligned}$$

With these numbers, the implied repo rate is

$$\text{IRR} = \left(\frac{\$122.0143}{\$120.8764} - 1\right) \times \left(\frac{360}{84}\right)$$
$$= 4.03\%$$

which you can find in column 13 of Exhibit 1.2.

---

1 Exhibit 1.2 is a report that is produced following the close of business each day. Thus, because the prices shown in Exhibit 1.2 are the closing prices, the next opportunity to trade is the next business day. In this case, because April 4 was a Monday, the assumed trade date would be Tuesday, April 5. Cash trades would settle on the next business day, which would be Wednesday, April 6.

Important Note The implied repo rate is a theoretical return. The calculation assumes that you are short a number of futures equal to the bond's conversion factor, C, for each \$100,000 bonds held long and that any coupon payments can be invested at the implied repo rate. Even then, you can only approximate the return because of variation margin payments on the futures contract. As prices fall, you make money on your short futures position, and these gains can be reinvested to increase the return on the position. As prices rise, you pay variation margin payments, and these losses must be financed, resulting in a lower return on the position. Of course, to the extent that the bonds are financed in the repo market, there may be offsetting collateral flows on the repurchase agreement. In this case, the difference between actual and theoretical return is likely to be small.

BUYING AND SELLING THE BASIS

Basis trading is the simultaneous or nearly simultaneous trading of cash bonds and bond futures to take advantage of expected changes in the basis. To "buy the basis" or to "go long the basis" is to buy cash bonds and to sell a number of futures contracts equal to the conversion factor for every \$100,000 par value cash bond. To "sell the basis" or to "go short the basis" is just the opposite: selling or shorting the cash bond and buying the futures contracts.

Because a bond's basis is defined as the difference between the bond's price and its converted futures price [that is, Basis = (Price – Factor × Futures)], a useful way of keeping basis trades straight is to remember that whatever position you take in the bond is the position you take in the basis. If you buy the bond and sell the futures, you are long the basis, and you will profit from an increase in the price of the bond relative to its converted futures price. If you sell the bond and buy the futures, you are short the basis. With a short basis position, you will profit if the bond price falls relative to its converted futures price.

In practice, traders can buy or sell the basis in either of two ways. The first is to execute the cash and futures trades separately, which is known as "legging into the trade." For example, to buy the basis, you would buy the bonds in the cash market at the lowest price available and sell the appropriate number of futures contracts at the highest available price in the bond futures market. The second approach to trading the basis is to execute the trade as a spread in the EFP (exchange of futures for physicals) market. Such a transaction in the EFP market simultaneously establishes a position in cash bonds and bond futures at the agreed-upon spread. The main advantage of the EFP market is that it limits the execution risk of establishing a spread position because traders directly bid and offer on the basis itself.

Consider, for example, the June 2001 basis of the 7-7/8% of 2/15/21 just before the close of futures trading on April 5, 2001. The June 2001 conversion factor for this bond was 1.2138. Futures were trading at 103-30/32nds, and, in the EFP market, the 7-7/8% basis was bid at 20/32nds and offered at 21/32nds. This means that someone was willing to pay at least 20/32nds for the basis of the 7-7/8% and that someone was willing to sell the basis of the 7-7/8% at a price as low as 21/32nds.

In this example, if a trader "lifted the offer" and paid 21/32nds for $10 million of the 7-7/8 basis, the trader would have simultaneously established a *long* position in $10 million par amount of the 7-7/8% and a *short* position in 121 [= $10,000,000 × (1.2138/$100,000)] bond futures contracts. The price paid for the bond would be 21/32nds higher than the product of the bond's conversion factor and the price at which the futures were sold. On the other hand, if a trader "hit the bid" and received 20/32nds for $10 million of the 7-7/8% basis, the trader would have simultaneously established a *short* position in $10 million par value of the bonds and a *long* position in 121 bond futures contracts. The price received for the bond would be 20/32nds higher than the product of the bond's conversion factor and the price paid for the futures contracts.

Once an EFP trade has been done, prices have to be set for both the cash bond and the bond futures. In practice, the futures price is set first by the EFP broker at a level that is close to the current market. Then the cash price of the bond is calculated as a residual to achieve the agreed-upon value of the spread. For example, if the trader bought the basis in the EFP market for 21/32nds (step 1), and the 121 futures were sold in the futures market at a price of 103-30/32nds (step 2), the cash price of the bond *net* of accrued interest would be calculated (step 3) as

$$\text{Bond Invoice Price} = (\text{Basis} + \text{Conversion Factor} \times \text{Futures Price})$$
$$= (21/32\text{nds} + 1.2138 \times 103\text{-}30/32\text{nds})$$
$$= (0.65625 + 1.2138 \times 103.9375)$$
$$= 126.815588$$

which produces a basis of almost exactly 21/32nds.

EXHIBIT 1.5

EFB Basis Quotes

2 YR	99.156(05)-16+
5YR	- - - (103.20+
10YR	

B58	516					
B50	N16					
B56	517	63 /	65	10	X	5
B65	817	59 /	60	5	X	5
B62	518					
B63	N18	48 /		5	X	
B64	219	45 /	49	5	X	5
B83	819					
B66	220					
B67	520	35+/		10	X	
B68	820	34 /		10	X	
B69	221	24 /	25+	5	X	5
B70	521	24+/	27+	5	X	5
B93	821	23 /		10	X	
B95	N21	22+/	23+	25	X10	
B84	822	17+/	18	5	X	5
B74	N22	18 /	19+	5	X	5
B71	223	17+/	18	10	X10	
B76	823	14 /	15	10	X	5
B77	N24	21+/		10	X	
B78	225	20 /	22	5	X	5

Source: *Garban.* (Used with permission from Gaban LLC.)

Exhibit 1.5 shows EFP basis quotes provided by Garban, which is one of the active bond brokers in New York. The page shows some of the more actively traded issues eligible for delivery into the bond contract and, for each issue, lists the best bid and offer available along with the size of the bid and offer. For example, at 3 p.m. (New York time) on April 27, 2001, the June basis of the 6-1/4% of 8/23 was bid at 14/32nds and offered at 15/32nds. The "size" column indicates that the bid was good for $10 million and the offer for $5 million.

The main difference between legging into a basis trade and executing a basis trade in the EFP market, apart from execution risk, are the prices at which the two legs of the spread trade are executed. The difference can have a small effect on the realized value of the spread.

If the trader legs into the position, the cash and futures trades are done at their respective *market* prices, and the resulting value of the basis is calculated as a residual. In contrast, if the trader undertakes the trade in the EFP market, the value of the basis and the futures prices are established first, and the invoice price for the cash bonds is calculated as a residual.

For example, if the trader could buy $10 million of the 7-7/8% of 2/21 at a market price of 126-25+/32nds and sell 121 bond futures at a market price of 103-30/32nds, the resulting value of the basis would be

$$
\begin{aligned}
\text{Basis} &= \text{Bond Price} - \text{Conversion Factor} \times \text{Futures Price} \\
&= 126.796875 - 1.2138 \times 103.9375 \\
&= 0.637538 \\
&= 20.40/32\text{nds}
\end{aligned}
$$

which is the value of the basis as reported in column 6 of Exhibit 1.2, and which is slightly lower than the 21/32nds basis achieved in the EFP example. If the cash price of the bond were 126-26, or 126-26/32nds, the resulting basis would be 20.9/32nds.

Why Use the Bond's Conversion Factor?   Perhaps the best reason to use the bond's conversion factor is that a bond's conversion factor defines its basis. If futures and bonds are combined in a ratio equal to the bond's conversion factor, a change in the bond's basis of any given amount will yield the same profit regardless of whether the change in the basis comes from a change in the price of the bond or a change in the futures price, and regardless of whether bond and futures prices generally rise or generally fall.

As we will see in Chapters 2 and 3, however, a basis position typically has a bullish or bearish tilt. This is because a bond's conversion factor only *approximates* the number of futures required for each $100,000 par value of the cash bonds to remove the directional bias. A trader can, of course, overcome this drawback by using a better hedge ratio to construct spread positions. This approach has its own drawback, though, because the resulting profit or loss in the position will no longer track changes in the bond's basis as closely.

SOURCES OF PROFIT IN A BASIS TRADE

A basis trade has two sources of profit. These are

- Change in the basis

■ Carry

A long basis position profits from an increase in the basis. Further, if net carry on the bond is positive, a long basis position earns the carry as well. On the other hand, a short position profits from a decrease in the basis but loses the carry if carry is positive.

The profit and loss characteristics of long and short basis trades are best illustrated with an example of each.

Buying the Basis   Suppose that on April 5, 2001, June 2001 bond futures are trading at 103-30/32nds. At the same time, the 7-1/2% of 11/16 are trading at 120-20/32nds for a basis of 40.4/32nds. You think that 40.4/32nds is a narrow basis at this time in the delivery cycle and that a long basis position is likely to be profitable. Exhibit 1.2 shows that the 7-1/2% of 11/16 had a conversion factor of 1.1484. Suppose that the repo rate for the 7-1/2% of 11/16 is 4.5%. Your opening trade would be

On 4/5/01 (Settle 4/6/01)

Buy $10 million of the 7-1/2% of 11/16 at 120-20/32nds

Sell 115 June 2001 futures at 103-30/32nds

Basis = 40.4/32nds

By April 19, your views have been borne out, and you want to unwind the position. Your closing trade would be

On 4/19/01 (Settle 4/20/01)

Sell $10 million of the 7-1/2% of 11/16 at 116-21/32nds

Buy 115 June 2001 futures at 100-16/32nds

Basis = 39.7/32nds

Profit/Loss

Bonds

Buy $10 million of 7-1/2% of 11/16 at 120-20/32nds

Sell $10 million of the 7-1/2% of 11/16 at 116-21/32nds

Loss = 127/32nds × $3,125.00 = ($396,875.00)

Futures

Sell 115 June bond futures at 103-30/32nds

Buy 115 June futures at 100-16/32nds

Gain = 110/32nds × 115 × $31.25 = $395,312.50

Coupon interest earned (14 days)

$10,000,000 × (.075/2) × (14/181) = $29,005.52

RP interest paid (14 days)[2]

$12,356,700 \times .045 \times (14/360) = ($21,624.23)$

Summary P/L

7-1/2% of 11/16	($396,875.00)
June 2001 futures	$395,312.50
Coupon income	$ 29,005.52
RP interest	($ 21,624.23)
Total	$ 5,818.80

ALTERNATIVE SUMMARY P/L

You can see from the example that even though you lost money on the cash bond and futures transactions, you still made money on the trade. Put differently, you lost money on a change in the bond's basis but more than made up for it in positive carry. We find it useful to restate the P/L for a basis trade in terms of these two components: the change in the basis and carry. For this particular trade, these would be

Change in the basis	($1,562.50)
Carry	$7,381.29
Total	$5,818.79

where the change in the basis is the combined value of what you made on the 7-1/2% and lost on the June 2001 futures, while carry is the combined value of coupon income received and RP interest paid.

As a rough check on your trade construction, you can compare what you realized on the change in the price relationship between cash bonds and bond futures with what you should have made. The basis narrowed from 40.4/32nds to 39.7/32nds, for a change of –0.7/32nds. For a basis position of $10 million, each 32nd is worth $3,125. Thus, your profit from the change in the basis should have been –$2,188 [= –0.7/32nds × $3,125]. The difference between the theoretical value and what you realized is due simply to rounding in the number of futures contracts. You can deal only in whole contracts, and so you had to sell 115 futures rather than 114.84, which is the exact number needed to replicate the bond's basis.

---

2 Calculated on the basis of the full price, or cash price plus accrued interest.

Selling the Basis   In contrast to the basis of the 7-1/2%, you believe that the basis of the 7-5/8% of 2/15/25 on April 5 is too wide and will narrow more than enough over the next few days to offset any negative carry in a short basis position. From Exhibit 1.2, we know that the conversion factor of the 7-5/8% of 2/15/25 is 1.2033. Suppose that the reverse repo rate for the 7-5/8% of 2/25 is 4.5%. Your opening trade is

On 4/5/01 (Settle 4/6/01)
Sell $10 million of the 7-5/8% of 2/25 at 125-22.5/32nds
Buy 120 June 2001 futures at 103-30/32nds
Basis = 20.3/32nds

By April 19, the basis has narrowed enough to close out the position. Your closing trade is

On 4/19/01 (Settle 4/20/01)
Buy $10 million of the 7-5/8% of 2/25 at 121-15/32nds
Sell 120 June 2001 futures at 100-16/32nds
Basis = 17.2/32nds

Profit/Loss
Bonds
   Sell $10 million of the 7-5/8% of 2/25 at 125-22.5/32nds
   Buy $10 million of the 7-5/8% of 2/25 at 121-15/32nds
   Gain = 135.5/32nds × $3,125.00 = $423,437.50

Futures
   Buy 120 June 2001 futures at 103-30/32nds
   Sell 120 June 2001 futures at 100-16/32nds
   Loss = 110/32nds × 120 × $31.25 = ($412,500.00)

Coupon interest paid (14 days)
   $10,000,000 × (.07625/2) × (14/181) = ($29,488.95)

Reverse RP interest earned (14 days)
   $12,675,630 × .045 × (14/360) = $22,182.35

Summary P/L

7-5/8% of 2/25	$423,437.50
June 2001 futures	($412,500.00)
Coupon interest	($29,488.95)

Reverse RP interest	$22,182.35
Total	$3,630.90
Alternative Summary P/L	
Change in the basis	$10,937.50
Carry	($7,306.60)
Total	$3,630.90

RP VERSUS REVERSE RP RATES

RP stands for repurchase, or "repo." Standard industry practice in the U.S. Treasury bond market is to finance long securities positions through the use of repurchase agreements. Formally, at least, a *repurchase agreement* is an arrangement in which a bond is sold today at one price and bought back at a later date, often the next day, at a predetermined price that is usually higher. The effect of this transaction is to finance the position, and the difference in the two prices is the cost of financing the position. When the cost is expressed in annual percentage terms, the resulting figure is the RP, or *repo*, rate. Note that because the repurchase price is set in advance, the RP rate is a comparatively risk-free short-term rate of return.

In a reverse repo, a bond is "reversed in" at one price and sold back later at a predetermined price that is usually higher. The effect of this transaction is to lend money at a comparatively risk-free short-term rate.

Repo transactions can be either overnight or for a set term. If the repurchase is set for the next day, the repo is overnight. If the repurchase is set for any longer period of time, the repo is *term*.

Under normal circumstances, the reverse repo rate tends to trade between 10 to 25 basis points below the repo rate. That is, the rate at which you can finance long positions in Treasuries is about 10 to 25 basis points higher than the rate at which you can invest money short-term.

The difference can have a substantial effect on the profitability of basis trades. Suppose, for example, that the reverse repo rate in the example of selling the basis had been 4.25%, or 25 basis points lower than the repo rate. At this rate, our income from reverse RP interest would have been only $20,950 [= $12,675,630 × .0425 × (14/360)] instead of $22,182.35. As a result, the trader's profit from selling the basis would have been $1,232.35 less than was shown in the example. Had the bond been "on special," which we will discuss in Chapter 6, and the reverse repo rate had been as low as, say, 1.00%, the trade would have produced a loss of $13,622.04 instead of a gain.

CHAPTER 2

What Drives the Basis?

From a strict carry standpoint, futures prices usually are too low. Those who buy bonds and sell futures cannot make enough in carry to compensate for the lower futures price. Those who sell bonds and buy futures seem as if they will more than make up for the carry they lose. In a nutshell, basis tends to exceed carry and has done so persistently since Treasury futures began trading.

The players in the bond market are some of the brightest people in the financial world, and so we cannot chalk up the difference to ignorance or stupidity. Instead, we should expect to find that those who sell futures are getting something other than carry in return. On the other side of the trade, of course, those who buy futures must be giving up whatever the shorts expect to gain. For those who are long futures, then, the difference between basis and carry is what they receive for whatever it is they are giving up.

What accounts for the difference? The answer lies in the short's rights to choose which bond to deliver and when to deliver it. These rights make up a valuable set of strategic delivery options that must be reflected in any bond's basis.

THE SHORT'S ALTERNATIVES

If there were only one bond that could be delivered into the futures contract and only one day on which delivery could be made, understanding the bond basis would be a breeze. Competitive forces would cause the bond basis for the one deliverable bond to equal net carry, and the relationship between the basis and the time to delivery would look like the graph in Exhibit 1.4.

As it is, there were 33 bonds that were eligible on April 5, 2001, for delivery into the Board of Trade's June 2001 bond futures contract, each with its own basis, carry, conversion factor, yield, and implied repo rate. Further, the Treasury periodically introduces bonds with new coupons and maturities into the eligible set of deliverable bonds. A basis trade can involve any one of these eligible issues.

Moreover, the delivery window is a full month long. Delivery can be made on any business day of the contract month. This includes seven business days after the futures have stopped trading.

Under the rules that govern the Chicago Board of Trade's bond futures contract, the one who is short the contract is the one who decides which bond to deliver and when in the delivery month to deliver it. The short strives, of course, to pick both the bond and the delivery day that work to his or her best advantage.

Our objective in this chapter is to show why the short's ability to shift out of one bond into another is worth something, as is the short's right to deliver early in the delivery month rather than late. The value of these rights is what accounts for the difference between basis and carry. Moreover, changes in the values of these rights account for changes in the difference between basis and carry. We provide a complete description of the short's strategic delivery options in Chapter 3 and of how we value them in Chapter 4.

SEARCH FOR THE CHEAPEST BOND TO DELIVER

The search for the best bond to deliver is, in the language of futures, the search for the "cheapest to deliver." Because the bond that is cheapest to deliver (CTD) can change, many of the interesting questions for basis traders revolve around this search.

The key concepts covered in this section are

- Deliverable set
- Cheapest to deliver

The Deliverable Set   Under the rules of the Chicago Board of Trade, any U.S. Treasury bond is eligible for delivery into the bond futures contract if it has, as of the first delivery day of the contract month, at least 15 years left to maturity. As mentioned, on April 5, 2001, there were 33 such bonds that were eligible for delivery into the June 2001 contract. These are shown in Exhibit 2.1.

EXHIBIT 2.1

Choosing the Cheapest to Deliver Bond and the Best Time to Deliver It

Jun 01 futures = 103-30. 85 days to last delivery
(Closing prices for April 4, 2001, trade on April 5, settle on April 6)

| Issue | | Closing Price | Yield | Conversion Factor | Basis (32nds) | Carry (32nds) | BNOC (32nds) | Implied RP | | Term RP | Implied Less Term RP |
Coupon	Maturity							First del.	Last del.		
5 3/8	02/15/31	98-08	5.494	0.9140	104.04	7.02	97.02	-15.71	-8.68	4.45	-13.13
6 1/4	05/15/30	109-14	5.589	1.0339	63.25	9.55	53.70	-5.88	-2.10	4.43	-6.53
6 1/8	08/15/29	107-02	5.623	1.0169	43.79	8.90	34.89	-2.51	0.21	4.54	-4.33
5 1/4	02/15/29	94-18	5.639	0.8996	33.93	6.68	27.25	-1.67	0.71	4.54	-3.83
5 1/4	11/15/28	94-15	5.647	0.8999	29.93	6.40	23.53	-0.85	1.23	4.54	-3.31
5 1/2	08/15/28	97-30	5.648	0.9336	28.85	7.38	21.46	-0.33	1.63	4.54	-2.91
6 1/8	11/15/27	106-14	5.654	1.0163	25.79	8.74	17.04	0.82	2.41	4.54	-2.13
6 3/8	08/15/27	109-25	5.656	1.0491	23.69	9.82	13.87	1.43	2.86	4.54	-1.68
6 5/8	02/15/27	113-03	5.655	1.0811	23.26	10.55	12.72	1.68	3.05	4.54	-1.49
6 1/2	11/15/26	111-10+	5.657	1.0645	21.97	9.83	12.14	1.79	3.09	4.54	-1.45
6 3/4	08/15/26	114-21+	5.653	1.0965	22.54	10.93	11.61	1.89	3.20	4.54	-1.34
6	02/15/26	104-18	5.655	1.0000	20.00	8.83	11.17	1.85	3.12	4.54	-1.42
6 7/8	08/15/25	116-01	5.654	1.1105	19.48	11.39	8.08	2.50	3.61	4.54	-0.93
7 5/8	02/15/25	125-22+	5.650	1.2033	20.32	13.65	6.67	2.76	3.83	4.54	-0.71
7 1/2	11/15/24	124-00	5.646	1.1866	21.37	12.85	8.51	2.49	3.63	4.54	-0.91
6 1/4	08/15/23	107-18	5.649	1.0303	15.22	9.65	5.57	2.91	3.85	4.54	-0.69
7 1/8	02/15/23	118-16	5.641	1.1349	17.32	12.40	4.92	3.02	3.99	4.54	-0.55
7 5/8	**11/15/22**	**124-20**	**5.639**	**1.1936**	**18.09**	**13.56**	**4.53**	**3.09**	**4.06**	**4.54**	**-0.48**
7 1/4	08/15/22	119-28	5.637	1.1481	17.42	12.86	4.56	3.07	4.03	4.54	-0.51
8	11/15/21	128-23+	5.626	1.2325	20.20	14.91	5.30	2.95	3.99	4.54	-0.55
8 1/8	08/15/21	130-04+	5.620	1.2456	21.63	15.84	5.80	2.84	3.95	4.54	-0.59
8 1/8	05/15/21	129-30	5.620	1.2438	21.12	15.41	5.71	2.88	3.96	4.54	-0.58
7 7/8	02/15/21	126-25+	5.618	1.2138	20.40	15.12	5.28	2.92	3.99	4.54	-0.55
8 3/4	08/15/20	136-28	5.604	1.3093	25.27	18.16	7.10	2.63	3.85	4.54	-0.69
8 3/4	05/15/20	136-22+	5.597	1.3069	27.75	17.70	10.06	2.22	3.56	4.54	-0.98
8 1/2	02/15/20	133-18+	5.595	1.2771	26.87	17.44	9.43	2.27	3.60	4.54	-0.94
8 1/8	08/15/19	128-28	5.589	1.2320	26.37	16.26	10.10	2.14	3.50	4.54	-1.04
8 7/8	02/15/19	137-02+	5.570	1.3089	33.10	19.02	14.08	1.57	3.18	4.54	-1.36
9	11/15/18	138-11	5.557	1.3195	38.34	18.97	19.37	0.86	2.68	4.54	-1.86
9 1/8	05/15/18	139-07	5.545	1.3272	40.73	19.59	21.15	0.60	2.52	4.54	-2.02
8 7/8	08/15/17	135-24+	5.525	1.2931	43.65	19.46	24.19	0.04	2.18	4.54	-2.36
8 3/4	05/15/17	134-06+	5.517	1.2775	45.53	18.54	26.99	-0.36	1.87	4.54	-2.67
7 1/2	11/15/16	120-20	5.512	1.1484	40.42	14.00	26.42	-0.57	1.63	4.54	-2.91

Source: JPMorgan

The bonds are listed from newest to oldest, and a quick glance down the list provides an interesting thumbnail history of yields in the Treasury bond market. The Treasury sets the coupon on a new issue so that the bond will trade just below but as close to par as possible. Thus, by following the coupons from top to bottom, you can trace out a reverse history of interest rates on 30-year Treasury bonds over the years from 2001 back through 1986. For example, the most recently issued bond, issued in February 2001, has a coupon of 5-3/8 and matures in February 2031. The oldest bond in the deliverable set, issued in November of 1986, has a coupon of 7-1/2 and matures in November 2016. A glance at the coupons shows that Treasury bond yields were highest in 1988, when the Treasury issued bonds with coupons of 9-1/8 and 9.

Outstanding Supplies   Exhibit 2.2 shows the outstanding supplies of the 33 deliverable issues by maturity. Exhibit 2.2 also shows the deliverable yield curve as of the close of business on April 4. The cheapest to deliver bond—the 7-5/8% of 11/22—is singled out from the deliverable issues. The total public supply of each issue is measured by the height of each bar. The dark shading indicates how

E X H I B I T   2.2

Supplies of Deliverable Treasury Bonds; April 4, 2001

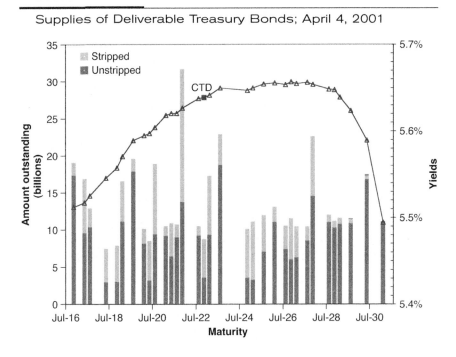

much is available as whole bonds, while the light shading shows how much of the issue has been stripped.

As time passes, the characteristics of the deliverable set change. Older issues drop out of the deliverable set. New issues are added to the deliverable set. Treasury buyback programs can reduce the total amount outstanding. The amount of an issue that is available in unstripped form can rise or fall as bonds are reconstituted or stripped further.

Using the Implied Repo Rate to Find the Cheapest to Deliver

The cheapest bond to deliver is not the bond with the lowest market price. The Chicago Board of Trade's system of conversion factors tends to put all deliverable bonds on roughly equal footing by scaling the futures price up or down to reflect higher and lower coupons. Their footing is not exactly equal, however, and the short will find some bonds more profitable or less costly to deliver than others.

Of the entire set of eligible bonds, the cheapest bond to deliver is the bond that maximizes the net return to buying the cash bond, carrying the bond to delivery, and delivering the bond into the bond futures contract.

Industry Practice Under most circumstances, a very reliable way to find the cheapest to deliver is to find the bond with the highest implied repo rate. The implied repo rate, as shown in Chapter 1, is the hypothetical rate of return to buying the cash bond and delivering it into the futures contract.

Exhibit 2.1 shows the implied repo rates for all eligible bonds as of April 5, 2001. The implied repo rates for the last delivery day range from –8.68% for the 5-3/8% of 2/15/31 to 4.06% for the 7-5/8% of 11/15/22. By this measure, the cheapest bond to deliver on April 5 would have been the 7-5/8%. The 5-3/8%, with an implied repo rate of −8.68%, would have been more costly to buy, hold, and deliver.

The intuition behind using the implied repo rate as a guide to the cheapest to deliver is apparent in the way it is calculated. That is, the formula for calculating the implied repo rate when there is no intervening coupon payment is

$$IRR = \left(\frac{\text{Invoice Price}}{\text{Purchase Price}} - 1 \right) \times \left(\frac{360}{\text{Days}} \right)$$

which allows us to see that the bond with the highest ratio of invoice price to purchase price is the bond with the highest implied repo rate. Put differently, the bond with the lowest purchase price relative to its invoice price is the bond that is best to deliver.

Repo Specials   A somewhat better guide to finding the cheapest to deliver is the spread or difference between a bond's implied repo rate and its own term repo rate. The difference, which would be negative for all bonds, is a measure of the cost of the strategic delivery options. And the bond for which this number is least negative (largest algebraically) is the cheapest to deliver.

To be sure, if all bonds in the deliverable set can be financed at the same term repo rate to delivery, this refinement in the search for the cheapest to deliver adds nothing. In that case, the bond with the highest implied repo rate is also the bond for which this spread between implied and term repo rates is least negative. Thus, the two rules yield the same result.

In practice, though, some bonds can be financed at special repo rates, which are lower than general collateral rates. As a result, the bond for which the spread between implied and term repo is the least negative need not be the bond with the highest implied repo rate. This rule rarely kicks in, but it can and does, especially when recently auctioned issues, which are more likely to trade on special, become attractive candidates for delivery.

Why Not Basis Net of Carry?   An alternative rough-and-ready way to find the CTD is to compare a bond's basis with its total carry to delivery. The difference is called the "net basis," or "basis net of carry." As shown in Exhibit 2.1, the 7-5/8% of 11/15/22 had a basis of 18.09/32nds on April 5 and estimated total carry to the last delivery day of 13.56/32nds. Thus, the basis of the 7-5/8% was trading at "4.53/32nds over carry." By contrast, the 5-3/8% of 2/15/31 had a basis of 104.04/32nds with total carry to the last delivery day of 7.02/32nds. Thus, the basis of the 5-3/8% of 2/15/31 was trading at 97.02/32nds over carry.

The net cost of buying the 7-5/8% and delivering them into the futures contract would be 4.53/32nds, while the net cost of doing the same thing with the 5-3/8% would be 97.02/32nds. By this measure, then, the 7-5/8% would be the cheaper bond to deliver.

The chief drawback to using this approach to find the CTD is that it can give incorrect rankings when the prices of two competing bonds are different. A bond's basis net of carry does not take into account the actual market price of the bond. If two bonds were to have the same basis net of carry, the bond with the higher price would be the cheaper of the two bonds to deliver.

Exhibit 2.3 compares the three approaches to ranking the cheapness of competing deliverables. In this example, both ways of

EXHIBIT 2.3

Measures of Cheapness to Deliver
(Trade Date: April 5, 2001)

Implied RP	Issue Coupon	Issue Maturity	Implied Less Term	Issue Coupon	Issue Maturity	BNOC	Issue Coupon	Issue Maturity
4.06	**7 5/8**	**11/15/22**	**-0.48**	**7 5/8**	**11/15/22**	**4.53**	**7 5/8**	**11/15/22**
4.03	7 1/4	08/15/22	-0.51	7 1/4	08/15/22	4.56	7 1/4	08/15/22
3.99	8	11/15/21	-0.55	8	11/15/21	4.92	7 1/8	02/15/23
3.99	7 1/8	02/15/23	-0.55	7 1/8	02/15/23	5.28	7 7/8	02/15/21
3.99	7 7/8	02/15/21	-0.55	7 7/8	02/15/21	5.30	8	11/15/21
3.96	8 1/8	05/15/21	-0.58	8 1/8	05/15/21	5.57	6 1/4	08/15/23
3.95	8 1/8	08/15/21	-0.59	8 1/8	08/15/21	5.71	8 1/8	05/15/21
3.85	6 1/4	08/15/23	-0.69	6 1/4	08/15/23	5.80	8 1/8	08/15/21
3.85	8 3/4	08/15/20	-0.69	8 3/4	08/15/20	6.67	7 5/8	02/15/25
3.83	7 5/8	02/15/25	-0.71	7 5/8	02/15/25	7.10	8 3/4	08/15/20
3.63	7 1/2	11/15/24	-0.91	7 1/2	11/15/24	8.08	6 7/8	08/15/25
3.61	6 7/8	08/15/25	-0.93	6 7/8	08/15/25	8.51	7 1/2	11/15/24
3.60	8 1/2	02/15/20	-0.94	8 1/2	02/15/20	9.43	8 1/2	02/15/20
3.56	8 3/4	05/15/20	-0.98	8 3/4	05/15/20	10.06	8 3/4	05/15/20
3.50	8 1/8	08/15/19	-1.04	8 1/8	08/15/19	10.10	8 1/8	08/15/19
3.20	6 3/4	08/15/26	-1.34	6 3/4	08/15/26	11.17	6	02/15/26
3.18	8 7/8	02/15/19	-1.36	8 7/8	02/15/19	11.61	6 3/4	08/15/26
3.12	6	02/15/26	-1.42	6	02/15/26	12.14	6 1/2	11/15/26
3.09	6 1/2	11/15/26	-1.45	6 1/2	11/15/26	12.72	6 5/8	02/15/27
3.05	6 5/8	02/15/27	-1.49	6 5/8	02/15/27	13.87	6 3/8	08/15/27
2.86	6 3/8	08/15/27	-1.68	6 3/8	08/15/27	14.08	8 7/8	02/15/19
2.68	9	11/15/18	-1.86	9	11/15/18	17.04	6 1/8	11/15/27
2.52	9 1/8	05/15/18	-2.02	9 1/8	05/15/18	19.37	9	11/15/18
2.41	6 1/8	11/15/27	-2.13	6 1/8	11/15/27	21.15	9 1/8	05/15/18
2.18	8 7/8	08/15/17	-2.36	8 7/8	08/15/17	21.46	5 1/2	08/15/28
1.87	8 3/4	05/15/17	-2.67	8 3/4	05/15/17	23.53	5 1/4	11/15/28
1.63	7 1/2	11/15/16	-2.91	7 1/2	11/15/16	24.19	8 7/8	08/15/17
1.63	5 1/2	08/15/28	-2.91	5 1/2	08/15/28	26.42	7 1/2	11/15/16
1.23	5 1/4	11/15/28	-3.31	5 1/4	11/15/28	26.99	8 3/4	05/15/17
0.71	5 1/4	02/15/29	-3.83	5 1/4	02/15/29	27.25	5 1/4	02/15/29
0.21	6 1/8	08/15/29	-4.33	6 1/8	08/15/29	34.89	6 1/8	08/15/29
-2.10	6 1/4	05/15/30	-6.53	6 1/4	05/15/30	53.70	6 1/4	05/15/30
-8.68	5 3/8	02/15/31	-13.13	5 3/8	02/15/31	97.02	5 3/8	02/15/31

using the implied repo rate produced the same ranking. The only issues that were on special in the term repo market were the 6-1/4% of 5/30 and the 5-3/8% of 2/31, which were so expensive to deliver that their specialness in the repo market was not enough to improve their relative rankings.

And, while the cheapest to deliver bond also had the lowest basis net of carry, this measure of cheapness produced different relative rankings further down the list. For example, the third cheapest bond was the 8% of 11/21 even though its basis net of carry was larger than those for the 7-1/8% of 2/23 and the 7-7/8% of 2/21.

THE BEST TIME TO DELIVER A BOND

In addition to helping identify the cheapest bond to deliver, implied repo rates can help determine the best time within the contract month to deliver the bond. In Exhibit 2.1, we show the implied repo rates for delivery on both the first and last business days of June 2001. Notice that for any given bond or note, the implied repo rate for delivery on the last day is higher than the implied repo rate for delivery on the first day. Thus, because the hypothetical rate of return to the longer holding period is higher, the short almost certainly would choose to make delivery on the last business day of September.

Positively Sloped Yield Curves   The higher implied repo rates shown in Exhibit 2.1 for the last delivery day are the result of a positively sloped yield curve. If long-term yields are higher than short-term yields, the short's decision about when to make delivery is fairly simple. There are two forces working on the decision, both tending to make the short choose the last possible delivery day.

First, if the yield curve has a positive slope, carry for someone who is long bonds and short futures is positive. Every day that goes by is money in the bank. The implied repo rates simply confirm this.

Second, the short who makes delivery gives up any remaining value in the options to change the deliverable bond. The market value of these options is the difference between the basis of the cheapest to deliver and its remaining carry to the last delivery day. This difference, or premium, can amount to several 32nds, even for the cheapest to deliver bond. Only a rare "wild card" opportunity might cause the short to give up the current basis net of carry and make delivery early. (See Chapter 3 for details.)

Negatively Sloped Yield Curve   The short's problem is more complex if carry is negative. Every day that goes by is a drain, because what is being made in the form of coupon income is not enough to make up for the cost of financing the position in the RP market.

The way to avoid the negative carry, of course, is to make delivery early. The chief problem with early delivery, however, is that the short must give up the remaining value of the various delivery options.

Early delivery is worthwhile only under fairly extreme circumstances. It is profitable if the value of negative carry dominates the value of the remaining delivery options. Using the past as a guide, we find that the RP rate has had to be significantly higher than long-term bond yields to justify making early delivery.

Consider the delivery patterns shown in Exhibit 2.4 for the March 2001 contracts. Given the peculiar shape of the yield curve

EXHIBIT 2.4

Treasury Deliveries; March 2001

Delivery	Issue		Number of
Date	Coupon	Maturity	Contracts
2-year notes			
3/14/01	5.125	12/31/02	200
3/15/01	5.125	12/31/02	805
3/16/01	5.125	12/31/02	2153
3/19/01	5.125	12/31/02	551
3/20/01	5.125	12/31/02	125
3/21/01	5.125	12/31/02	500
3/23/01	5.125	12/31/02	105
3/26/01	5.125	12/31/02	435
3/27/01	5.125	12/31/02	353
3/29/01	5.125	12/31/02	791
4/3/01	5.125	12/31/02	1216
5-year notes			
3/30/01	6.75	5/15/05	20,934
10-year notes			
3/30/01	5.5	2/15/08	17884
Bonds			
3/30/01	8.75	5/15/20	9,567
3/30/01	8.75	8/15/20	3,860

Source: CFTC at www.cftc.gov

at the time (inverted from zero to roughly 2 years, positively sloped thereafter), the carry for deliverable 2-year notes was negative, but for 5-year, 10-year, and bonds, it was positive (or negligible). As a result, shorts began delivering 2-year notes in the middle of the month and continued delivering throughout the remainder of the month. Deliveries for the other three contracts all took place on the last possible day.

RULES OF THUMB

The cheapest bond to deliver changes from time to time, usually because the level of yields or the slope of the yield curve changes, and occasionally because a new bond or note is added to the eligible set through the Treasury's auction of new debt. On any given day, of course, the implied repo rate can pinpoint accurately the cheapest bond to deliver but gives no insight into why the cheapest to deliver changes from one bond to another.

This section describes the forces that cause the cheapest bond to deliver to change. The choice of the cheapest to deliver can be characterized in terms of duration and yield.

The two general rules of thumb that will help you organize your thinking on the business of cheapest to deliver are as follows:

Duration. For bonds trading at the same yield *below* 6%, the bond with the lowest duration will be the cheapest to deliver. For bonds trading at the same yield *above* 6%, the bond with the highest duration will be the cheapest to deliver.

Yield. For bonds with the same duration, the bond with the highest yield will be the cheapest to deliver.

Relative Durations The important thing to know about a bond's duration is that it represents the percentage change in the price of the bond for a given change in the bond's yield.[1] For the same change in yields, then, the prices of high-duration bonds change relatively more than the prices of low-duration bonds.

Why is this important? The Chicago Board of Trade's conversion factors are the approximate prices at which bonds eligible for delivery would yield 6%. As a result, the conversion factors are roughly neutral at 6% yields. If all deliverable bonds were trading

---

1 The best explanation of duration that we know is contained in Robert Kopprasch's "Understanding Duration and Volatility," Salomon Brothers Inc., September 1985.

EXHIBIT 2.5

Relative Duration and Cheapest to Deliver

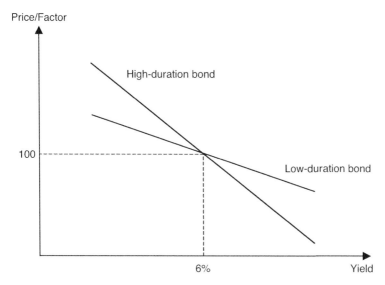

at 6%, their converted prices (that is, their prices divided by their respective conversion factors) would all equal 100. Anyone making delivery would be indifferent between any two eligible bonds.

Exhibit 2.5 shows a simple two-bond example in a graph of the converted prices of a high-duration bond against the converted prices of a low-duration bond. Note that if both bonds yield exactly 6% (and if we ignore the rounding to the nearest calendar quarter that is used in determining conversion factors), both bonds would have converted prices of 100 on the first delivery day of the month. In such a case, the short would be indifferent between the two bonds. Each is just as cheap to deliver as the other.

At yields above and below 6%, however, duration plays a factor. Consider yields below 6%. As yields fall from 6%, the prices of both bonds rise, but the price of the low-duration bond rises relatively less than the price of the high-duration bond. Thus, as yields fall below 6%, the low-duration bond becomes the cheaper to deliver.

In contrast, as yields rise above 6%, the price of the high-duration bond falls relatively more than the price of the low-duration bond. As a result, the high-duration bond becomes the cheaper bond to deliver as yields rise above 6%.

Hence the first rule of thumb.

Relative Yields   Bonds do not all trade at identical yields. As shown in Exhibit 2.1, deliverable bond yields at the close of business on April 4 ranged from 5.512% on the 7-1/2% of 11/16 (with roughly 15 years left to maturity) to 5.657% on the 6-1/2% of 11/26 (with roughly 25 years left to maturity) to 5.494% on the 5-3/8% of 2/31 (with nearly 30 years left to maturity). Bond yields depend on any number of things, including the slope of the yield curve, the size of the coupon, the bond's availability for trading, its specialness in the repo market, and so forth. Whatever the reasons, though, it is possible to find bonds with roughly the same duration trading at different yields.

Naturally enough, for any two bonds with the same duration, the bond with the higher yield would have the lower converted price and would be the cheaper bond to deliver.

Hence the second rule of thumb.

THE BOND BASIS IS LIKE AN OPTION

We can use the rules of thumb to gain a better understanding of the way the bond basis behaves. In particular, they allow us to liken any one bond's basis to one of a number of conventional and well-known option strategies.

Exhibit 2.6 shows the relationship between the converted cash prices of three bonds—the 5-1/2% of 8/28, the 7-5/8% of 11/22, and the 8-7/8% of 8/17—and the yield of the 7-5/8%. For the purposes of this illustration, we will suppose that these bonds are the only three that can be cheapest to deliver. For yields below 4.98%, the price of the 8-7/8% divided by its factor is lower than for any other bond and so will be cheapest to deliver at expiration. For yields above 4.98% but below 6.13%, the 7-5/8% have the lowest converted cash price and will be cheapest to deliver at expiration. For yields above 6.13%, the 5-1/2% have the lowest converted cash price at expiration and so will be cheapest to deliver.

At expiration, as long as the relative yield relationships between these three bonds behave as expected, the relationship between the futures price at expiration and the yield of the 8-7/8% can be found by tracing out a line that connects the lowest segment of each of the three price/yield curves. Except for small amounts of carry, the futures price if yields are below 4.98% will equal the price of the 8-7/8% divided by their conversion factor. At yields between 4.98% and 6.13 %, the futures price will equal the price of the 7-5/8%

EXHIBIT 2.6

Cash/Futures Price Relationships
(With Crossover Points on April 5, 2001)

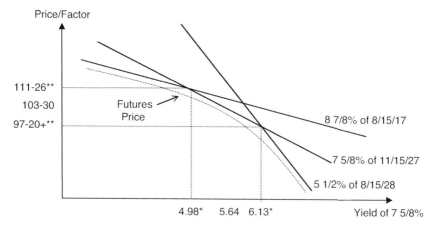

*Approximate crossover yields as of 4/5/01
**Approximate crossover futures prices as of 4/5/01

Issue	Yield
5 1/2% of 8/15/28	5.65
7 5/8% of 11/15/22	5.64
8 7/8% of 8/15/17	5.53

divided by their factor. Above 6.13%, the futures price at expiration will equal the converted price of the 5-1/2%.

Before expiration, we expect the futures price to track the smoothly curved dashed line that lies below the lowest converted cash price of the three competing bonds. Just how much below depends, as we show in Chapter 3, on how volatile yields and yield spreads are expected to be and therefore on how likely it is that there will be a change in the cheapest to deliver. Once we know this relationship, however, it is easy to see where some of the key delivery options are in the bond basis.

The Basis of a High-Duration Bond Is Like a Call Consider first what the basis of a high-duration bond like the 5-1/2% of 8/28 is likely to be at different yield levels. As Exhibit 2.7 shows, if yields are well above Y_C, the 5-1/2% are cheapest to deliver and likely to remain so. With a very small chance that the 5-1/2% will not be cheapest to deliver at expiration, the futures price before expiration can be expected to track very closely the converted price of the 5-1/2% net of carry. As yields fall, however, the likelihood that the

E X H I B I T   2.7

Basis of 5-1/2% Is Like a Call Option on Bond Futures

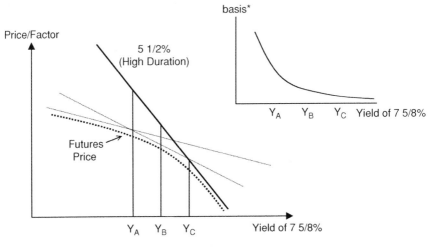

*Basis = Price − Factor × Futures

5-1/2% will not be cheapest to deliver at expiration rises. In fact, if yields fall below Y_C, the 5-1/2% will be replaced by the 7-5/8% as cheapest to deliver. If yields fall below Y_A, both the 5-1/2% and the 7-5/8% would be supplanted by the 8-7/8% as cheapest to deliver. Thus, as yield levels fall, the basis of the 5-1/2%, which is approximately the distance between the converted price/yield curve of the 5-1/2% and the dashed futures price curve in Exhibit 2.7, rises.[2] As yields rise, the basis of the 5-1/2% falls.

The relationship between the basis of the 5-1/2% and the level of yields is isolated in the upper right-hand corner of Exhibit 2.7. This is also the picture that one would draw to illustrate the relationship between a call option on a bond or a bond futures contract and the level of yields. As yields fall, bond and bond futures prices rise, and so would the value of any bond call. Thus, we can conclude that the basis of a high-duration bond like the 5-1/2% behaves like a bond call.

The Basis of a Low-Duration Bond Is Like a Put   Exhibit 2.8 focuses on the basis of a low-duration bond like the 8-7/8%. At low yields, the 8-7/8% is cheapest to deliver and its basis is small.

---

2 The distance between the converted cash price line of the 5-1/2% and the futures price line equals the basis of the 5-1/2% divided by its conversion factor.

E X H I B I T   2.8

Basis of 8-7/8% Is Like a Put Option on Bond Futures

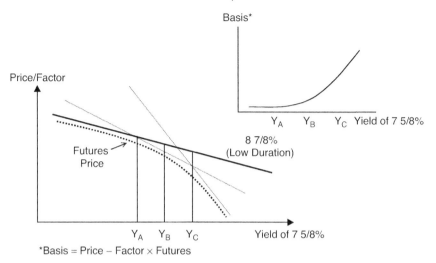

*Basis = Price − Factor × Futures

As yields rise, however, the 8-7/8% becomes expensive to deliver, and its basis increases. The same thing would happen to the value of a put option on a bond or bond futures contract. As yields rise, bond and bond futures prices fall, and the value of all put options would rise. Thus, the basis of a low-duration bond like the 8-7/8% can be likened to a bond put.

The Basis of a Middling-Duration Bond Is Like a Straddle
Because of its position in the middle of the deliverable pack, the basis of the 7-5/8% behaves much like a straddle, which is a combination of a call and a put. As Exhibit 2.9 shows, its basis is smallest when yields are around Y_B and tends to increase as yields either rise or fall from this neighborhood. This, of course, is just how the value of a straddle behaves.

SHIFTS IN THE CHEAPEST TO DELIVER

Because the level of yields is such an important force in determining the cheapest to deliver, we find it useful to do "what if" exercises to reckon the effect of increases and decreases in the level of yields on the bases of competing eligible bonds. The results of one such exercise are shown in Exhibit 2.10, which presents the basis net of carry at futures expiration for all eligible bonds and notes.

E X H I B I T   2.9

Basis of 7-5/8% Is Like a Straddle on Bond Futures

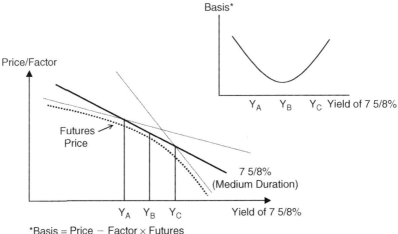

*Basis = Price − Factor × Futures

The construction of Exhibit 2.10 begins in a fairly straightforward way with whatever the current distribution of yields on eligible bonds or notes happens to be. We then ask what each bond's basis net of carry would be at the expiration of futures trading if the yield of the current on-the-run bond (in this case, the 5-3/8% of 2/31) were to

- Stay where they were at the close of business on April 4
- Increase by 60 basis points in 10 basis point increments
- Decrease by 60 basis points in 10 basis point increments

In this kind of exercise, we must assume something about the relationship between changes in the yield of the reference bond and change in the yields of other bonds in the deliverable set. In Exhibit 2.10, we use an estimated yield beta for each bond to capture the tendency of the curve to steepen as yields fall and to flatten as yields rise.

We answer these questions by calculating first what each bond's price would be at the expiration of futures trading and then dividing each bond's price net of carry to the last delivery day (that is, each bond's forward price as of the last delivery day) by its own conversion factor. The bond with the lowest converted price net of carry to delivery is taken to be the cheapest to deliver if the assumed set of yields were to prevail.

Once we have identified the cheapest to deliver at any given level of yields, we calculate a hypothetical futures price by assuming that the basis net of carry of the cheapest to deliver equals the value of the end-of-month switch option (more on this in Chapter 3). Because basis net of carry is defined as

$$\text{Basis Net of Carry} = \text{Bond Price} - \text{Carry} - \text{Factor} \times \text{Futures Price}$$

we can calculate the futures price at expiration as

$$\text{Futures} = \frac{(\text{CTD Price} - \text{Carry} - \text{DOV})}{\text{CTD Factor}}$$

where DOV is our estimate of the value of the end-of-month switch option. This is the option that has value during the eight business days after the invoice price is fixed until delivery. Armed with this hypothetical futures price, we simply calculate the bases net of carry for all of the non-cheap bonds in the usual way.

The results of these exercises are instructive. On April 4, 2001, bond yields were trading around 5.5%. On that day, judging by the implied repo rates shown in Exhibit 2.1, the cheapest to deliver bond was 7-5/8% of 11/22. The cheapness of this issue is confirmed in the center column of Exhibit 2.10. The center column corresponds to no change in the level of yields. There we see that the basis net of carry of the 7-5/8% is shown to be 1+ (that is, 1.5/32nds) if yields are unchanged between April 4 and the expiration of futures trading on June 20. This is the lowest basis net of carry for any of the bonds in the deliverable set. Exhibit 2.10 shows that two other bonds would be equally cheap to deliver if yields remain unchanged. The basis net of carry for the 8% of 11/21 and the 8-1/8% of 5/21 is also 1+. The asterisk identifies the true cheapest to deliver issue for each yield scenario.

Just how secure are the 7-5/8% as cheapest to deliver? Consider what happens to the issue's projected basis as yields fall. By following the asterisk, you can see that if yields fall 10, 20, 30, or 40 basis points, the 8-1/8% will be the cheapest to deliver (as they will prove to be if yields remain unchanged). If yields fall 50 basis points, however, the 8-1/8% will be replaced by the 8-3/4% of 8/20. And if yields fall 60 basis points, the cheapest to deliver would be the 8-7/8% of 2/19.

As yields rise, we find that the cheapest to deliver marches steadily out along the maturity spectrum. In particular, we find the cheapest to deliver shifting to the 6-1/4% of 8/23 (yields up 10 or 20

EXHIBIT 2.10

BNOC Scenario Analysis, June 2001 Bond Futures
(April 5, 2001, Horizon date 6/20/01)

Issue		Base Yield	Yield Change (Basis Points)*				
			-60	-50	-40	-30	-20
5 3/8	2/15/31	5.523	161+	147	134	122	111
6 1/4	5/15/30	5.616	108	95+	84+	74+	65+
6 1/8	8/15/29	5.651	84	72+	62+	53	45
5 1/4	2/15/29	5.664	79	67+	57	47+	39
5 1/4	11/15/28	5.671	75	63+	53+	44	35+
5 1/2	8/15/28	5.671	71+	60+	50+	42	33+
6 1/8	11/15/27	5.678	60+	50+	41+	33+	26+
6 3/8	8/15/27	5.680	55	45+	37	29+	23
6 5/8	2/15/27	5.680	49	40	32+	25+	19+
6 1/2	11/15/26	5.681	47	38+	31	24+	19
6 3/4	2/15/26	5.682	42	34	27	21	16
6	2/15/26	5.682	43+	35+	28+	22+	17
6 7/8	8/15/26	5.680	33	26+	20+	16	11+
7 5/8	2/15/25	5.676	24	18+	14	10+	7+
7 1/2	11/15/24	5.673	24+	19	15	11+	8+
6 1/4	8/15/23	5.675	24+	19	14+	11	8
7 1/8	2/15/23	5.667	16+	12+	9	7	5
7 5/8	11/15/22	5.664	11+	8	5+	4	2+
7 1/4	8/15/22	5.663	14	10	7+	5+	4
8	11/15/21	5.654	6	3+	2	1	1
8 1/8	8/15/21	5.649	5	2+	1+	1	1
8 1/8	5/15/21	5.649	4	1+	0+*	0*	0*
7 7/8	2/15/21	5.644	7	4+	3	2+	2+
8 3/4	8/15/20	5.623	2	0+*	0+	1	2+
8 3/4	5/15/20	5.624	2+	1+	1+	2+	3+
8 1/2	2/15/20	5.620	4+	3	3	3+	4+
8 1/8	8/15/19	5.615	5+	4+	4	4+	5
8 7/8	2/15/19	5.598	1*	1	2	4	6
9	11/15/18	5.584	4+	5	6	8	11
9 1/8	5/15/18	5.569	3+	4+	6+	9+	12+
8 7/8	8/15/17	5.551	1+	3+	6	10	14
8 3/4	5/15/17	5.543	2	4+	7+	11+	15+
7 1/2	11/15/16	5.538	5+	7+	10	13	16+

§ *Yield changes shown are for on-the-run bond. Projections assume nonparallel yield changes for*
Source: JPMorgan

basis points), the 6% of 2/26 (yields up 30 or 40 basis points), and the 5-1/4% of 2/29 (yields up 50 or 60 basis points).

A Check on the Duration Rule of Thumb Note carefully at this point that the projected shifts in the cheapest to deliver conform well to our duration rule of thumb. In the face of falling yields, the bonds that are projected to become cheapest to deliver have lower durations than do the 7-5/8%. Their coupons are higher and their maturities shorter, both contributing to their lower duration.

In the face of rising yields, the bonds that are projected to become cheapest to deliver have higher durations than do the 7-

Yield Change (Basis Points)*							
-10	0	10	20	30	40	50	60
100+	91	83	75+	69+	64	61+	59
56+	49	43	37+	33+	30+	29+	29+
37	29+	24	19+	16	13+	13	13+
30+	23	17+	12	7+	4+	3+	2+
27+	20+	14+	9+	5	2	1*	0+*
25+	18+	13+	8+	4+	2	1	0+
19+	13+	9+	5+	3	1+	2	3
16+	11	7	4	2	0+	2	3+
14	9	6	3+	2	1+	3+	6
13+	8+	5+	3	2	1+	3+	5+
11	6+	4	2+	1+	1+	4	7
12	7+	4+	2+	1*	0+*	2	4+
8	5	3+	2+	2+	3+	7	11
5	3	3	3+	5	7+	12+	17+
6	4+	4+	5	6	8+	13+	19
5	2+	2*	1+*	2	3+	7	11
3	2	3	4	6	8+	14	19+
1+	1+	2+	4+	7+	11	17+	24
2+	2	3	4+	6+	10	15+	21+
1	1+	3+	6+	10	14+	21+	29
1	2	4	7	11	16	23+	31
0+*	1+*	4	7	11	16	23+	31
2+	3	5+	8	11+	16+	23+	30+
3+	5+	9	13	18	24	33	41+
5	7	10+	15	20	26	34+	43+
5+	7+	11	15	19+	25+	34	42+
6	7+	11	14+	19	24+	32+	40+
8+	11	15+	20+	26+	33+	42+	52
13+	16+	23+	26+	32+	40	49+	59+
16	19+	25	31	37+	45+	56	66
17+	22	28+	34+	42	50	61	71+
19+	24+	30+	37+	45	53	64	74+
20	24	29+	35	41+	48+	58	67

other bonds based on historical yield betas.

5/8%. As it happens, in all cases the coupons are lower and the maturities longer, both of which contribute to higher durations.

Effect of Changing Yields on a Bond's Basis Exhibit 2.10 provides us with a rough-and-ready way to determine the effect of changes in the level of yields on the basis net of carry for any given deliverable issue. The expensiveness of the 7-5/8% of 11/22 as yields either rise or fall is measured by its hypothetical net basis at expiration. For example, if yields were 60 basis points lower at expiration than they were on April 4, the projected basis of the 7-5/8% is shown to be 11+, or 11.5/32nds. If yields were 60 basis points higher, the projected basis of the 7-5/8% would be 24/32nds. Thus, a large enough change in yields in either direction from their April 4 levels would tend to increase the basis of the 7-5/8%. Thus, as our duration rule of thumb suggests, the basis of the 7-5/8% can be likened to a straddle or a strangle—a combination of a long call and a long put—which rises in value if yields either rise or fall.

The basis of a bond like the 8-7/8% of 2/19, a comparatively low-duration bond, behaves quite differently. A decrease in yields from the April 4 levels tends to decrease its basis, while an increase in yields tends to increase its basis. In this way, the basis of the 8-7/8% behaves like a put option on bonds, which gains in value as yields rise and bond prices fall.

A bond like the 5-1/2% of 8/28, a comparatively high-duration bond, behaves differently still. A decrease in yields tends to increase its basis, while any increase in yields tends to decrease its basis. In this way, the basis of the 5-1/2% is like a call option on bonds, gaining in value as yields fall and bond prices rise.

HISTORY OF THE MOST DELIVERED BOND

Our duration rule of thumb is borne out more or less well by the history of bond deliveries into the futures contract. In Exhibit 2.11, we show the history of the most delivered bond for each delivery month beginning with March 1987. From March 1987 through December 1999, the hypothetical yield used to calculate conversion factors was 8%. Beginning with the March 2000 contract, the hypothetical yield has been 6 %.

This change in the hypothetical coupon explains an interesting break in the series. Government bond yields tended to trade above 8% through much of the 1980s and the first year or two of the 1990s. After that, bond yields tended to fall, and as they did, deliveries tended to involve lower and lower-duration bonds. At one point, beginning in June of 1995, yields had fallen so low that the 11-1/4% of 2/15, the lowest duration bond in the deliverable set, became the cheapest to deliver and held that position almost without a break until December 1999. For all practical purposes, then, during the second half of the 1990s, the bond contract was dominated by a single low-duration bond.

Because this tended to rob the contract of its usefulness as a proxy for the long end of the Treasury curve, the Chicago Board of Trade finally broke with tradition and lowered the hypothetical

EXHIBIT 2.11

History of the Most Delivered Bond

Contract Month	Coupon	Maturity	Issue Price	Yield	Modified Duration
3/31/87	14	11/15/11	158.0	8.39	9.29
6/30/87	12	8/15/13	130.2	8.98	9.30
9/30/87	7 1/4	5/15/16	75.4	9.83	9.57
12/31/87	7 1/4	5/15/16	82.0	9.02	10.39
3/31/88	10 3/8	11/15/12	112.6	9.09	9.25
6/30/88	7 1/4	5/15/16	82.2	9.01	10.37
9/30/88	7 1/4	5/15/16	81.8	9.05	10.10
12/30/88	7 1/4	5/15/16	82.1	9.02	10.32
3/23/89	7 1/4	5/15/16	80.1	9.27	9.92
6/30/89	10 3/8	11/15/12	120.0	8.41	9.70
9/29/89	12	8/15/13	132.8	8.71	9.40
12/29/89	12	8/15/13	136.5	8.41	9.32
3/30/90	11 3/4	11/15/14	126.2	9.07	9.10
6/29/90	7 1/2	11/15/16	89.7	8.49	10.57
9/28/90	7 1/2	11/15/16	84.8	9.02	9.95
12/31/90	12	8/15/13	132.3	8.71	9.01
3/28/91	7 1/2	11/15/16	91.2	8.34	10.38
6/28/91	7 1/2	11/15/16	89.3	8.53	10.43
9/30/91	7 1/2	11/15/16	95.6	7.90	10.64
12/31/91	7 1/2	11/15/16	100.2	7.48	11.10
3/31/92	7 1/2	11/15/16	94.5	8.02	10.49
6/30/92	7 1/2	11/15/16	96.4	7.84	10.78
9/30/92	7 1/2	11/15/16	101.0	7.41	10.83
12/31/92	9 1/4	2/15/16	119.7	7.45	10.22
3/31/93	9 1/4	2/15/16	125.3	7.01	10.65
6/30/93	9 1/4	2/15/16	130.3	6.64	10.63
9/30/93	11 3/4	11/15/14	159.9	6.50	9.94
12/31/93	11 3/4	11/15/14	154.1	6.84	9.88
3/31/94	13 1/4	5/15/14	156.0	7.72	8.92
6/30/94	8 7/8	8/15/17	111.7	7.78	10.11
9/30/94	9	11/15/18	110.3	8.02	10.07
12/30/94	8 7/8	8/15/17	108.9	8.02	9.87
3/31/95	8 3/4	5/15/17	112.5	7.57	10.07
6/30/95	11 1/4	2/15/15	150.1	6.64	9.57
9/29/95	11 1/4	2/15/15	151.0	6.56	9.72
12/29/95	11 1/4	2/15/15	160.0	5.95	9.76
3/29/96	11 1/4	2/15/15	147.0	6.79	9.49
6/28/96	11 1/4	2/15/15	144.3	6.97	9.17
9/30/96	7 1/4	5/15/16	102.2	7.04	10.21
12/31/96	11 1/4	2/15/15	147.7	6.67	9.16
3/31/97	11 1/4	2/15/15	140.6	7.18	9.06
6/30/97	11 1/4	2/15/15	145.3	6.80	8.97
9/30/97	11 1/4	2/15/15	150.4	6.40	9.22

(Continued)

E X H I B I T   2.11

History of the Most Delivered Bond (*Continued*)

Contract Month	Coupon	Maturity	Issue Price	Yield	Modified Duration
12/31/97	11 1/4	2/15/15	156.7	5.93	9.16
3/31/98	11 1/4	2/15/15	156.3	5.92	9.25
6/30/98	11 1/4	2/15/15	160.3	5.62	9.12
9/30/98	11 1/4	2/15/15	170.2	4.94	9.43
12/31/98	11 1/4	2/15/15	165.3	5.21	9.08
3/31/99	11 1/4	2/15/15	155.9	5.81	8.96
6/30/99	11 1/4	2/15/15	149.7	6.23	8.57
9/30/99	11 1/4	2/15/15	146.7	6.42	8.59
12/31/99	11 1/4	2/15/15	141.3	6.83	8.21
3/31/00	8 3/4	5/15/17	126.4	6.22	9.50
6/30/00	7 7/8	2/15/21	118.8	6.24	10.72
9/29/00	8 1/8	5/15/21	123.3	6.12	10.72
12/29/00	9 1/4	2/15/16	138.0	5.52	8.96
3/30/01	8 3/4	5/15/20	136.9	5.58	10.41

yield for calculating conversion factors to 6%. This change immediately lowered the crossover points for bonds in the deliverable set. At the same level of yields, higher-duration bonds were cheaper to deliver than they had been. As a result, beginning with the March 2000 contract month, deliveries began to involve bonds that were further out in the maturity spectrum.

Examples of Buying and Selling the Cheapest to Deliver Basis

One way to get a clear understanding of the options that the long cedes to the short is to consider the potential gains and losses on long and short basis positions. In a long basis position, you are long the bonds and short an appropriate number of futures. In a short basis position, you are short the bonds and long an appropriate number of futures. As you will see, the long basis position is the safer of the two because it is the position that is short the futures and so is the position that enjoys a long position in the strategic delivery options.

Suppose, for example, that you decide to buy the basis of the 7-5/8% of 11/22 on April 5, 2001. Its basis at the close on April 4 was 18.09/32nds, and Exhibit 2.1 shows that there were 85 days remaining to the last delivery day. Given a term repo rate of 4.54%, total carry to last delivery would have been 13.56/32nds. Of the total basis of 18.09/32nds, the trader who buys the basis would get back 13.56 in carry. Thus, the net cost of buying the basis of the 7-5/8% was 4.53/32nds if held to the last trading day. In other words, the trader who buys the basis would pay 4.53/32nds for the right to participate in the delivery options.

Now then, in light of the basis net of carry estimates shown in Exhibit 2.10, we can get an idea of what the trader stands to make or lose if the position is unwound on the last trading day. If yields do not change, the basis net of carry of the 7-5/8% is expected to be about 1.5/32nds. (The bond's basis would be this amount plus any carry remaining between futures expiration and last delivery day.) In this case, the trader will have lost abut 3/32nds on the trade [= 4.5/32nds − 1.5/32nds].

The trade can make money, however, if yields rise or fall enough. For example, if yields fall 60 basis points, the projected basis net of carry of the 7-5/8% at expiration is 11.5/32nds. In this case, the trader will have made about 7/32nds [= 11.5/32nds − 4.5/32nds]. And if yields rise 60 basis points, the projected basis net of carry of the 7-5/8% at futures expiration is shown as 24/32nds. In this case, the trader will have made 19.5/32nds [= 24/32nds − 4.5/32nds].

In buying the basis, then, you have a position that will cost you money if yields do not change much between the time the trade is put on and the time the futures contract reaches expiration. Your position can make money if yields change enough, however, and can make a great deal if yields change a lot.

Options traders will recognize such a profit/loss profile. Buyers of options tend to lose money in quiet markets and to make money in volatile markets. In this sense, then, the person who is short a bond futures contract has a lot in common with the person who buys options. The chief difference between the two is that the seller of the futures contract has bought embedded options rather than explicit options.

If we turn the preceding trade around and sell the basis rather than buy it, we have a position that resembles a short option position. If yields remain unchanged, you would take in a net of 3/32nds on the short basis position (assuming the same repo rate of 4.54%). This is about as much as you can hope to make on the sale of the basis. If yields either rise or fall, however, the short basis position can lose money, and there is no particular limit on what the position might lose. In this sense, the seller of the basis (the buyer of the futures) has sold an option on interest rate volatility.

THE IMPORTANCE OF EMBEDDED OPTIONS

The resemblance between the behavior of a bond's basis as yields rise or fall and the behavior of one or another kind of bond option position is no accident. Apart from carry, the single most important determinant of the price and behavior of bond futures prices is the value of the short's strategic delivery options. In Chapter 3, we describe the mechanics of the short's various options. In Chapter 4, we explain how the options can be valued.

The Short's Strategic Delivery Options

The person who is short a bond futures contract has two kinds of options—what to deliver and when to deliver it. In practice, these two options take on a variety of forms that owe their richness in part to the complexity of the rules that govern trading and deliveries in the Chicago Board of Trade's futures contracts and in part to the complexity of the Treasury securities market itself.

The short's option to choose the cheapest to deliver bond really represents a set of options, some of which can be exercised before trading in the futures contract expires and some between the time trading expires and the last delivery day of the month. By market convention, the options that can be exercised any time before trading expires are known collectively as the "switch" or "quality" option. The value of the switch option depends on the following:

- Changes in yield levels
- Changes in yield spreads
- Anticipated new issues

We will deal with each separately.

The options that can be exercised during the week or so between the expiration of trading and the last delivery day in a contract month are known as the "end-of-month" option. Although the end-of-month option also revolves around changes in the cheapest to deliver, the reason why it works stems from the fact that the futures price is no longer free to vary with market forces. As a result, we find that absolute price volatility (basis point values, or BVP) rather than relative price volatility (duration) is what counts for the end-of-month option.

The short's option to choose the best time to deliver also represents a set of possible options that are driven by forces such as negative carry, volatility after the market closes, and the Chicago Board of Trade's daily price limits.

You should know as you work through the following sections that the order in which we present these three broad types of strategic delivery options is a good reflection of their relative importance to the behavior of bond and note futures prices. The switch option is far and away the most valuable of the options under almost all circumstances. The end-of-month option is the next most important, and the timing options usually contribute nothing at all.

This chapter provides a catalogue complete with descriptions of the full range of the short's strategic delivery options. We explain how to value the strategic delivery options and compare their values for the bond and note contracts in Chapter 4.

We set the stage here with a description of the Chicago Board of Trade's delivery process and key dates and times around the delivery month.

STRUCTURE OF THE DELIVERY PROCESS

A solid understanding of the timing options that are embedded in the bond and note contracts requires familiarity with the details of the three-day delivery process and the key dates in the contract month.

Delivery Process

The delivery process requires three days, which are known in the street as Tender Day, Notice Day, and Delivery Day (see Exhibit 3.1). The process is highly structured, and each day contains one or more important deadlines.

Tender Day   Tender Day, or Position Day (the Board of Trade's official designation), is the day on which the short gives official notice that delivery will be made. The exchange's deadline for getting delivery notices from clearing members is 8 p.m. Chicago time. Most clearing members set earlier deadlines (typically one to three hours earlier) for getting delivery notices from their customers. Notice that the deadline for submitting a notice of delivery

EXHIBIT 3.1

CBOT Delivery Process (Chicago Time)

Tender (Position) Day	7:20 a.m.	Futures Market opens
	2:00 p.m.	Futures Market closes
	5:00 (8:00) p.m.	Clearing member's deadline for short to give delivery notice (Exchange deadline in parentheses)
Notice (Intention) Day	7:20 a.m.	Clearing member's deadline for advising long
	1:00 p.m.	Deadline for short to nominate bond to be delivered; long advised
	2:00 p.m.	Deadline for long to give bank information to short
Delivery Day	9:00 a.m.	Deadline for short to deliver bond to clearing member's bank
	1:00 p.m.	Deadline for short's clearing member to deliver bond and for the long to pay for the bond

is several hours after the close of trading for the day in the futures market, a timing lag that is the source of the "wild card" option.

Notice Day   The second day in the delivery process is called Notice Day in the street and Intention Day by the Chicago Board of Trade. This is the day the short must say precisely which bond will be used for delivery. The exchange deadline for stating the specific issue is 2 p.m. (and the clearing member's deadline is one hour earlier), which is almost a full day after the delivery notice is filed. This one-day lag is the source of a one-day switch option.

Delivery Day   The third day in the delivery process is called Delivery Day by everyone. The exchange's deadline for delivering the bond to the long's bank is 1 p.m. Chicago time, and the penalties for missing this deadline can be severe. The Chicago Board of Trade retains the right to impose a fine on the short for failing to deliver the nominated bond to the long's bank. Further, the short must make do with whatever bond the exchange chooses to deliver, which need not be the cheapest to deliver. Such a penalty is far more serious than the cost of failing to deliver in the cash market for Treasuries and is sufficiently large to limit the flexibility of the short in exercising the end-of-month option.

Because the penalties for failing to deliver on time are high, it is common (and recommended) for shorts intending to deliver to have physical possession of the cheapest to deliver bond at least two days before delivery day. This usually requires that the short does not finance the bond through a normal repo transaction for the last two days before delivery. Instead, to ensure that the short has the bond "in the box," the position is financed either at uncollateralized lending rates or through a transaction known as a *triparty repo agreement*. In a triparty repo transaction, the bond is lent to another party but is held in custody by the short's clearing member. This ensures that the bond is available for delivery to the exchange on delivery day.

Delivery Month

Deliveries can be made on any business day during the contract month (see Exhibit 3.2). What this means in practice is that the first Tender Day actually falls on the second business day before the beginning of the contract month. This two-day outcropping provides a variant of the wild card play, stemming in this case from the daily price limits that apply outside the contract month.

Further, because trading in Treasury bond, 10-year, and 5-year note futures stops on the eighth business day before the end of the contract month, deliveries can be made on any day during the seven business days that follow the expiration of trading. The weeklong lag between the close of trading and the last possible delivery day is the source of the "end-of-month option."

This comparatively complicated set of arrangements—taken together with the widely varied set of bonds that are eligible for delivery—gives the short plenty of room to maneuver.

THE SWITCH OPTION

The switch option is driven by any change in the cheapest to deliver any time before futures contract trading expires. During this time, the futures price is free to vary with market forces and to reflect changes in the cheapest to deliver. In Chapter 2, we showed that a change in the cheapest to deliver can happen because of a change in the level of yields. We also noted that relative yields matter, and we will show here that changes in yield spreads can cause the cheapest to deliver to change as well. The switch option can also be affected by the possibility that a newly issued bond or note will be the cheapest to deliver.

E X H I B I T   3.2

Contract Month in Chicago
(Actual Dates for March 2004 Contract)

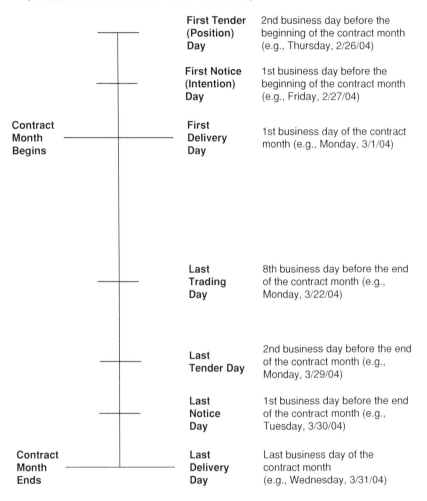

	First Tender (Position) Day	2nd business day before the beginning of the contract month (e.g., Thursday, 2/26/04)
	First Notice (Intention) Day	1st business day before the beginning of the contract month (e.g., Friday, 2/27/04)
Contract Month Begins	**First Delivery Day**	1st business day of the contract month (e.g., Monday, 3/1/04)
	Last Trading Day	8th business day before the end of the contract month (e.g., Monday, 3/22/04)
	Last Tender Day	2nd business day before the end of the contract month (e.g., Monday, 3/29/04)
	Last Notice Day	1st business day before the end of the contract month (e.g., Tuesday, 3/30/04)
Contract Month Ends	**Last Delivery Day**	Last business day of the contract month (e.g., Wednesday, 3/31/04)

Parallel Changes in Yield Levels

The bond that is cheapest to deliver is systematically related to the level of yields. Exhibit 3.3, which we have reproduced from Chapter 2, shows that the different *relative* sensitivities of the prices of deliverable bonds tend to cause high-duration bonds to be cheap to deliver when yields are high, low-duration bonds to be cheap to deliver when yields are low, and middling-duration bonds to be cheap to deliver when yields are at middling levels.

EXHIBIT 3.3

Cash/Futures Price Relationships

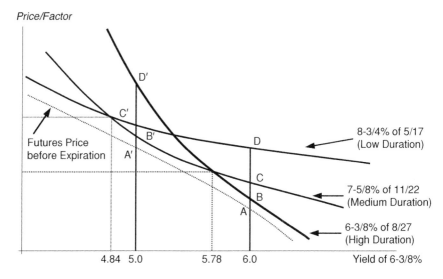

Price/Factor

8-3/4% of 5/17 (Low Duration)

7-5/8% of 11/22 (Medium Duration)

6-3/8% of 8/27 (High Duration)

Futures Price before Expiration

4.84   5.0   5.78   6.0   Yield of 6-3/8%

This systematic relationship between the level of yields and the cheapest to deliver imparts familiar option properties to the bases of competing bonds. The basis of a high-duration bond, for example, tends to behave like a call option on bonds, rising in value as yields fall and bond prices rise. The basis of a low-duration bond, in contrast, tends to behave like a put option, and the basis of the middling-duration bond would behave like a straddle or strangle, which is a combination of a call and a put.

Exhibit 3.3 illustrates the effect of a change in yields on the values of the competing bonds' bases. For example, if the yield of the 6-3/8% of 8/27 is 6%, the converted price of the 6-3/8% equals B, and we see that the 6-3/8% are cheapest to deliver. Given the projected futures price relationship, we also see that the futures price would equal A. Now, if yields fall to 5%, the 6-3/8% would be replaced by the 7-5/8% of 11/22 as cheapest to deliver, and the futures price would only increase to A'. At the same time, the converted price of the 6-3/8% would increase to D'. Thus, as yields fall from 6% to 5%, the spread between the converted price of the 6-3/8% and the futures price would increase from AB to A'D'. Because the spread between a bond's converted price and the futures price equals

$$\frac{\text{Price}}{\text{Factor}} - \text{Futures} = \frac{\text{Basis}}{\text{Factor}}$$

we can conclude that the basis of the 6-3/8% of 8/27 behaves like a call option on a bond or bond futures contract. That is, as yields fall and bond prices rise, the value of the 6-3/8% basis rises.

The practical consequences of these price/yield relationships for those who trade bond futures or use bond futures to hedge can be very important. Compare, for example, the choice between buying the 6-3/8% and buying a bond futures contract as ways of establishing a long position in the bond market. If yields do in fact fall, the gain on the 6-3/8% would be greater than the gain on the futures contract because of the change in the cheapest to deliver. The difference in the performance of the two positions reflects the value of the short's right to substitute a cheaper bond when yields fall.

For someone who wishes to short the market, the short's right to substitute a cheaper bond imparts desirable profit-and-loss characteristics to bond futures. As yields fall, for example, the positive convexity in a conventional, noncallable Treasury bond causes losses to accelerate on a short bond position. On the other hand, the effect of changes in the cheapest to deliver may actually cause the losses on a short bond futures position to decelerate. In other words, bond futures can exhibit negative convexity, which reflects the behavior of the delivery options that are embedded in the futures contract.

To compensate for the difference in performance, a bond futures price must be lower than a bond forward price. For example, one would buy a bond futures contract only if the price paid is less than one would pay for the cheapest to deliver in the forward market. On the other side, the seller is willing to accept less. Just how much less depends on how much the delivery options are thought to be worth, which we discuss in Chapter 4.

> **Important Point** One consequence of the futures price being lower than the cheapest to deliver's forward price is that the cheapest to deliver's basis net of carry will be positive. A second consequence is that the cheapest to deliver's implied repo rate will be lower than the issue's term repo rate. Thus, the cheapest to deliver's basis net of carry can be read as a measure of the value the basis market places on the strategic delivery options. So can the difference between the cheapest to deliver's implied repo rate and the market repo rate.

Changes in Yield Spreads

Most of what we have said about changes in yield levels so far has been based on parallel shifts in the yield curve. In other words, we have supposed that all bond and note yields rise and fall by the same number of basis points. In practice, however, we find that yields do not rise or fall in parallel. Instead, we find a rather strong tendency for the deliverable yield curve to steepen as yields fall and to flatten as yields rise. Also, we find that yield spreads among deliverable bonds and notes can change a great deal when yields are neither rising nor falling.

A failure to take changes in yield spreads into account can lead to serious mispricings of bond and note futures. The systematic tendency for the slope of the yield curve to change as yields rise or fall, for example, tends to reduce the value of the strategic delivery options in bond futures. Nonsystematic changes in yield spreads, on the other hand, have the effect of increasing the value of the delivery options in bond and note futures.

Systematic Changes in Yield Spreads Exhibit 3.4 shows how the yield spread between the 6-3/8% of 8/27 and the 8-7/8% of 8/17 behaved as yields on the 6-3/8% ranged between 5.40% and 6.20% from September 2000 to September 2001. Note the very strong

E X H I B I T   3.4

Yield Spread Relationships
(September 2000–September 2001)

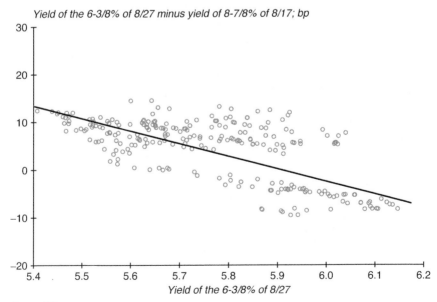

Yield of the 6-3/8% of 8/27 minus yield of 8-7/8% of 8/17; bp

Yield of the 6-3/8% of 8/27

Source: *JPMorgan*

systematic tendency for this yield spread to fall as the general level of yields rises. Because the 6-3/8% have the longer maturity, this can be also read as a flattening of an otherwise positively sloped yield curve as yields rise, or as a steepening of the yield curve as yields fall. If you look at the behavior of the 2017 to 2027 yield curve during this period, you find that each 10 basis point increase in the level of yields of the 6-3/8% of 8/27 produced a 2.3 basis point flattening in the yield curve.

How does this affect the behavior of the bond basis? Consider the setting shown in Exhibit 3.5. The converted prices of the 6-3/8% of 8/27 and of the 8-7/8% of 8/17 are measured along the vertical axis and the yield of the 6-3/8% along the horizontal axis. Given this setting, we show one converted price/yield relationship for the 6-3/8%, but we show two for the 8-7/8%. The lower of the two corresponds to the yield that we have labeled "Today's Yield Spread" and is the price/yield relationship that one would observe if the yield spread between the two issues never changed. That is, the lower price/yield relationship for the 8-7/8% is drawn on the assumption that all yields rise and fall by the same number of basis points. If this were true, we would expect the 6-3/8% and the 8-7/8% to be equally cheap to

EXHIBIT 3.5

Effect of Yield Spread Changes on 6-3/8% Basis

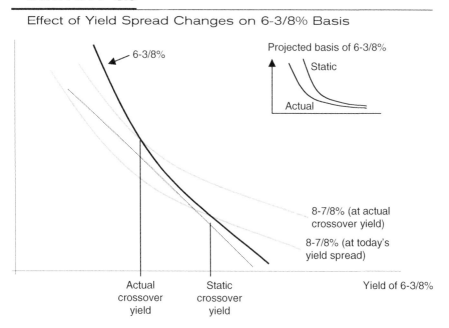

deliver at what we have labeled the "Static Crossover Yield." At yields above this, the 6-3/8% are cheapest to deliver. At yields below this, the 8-7/8% are cheapest to deliver. And the projected futures price would correspond to the lower of the two gray colored curves.

If, however, the deliverable yield curve steepens (6-3/8% of 8/27 yield increases relative to 8-7/8% of 8/17 yield) whenever yields fall, a drop in the yield of the 6-3/8% will be accompanied by a larger drop in the yield of the 8-7/8%, and so its price/yield relationship will shift upward relative to that of the 6-3/8%. In other words, a drop in yields will tend to cause the 8-7/8% to become expensive relative to the 6-3/8%. If this happens, we can see in Exhibit 3.5 that the actual crossover yield is lower than the static cross yield. We can also see that the projected futures price would correspond to the higher of the two gray colored curves.

The effect of the systematic change that we have observed in yield spreads as yields rise and fall is to reduce the value of the switch option in bond futures. In fact, the effect is very much like the effect that one would have on the price of a call option if the strike price were always raised somewhat as the underlying price rose, or if the strike price of a put were pushed down whenever the underlying price fell. Now, if we trace out the basis of the 6-3/8%, we find that it is everywhere smaller than it would be if yields always moved in parallel. And, although it is a little harder to detect in Exhibit 3.5, so would the basis of the 8-7/8%.

Nonsystematic Yield Spread Volatility   An increase in one bond or note's yield relative to other bonds or notes in the deliverable set will make it less expensive to deliver and, if the increase is large enough, can make it cheapest to deliver. Spreads among yields on issues in the deliverable set can be affected by several things. A steepening of the yield curve, for example, will increase the yields of the longer-dated issues in the set relative to the yield of the shorter-dated issues. A temporary squeeze on a particular issue might make it expensive to deliver. A surprise reduction in 30-year Treasury bond issuance might make long-duration bonds expensive to deliver.

Of these various possible reasons for changes in yield spreads, what matters most for the basis of Treasury bond and 10-year Treasury note contracts are changes in the slope of the yield curve within the deliverable sets.

Exhibit 3.6 illustrates an episode that caused a shift in the cheapest to deliver bond into the March 2000 Treasury bond contract. During the early part of January 2000, the spread between the yield

EXHIBIT 3.6

Nonsystematic Changes in Yield Spreads

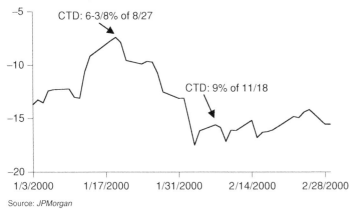

6-3/8% of 8/27 yield - 9% of 11/18 yield; bp

Source: *JPMorgan*

on the 6-3/8% of 8/27 and the 9% of 11/18 traded between −13 and −7 basis points (bp). During this time, the 6-3/8% of 8/27 were the cheapest to deliver. Then, in mid-January, the Treasury announced a buyback plan for Treasury bonds, causing the long-end of the bond curve to richen and the deliverable bond curve to flatten. When the yield spread between 8/27 and 11/18 Treasuries declined to −17 bp, the 9% of 11/18 replaced the 6-3/8% of 8/27 as cheapest to deliver. As it happened in this episode, the yield curve flattened as yields were falling, not as yields were rising. Thus, this is an example of a nonsystematic change in yield spreads.

The effect of a change in yield spreads on a bond's basis is illustrated in Exhibit 3.7. As the chart shows, the 6-3/8% of 8/27 is initially cheapest to deliver and the converted price/yield relationship for this issue lies below that of the converted price/yield line for the 9% of 11/18.

If the yield curve flattens, however, the converted price of the 6-3/8% of 8/27 increases relative to that of the converted price of the 9% of 11/18. And if the yield curve flattens enough, the 8/27 Treasury will richen enough to allow the 9% of 11/18 to become cheapest to deliver.

The effect of the change in the slope of the yield curve on the bases of the two issues is also apparent in Exhibit 3.7. At the outset, when the 6-3/8% of 8/27 is cheapest to deliver, its basis is comparatively small and reflects mainly the value of carry. The basis of the

EXHIBIT 3.7

Effect of Change in Yield Spreads on the
Cheapest to Deliver

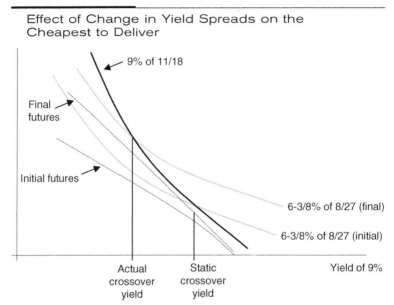

11/18 issue, which is expensive to deliver, is comparatively large. With the rotation of the yield curve, the roles and bases of the two bonds are reversed. The basis of the 6-3/8% of 8/27 increases to reflect its new expensiveness, while the basis of the newly cheap 9% of 11/18 collapses.

As Exhibit 3.8 highlights, this is precisely what happened to 2027 and 2018 bond bases following the Treasury buyback announcement in early 2000. The basis net of carry of the 6-3/8% of 8/27 widened from 7/32nds to 28/32nds from January 13 to February 3 of 2000. During the same time period, the basis net of carry of the 9% of 11/18 declined from 50/32nds to 8/32nds.

The short's right to swap out of the 27-year bond and into an appropriate position in the 18-year bond is like a call option on the yield spread between the two issues. Such an option is valuable if yield spread changes are both likely enough and large enough to cause changes in the cheapest to deliver. We show in Chapter 6 that nonsystematic yield spread volatility has been a source of considerable delivery option value in the Treasury bond and 10-year Treasury note contracts over the past few years.

Anticipated New Issues   As long as a bond or note meets the Chicago Board of Trade's eligibility requirements on the first delivery day of the contract month, it can be delivered. Thus, any bond or note issued before the first delivery day may be eligible for delivery.

E X H I B I T   3.8

Basis Net of Carry of 11/18 and 8/27
Treasury

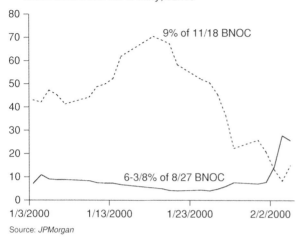

March 2000 basis net of carry; 32nds

Source: JPMorgan

The characteristics of a newly issued bond or note cannot be known with certainty, but they can be predicted with increasing accuracy and confidence as the event approaches. First, the date and maturity of the issue are fairly easy to pin down. The U.S. Treasury follows a regular funding cycle with auctions falling on regular dates. For example, 2-year and 5-year Treasuries currently are auctioned monthly; 10-year Treasuries are auctioned eight times a year with new issues in February, May, August, and November and reopenings in March, June, September, and December.

Second, the Treasury only rarely changes the maturity and call features of the bonds that it issues. For example, the Treasury switched from monthly to quarterly issuance of 5-year Treasuries in July 1998, and then back to monthly issuance in August of 2003. Similarly, in October of 2001, the Treasury surprised the market by announcing the suspension of 30-year Treasury bond issuance. In May 2005, the Treasury announced that it is considering resuming the issuance of 30-year bonds starting in February 2006.

In general, however, traders can predict the maturity of new Treasury issues with considerable precision. What is more difficult is predicting the coupon of the issue. The Treasury tends to set the coupon for a new issue so that the issue's initial price will be at or slightly below par. What can only be guessed is the level of yields at the time of the auction.

Even so, valuing the anticipated new issue option is no more difficult than valuing any of the other switch options. For example, if yields are high, the new issue's coupon will be high as well. High yields favor the delivery of high-duration issues, and the high coupon will tend to give the newly issued bond or note a low duration. Thus, the newly issued bond or note likely would not be the cheapest to deliver if yields are high. Similarly, if yields are low, the new issue would have a low coupon. But low yields favor the delivery of low-duration issues, and its coupon issue would tend to give the new issue a high duration.

Further, a new issue tends to trade at a slightly lower yield than seasoned bonds simply because it is "on the run" and liquid. The comparatively lower yield tends to make a new issue expensive to deliver.

As a result, the anticipated new issue option usually is worth comparatively little. The chief exception to this rule has occurred in the 5-year and 10-year Treasury note contracts in periods when yields were high but falling. The high yields meant that high-duration notes were favored for delivery while the falling yields meant that the "new guy" had both the lowest coupon and longest maturity combining to produce the highest duration of any note in the deliverable set. In these periods, the anticipated new issue played an important role in setting note futures prices.

The End-of-Month Option

Once trading in an expiring futures contract has closed on the last day of trading, the settlement price used in calculating delivery invoices is fixed. Even so, substantial changes in cash prices can occur during the seven business days between the last day of trading and the last delivery day. As a result, the cheapest bond to deliver may change between the time futures trading stops and the last possible delivery day. In a sufficiently volatile market, the deliverable bond can change more than once during this period.

The short's right to swap from an expensive bond into a newly cheap bond after the last day of trading is generally known as the "end-of-month" option.

The forces that drive the end-of-month option are quite a bit different from those that drive a change in the cheapest to deliver while futures are still trading. One peculiar result of these differences is that a change in yields that would make a bond cheap to deliver before the expiration of futures trading often will tend to make the bond expensive to deliver once futures trading has expired.

The resolution to this paradox is this. A high-coupon issue will have a high basis point value but will tend to have a low duration. On the other hand, a low-coupon issue will have a low basis point value but will tend to have a high duration. Thus, although a rise in interest rates will tend to make high-duration issues cheap to deliver before the close of trading, a rise in interest rates will tend to make high basis point value issues cheap to deliver. Because the high basis point issues will tend to have the lower durations, we may well find that a rise in rates will cause a low-duration issue to become cheap to deliver after trading in the futures contract has expired and the futures price is fixed. Of course, long maturity issues will tend to have both high durations and high basis point values, and so there can be exceptions to this paradox as well.

Hedge Ratios Fixing the settlement price at the expiration of futures trading has one immediate implication: Hedge ratios must be adjusted. Each short futures position that remains open after the close of trading calls for the delivery of $100,000 par value of eligible bonds irrespective of the bonds' market price. The correct ratio is then one-to-one after the close of trading rather than the C (conversion factor) futures contracts for each $100,000 par value of bonds that would be held in a conventional basis position. The reason for this sharp change in hedge ratios is that each bond's invoice price is fixed for good once the final bell has rung for the expiring contract.

During the week between the last day of trading and the last delivery day, the short can exploit the use of conversion factors with a vengeance. The resulting end-of-month option can be quite valuable, even though it lasts only a week. For that matter, it is the value of the end-of-month option that can prevent the cheapest to deliver's basis net of carry from approaching zero on the last trading day.

Payoff to the End-of-Month Option Suppose, for the purposes of this example, that the three bonds shown in Exhibit 3.9 are in the running for cheapest to deliver. Of the three, the 7-1/4% of 8/22 with a basis net of carry equal to zero on the last day of trading is

EXHIBIT 3.9

How the End-of-Month Option Works

Bond	Yield	Basis Net of Carry (32nds)	BPV (32nds)	Yield Change Needed to Become CTD
6-1/4% of 8/23	5.649	1.0	4.25	-4.0
7-1/4% of 8/22	5.639	0.0	4.50	0.0
8-3/4% of 8/20	5.602	1.5	4.70	7.5

the cheapest. The basis net of carry for the other two issues shown range from 1/32nd for the 6-1/4% of 8/23, to 1.5/32nds for the 8-3/4% of 8/20.

The key to understanding the payoff to the end-of-month option is that the invoice price for each deliverable bond is carved in stone once the closing bell has rung and the final settlement price for the expiring futures contract has been established. At this point, the net cost to delivering any of the eligible bonds into the futures contract is simply

Net Cost = Cash Price – (Factor × Final Futures Settlement Price) – Carry

For example, if one were to buy $100,000 par value of the 7-1/4% of 8/22 and sell one futures contract, both at the closing bell, the net cost including carry of delivering the 7-1/4% on the last delivery day would be zero. The net cost of doing the same transaction with the 8-3/4% would be 1.5/32nds, or about $46.88 per $100,000 par value of the bond.

Once the final futures settlement price is known, the only thing that can vary is the bond's cash price. But, as shown in Exhibit 3.9, the prices of the bonds that are vying to be cheapest to deliver do not display the same sensitivity to changes in yields.

For example, a 1-basis-point change in the yield of the 7-1/4% would cause its price to change by 4.5/32nds. A 1-basis-point change in the yield of the 8-3/4% would cause its price to change by 4.7/32nds. Thus, if yields rise, the price of the 8-3/4% will fall faster than the price of the 7-1/4%. If yields rise enough, the net cost of delivering the 8-3/4% might actually be lower than that for the 7-1/4%, and it could pay to swap out of the 7-1/4% and into the 8-3/4%. As shown in Exhibit 3.9, the increase in yields needed for the 8-3/4% to overtake the 7-1/4% as cheapest to deliver is 7.5 basis points [=1.5/(4.7 – 4.5)].

We can also see in Exhibit 3.9 that the price value of a basis point for the 6-1/4% is only 4.25/32nds. Thus, if yields fall, the price of the 6-1/4% will rise more slowly than the price of the 7-1/4%. If yields fall enough, the net cost of delivering the 6-1/4% might turn out to be lower than the net cost of delivering the 7-1/4%, and it could pay to swap out of the 7-1/4% and into the 6-1/4%. As Exhibit 3.9 shows, the crossover occurs with a drop in yields of 4 basis points [=1/(4.5 – 4.25)].

Several possible yield change outcomes are shown in Exhibit 3.10. With yields unchanged between the last day of trading and the last delivery day, the 7-1/4% would continue to have a basis net

EXHIBIT 3.10

Bond Price Less Invoice Price and Carry to Last Delivery Day

Bond	Yield Change (bps)						
	30	20	10	0	-10	-20	-30
1/4% of 8/23	-126.5	-84.0	-41.5	1.0	43.5	86.0	128.5
1/4% of 8/22	-135.0	-90.0	-45.0	0.0	45.0	90.0	135.0
3/4% of 8/20	-139.5	-92.5	-45.5	1.5	48.5	95.5	142.5

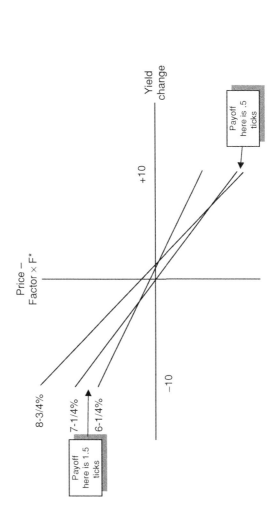

of carry (that is, a bond price net of invoice price and carry) equal to zero. In contrast, the net cost of delivering any of the other bonds would be positive.

If yields were to increase 10 basis points any time after the close of trading, however, the price of the 8-3/4% would fall 47/32nds [= 10 basis points × 4.7/32nds], while the price of the 7-1/4% would fall only 45/32nds. Thus, even though the 8-3/4% started out 1.5/32nds more expensive to deliver, it would become 0.5/32nds cheaper to deliver than the 7-1/4%. The relative cheapness of the 8-3/4% is determined by comparing its net cost of delivery of −45.5/32nds with the net cost of −45.0/32nds of delivering the 7-1/4%.

Therefore, if yields increase 10 basis points, the net payoff to swapping out of the 7-1/4% and into the 8-3/4% is 0.5/32nds.

If yields were to fall 10 basis points, on the other hand, the price of the 6-1/4% would increase only 42.5/32nds, while the price of the 7-1/4% would rise 45/32nds. Thus, even though the 6-1/4% is 1/32nds more expensive to deliver at the outset, it would become 1.5/32nds cheaper to deliver than the 7-1/4%.

In this case, swapping out of the 7-1/4% and into the 6-1/4% would produce a net payoff of 1.5/32nds.

What Does the Option Cost? The cost of playing the end-of-month option depends entirely on the basis net of carry of the cheapest to deliver bond at the close of trading in the expiring contract. In this example, the cost is zero because the basis net of carry for the 7-1/4% is zero. In a more likely setting, the basis net of carry, even for the cheapest to deliver, would be something greater than zero at expiration to reflect the value of the end-of-month option.

What Does the Payoff Look Like? Given the bonds and yields that we have used in this illustration, the payoff to the end-of-month option, which is shown in Exhibit 3.11, would look a lot like that of a long strangle. The cost of the option is zero, and the payoff to the end-of-month option would be positive as long as yields increase or decrease enough to cause a switch in the cheapest to deliver bond.

If yields rise more than 7.5 basis points, the 8-3/4% would kick in as cheapest to deliver, and the end-of-month option will be in the money. If yields were to fall more than 4 basis points, the 6-1/4% would become cheap to deliver, and again the end-of-month option would be in the money.

Of course, the size of the payoff depends on the size of the position. Consider, for example, a $100 million position in the 7-1/4% basis. At this size, the payoff to the end-of-month option is nearly

EXHIBIT 3.11

Projected End-of-Month Option Payoffs

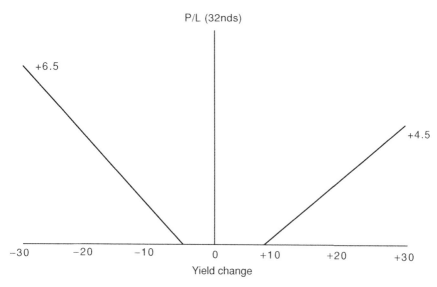

P/L (32nds)

+6.5

+4.5

−30   −20   −10   0   +10   +20   +30

Yield change

$5,000 for every 1 basis point increase in yields. This is roughly the same as that on a short position of 38 futures contracts. In the other direction, as yields are falling, the payoff to the end-of-month option is about the same as that on a long position of 51 futures.

Repeated Plays   It is worth noting that the end-of-month option can be exercised as often as opportunities permit. Once a switch from one bond to a cheaper bond has been made, all that is required to precipitate another exercise is a large enough change in yields in the right direction to produce another change in the cheapest to deliver.

A Word of Caution   The single greatest danger in exercising the end-of-month option is waiting too long. The penalty for failing to deliver into a bond futures contract can be severe, and so you want to be sure to have the bonds "in the box" in time to make delivery.

This means that the last possible day on which to make a switch is the second-to-last business day of the contract month. The next-to-last business day does not work. The rules of the Chicago Board of Trade require that bonds be delivered by 9 a.m. Chicago time the morning of delivery. Under regular settlement in a bond transaction, the bond is not received by the Fed wire until 2 p.m. the afternoon following the trade. Therefore, if you were to sell the 7-1/4% and buy the 8-3/4% on the next-to-last business day in the delivery month, you would not have the bonds in time to redeliver them into the bond contract.

Of course, even if you switch bonds in what seems like ample time to receive the new bonds, the seller of the bonds can still fail to deliver to you. To protect against such a "fail," the end-of-month option player can hold the original bonds until the new bonds have been received. That is, the end-of-month option player can plan to fail to deliver, which is substantially less costly in the cash market than is failure to deliver into the bond futures contract. Then, if the new bonds don't arrive on time, the worst that can happen is that the trader delivers the original bonds, and the valuable end-of-month option remains unexercised. In this way, the cost of a fail is a forgone opportunity to exercise a valuable end-of-month option.

Also, because you must have the bonds in the box the day before you make delivery, you cannot repo the bonds out (that is, finance the bonds through a repurchase agreement) the last day before delivery. The practical consequence of this is that you must finance the bond position at a rate that likely is substantially higher than the repo rate. This is a cost of buying the basis that must be reckoned with when you are evaluating any basis trade.

The problems that are posed by the delivery process underscore the importance of understanding both the futures market's requirements and the cash market's practices before undertaking to trade the basis.

A Minor End-of-Month Option   Notice of delivery must be given two business days before the bonds are actually delivered, but the short has almost a whole day after he or she gives notice of delivery to decide on the actual bond to deliver. Since the settlement price is already determined, the short has a very short-term option of the type he or she has after the last trading day. Because it lasts less than a day, it has almost no value.

TIMING OPTIONS

In addition to deciding which bond to deliver, the short decides when to make delivery. Delivery can take place on any business day in the delivery month. In all, there are three timing options, which we will call options on

- Carry
- Aftermarket price moves
- Limit moves

Only the second of these has a name that people widely recognize—that is, the "wild card" option.

As a practical matter, these options are not especially valuable, and we will give them the space in this chapter that their value warrants.

Carry   Generally, the decision to deliver at the beginning or end of the delivery month is influenced by the repo (financing) rate on the bond that is cheapest to deliver. If the repo rate is less than the current yield on the bond, carry will be positive. A position that is long bonds and short futures will have positive cash flow, and the inclination will be to defer delivery. This inclination is borne out by the higher implied repo rates to the last delivery day that are evident in Exhibit 2.1. Conversely, when carry is negative, it may pay to deliver at the beginning of the delivery month. The advantage in doing so is to avoid one month's worth of negative carry. The disadvantage, and what makes this problem so nettlesome when carry is negative, is that the short gives up the remaining value of the other strategic delivery options. As a result, the short might defer delivery even if carry is slightly negative. Evidence of these tensions was apparent in Exhibit 2.4, which shows deliveries during a month in which carry was positive for 5s, 10s, and bonds, but negative for 2s. All of the 5s, 10s, and bonds were delivered on the last business day of the month, while deliveries of the 2s were strung out over the month.

If the repo rate is higher than the current coupon yield, delivering at the beginning of the month rather than at the end saves a month's worth of negative carry. For example, if the repo rate were 100 basis points higher than the coupon yield, a month's negative carry amounts to about 8 basis points [= 100 basis points/12 months], or 0.08% of the futures invoice price.

Whether the right to avoid negative carry is worth anything depends on the likelihood of facing a negatively sloped yield curve. For example, during the period from late 1997 through 1998, the slope of the yield curve was sufficiently flat that early delivery, particularly in 2-year and 5-year futures occurred regularly.

The Wild Card   The wild card is one of the short's delivery options that is triggered by a large move in the cash market after trading has closed for the day. If this move happens during a delivery month, such a move can make it worth the short's while to deliver early, even at the cost of giving up a valuable basis position.

To understand how the wild card works, suppose that you are long $100 million of the 8-3/4% of 8/20, which is cheapest to deliver into the June 2001 bond futures contract. Given the issue's conversion factor of 1.3093, you would be short 1,309 futures contracts. Your long position in $100 million of the bonds is only enough to make delivery on 1,000 of these contracts. To make delivery on the rest, you would have to buy an additional $30.9 million of the bonds in the cash market. This is known as "covering the tail" and is the key to the success of the wild card play.

Once futures trading has closed for the day, the futures invoice price is fixed for the day as well. Trading in the cash bond market will continue, however. And if cash bond prices fall sharply after the close, the short may have a chance to "cover the tail" on his or her basis position at a cash price that is low enough to justify losing the value of the basis.

Suppose, for the sake of this example, that futures have closed at a price of 104-10/32nds and that the basis of the 8-3/4% of 8/20 is worth 6/32nds. If the short decides to deliver early, giving up this basis entails a loss of $187,500 [=6/32nds × $31.25 × (100 million/100,000)]. The invoice price net of accrued interest for delivering the 8-3/4% is 136.576356 [= 1.3093 × 104.3125]. To justify making delivery early, the short has to be able to buy the additional $30.9 million bonds enough below this price to make up for a loss of $187,500 on the basis.

In this example, the price would have to be 0.6068 price points [= ($187,500/$30,900) × 100], or just over 19/32nds below the futures invoice price. That is, the price of the 8-3/4% of 8/20 would have to fall to 135-31/32nds to just break even on the wild card. If the price fell further than this, playing the wild card would produce a gain.

Following is a simple rule of thumb for reckoning the break-even on the wild card:

$$(C - 1) \times (C \times F - P) = B$$

where

C	is the bond's conversion factor
F	is the closing futures price
P	is the aftermarket price of the bond in the cash market
B	is where you expect the bond's basis to open when trading resumes

On the left-hand side is the profit from covering the tail on the position. On the right-hand side is the sacrifice associated with giving up the bond's basis if you make early delivery.

For the 8-3/4%, the price of the bond in aftermarket trading would have to be 19.4/32nds [=6/32nds / 0.3093] lower than its futures invoice price. Given a basis of 6/32nds, the bond's price would have to fall a total of 25.4/32nds after the close of futures trading for the day.

If the conversion factor is greater than 1, a drop in the issue's price is required to make the wild card profitable. If the conversion factor is less than 1, an increase is required. The whole idea behind covering the tail in the cash market is that you need the bonds to make delivery on your short futures position. Once you have given notice that you intend to make delivery, though, you should be absolutely sure that the bonds or notes you are buying will be available to you in time to turn around and redeliver on your futures.

Limit Moves The expiring bond contract at the Chicago Board of Trade has no price limits in its delivery month. The first two notice days, however, occur in the preceding month and are governed by price limits.

The principal effect of a limit move is to accelerate the closing time for the market to the time at which the market last hits and stays at the limit. When this happens, the wild card play has more time to develop. Because these conditions are only in place for two days, this variant of the wild card option adds next to nothing to the option value of wild card opportunities.

CHAPTER 4

The Option-Adjusted Basis

Chapter 3 provided a richly detailed description of the kinds of delivery options enjoyed by the short. In this chapter, we use our understanding of these options to tackle the question of whether the short's strategic delivery option are fairly price and whether, by extension, the futures contracts are fairly priced. Hedgers, speculators, and arbitrageurs have a keen interest in the answer because the wisdom of using futures in lieu of the various alternatives depends at least in part on whether futures are bought or sold on advantageous terms.

We have four objectives in this chapter. First, we define the option-adjusted basis and how we use this to determine whether futures are rich or cheap. Second, we outline the general approach to the way we value the short's strategic delivery options. Third, we provide a checklist of the kinds of practical considerations that go into the valuation of these delivery options. And fourth, we provide a sample option-adjusted basis report.

Exhibit 4.1 provides a variety of ways of thinking about the basis. For the purpose of this chapter, the two relationships in Exhibit 4.1 that matter most are

$$\text{Option-Adjusted Basis} = \text{Actual Basis} - \text{Theoretical Basis}$$
$$= \text{BNOC} - \text{Theoretical Delivery Option Value}$$

and

$$\text{Market Price} - \text{Theoretical Price} = -\frac{(\text{Actual Basis} - \text{Theoretical Basis})}{\text{Factor}}$$

$$= -\frac{\text{Option-Adjusted Basis}}{\text{Factor}}$$

The first tells us that the basis is rich if the option-adjusted basis is positive. That is, the basis is rich if basis net of carry exceeds what you think is the value of the short's strategic delivery options. The second tells us that if the basis is rich—that is, if the option-adjusted basis is positive—then futures are cheap. In other words, if the basis market overvalues the short's strategic delivery options, the market undervalues the futures.

Whether futures are fairly priced revolves then around the question of whether the delivery options are fairly valued.

AN OUTLINE FOR PRICING THE SHORT'S DELIVERY OPTIONS

All of the short's delivery options depend for their value on the volatility of interest rate levels and interest rate spreads. The more volatile these are, the more valuable the delivery options.

E X H I B I T 4.1

Various Views of the Basis

Basis Definition

Actual Basis = Cash Price – [Factor x Futures Price]

Basis Relationships

Actual Basis = Carry + Market Delivery Option Value

Market Delivery Option Value = Basis Net of Carry (BNOC)

Theoretical Basis = Carry + Theoretical Delivery Option Value

Option-Adjusted Basis = Actual Basis – Theoretical Basis / Factor

                             = BNOC – Theoretical Delivery Option Value

Futures Price Relationships

Market Futures Price = [Cash Price – Actual Basis] / Factor

Theoretical Futures Price = [Cash Price – Theoretical Basis]

Market Futures Price – Theoretical Futures Price = – [Actual Basis – Theoretical Basis] / Factor

                             = – Option-Adjusted Basis / Factor

Option Structures

Exhibit 4.2 provides a simple schematic of the relationships between the various delivery options. From the trade date until the last trading day, the short enjoys the switch options that are driven by changes in the level and slope of the yield curve in a market where the futures price can still rise and fall with changes in the prices of deliverable issues.

From the last trading day to the last delivery day (or a couple of business days before the last delivery day), the short enjoys the end-of-month option. This option also depends on changes in the level and slope of the yield curve, but the futures price is fixed. As a result, the forces that impart value to the short's position are different from those that are at work before the expiration of futures trading, so the end-of-month option must be valued separately from the conventional switch options.

The timing options are in play from the first notice day until the end of the delivery month. There is the possibility that the short will want to deliver early in the month rather than late. In recent years, when the short end of the curve has, from time to time, been inverted enough to produce significant negative carry for 2-year and 5-year notes, deliveries have regularly taken place early in the month.

In our experience, however, we find that the incremental contribution of the timing options tends to be small. In what follows, therefore, we will skirt the complications that these options pose for valuing the basis and focus on the switch and end-of-month options.

EXHIBIT 4.2

Option Time Line

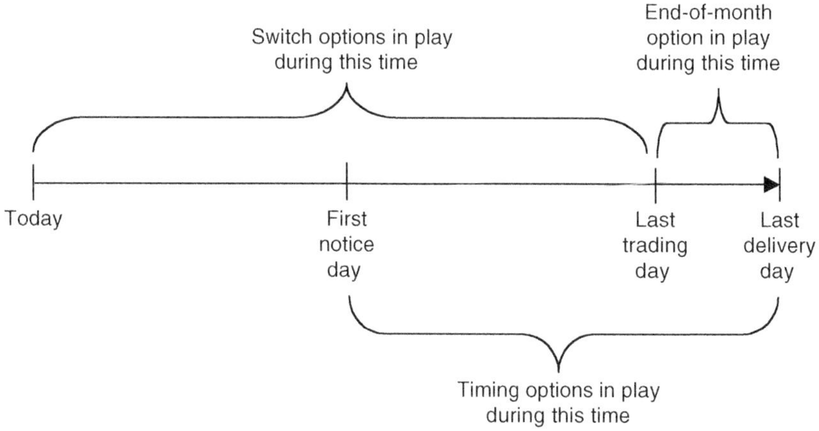

Valuing the Switch and End-of-Month Options

Exhibit 4.3 provides the simplest possible illustration of how to reckon the expected value of the strategic delivery options for any given deliverable issue. By the time futures trading expires on the last possible trading day, nine things can have happened to the yield curve. First, yields may have gone up, down, or stayed the same. Second, the curve may have steepened more, less, or just as much as was expected. In practice, you would use a more complex set of possible scenarios, but these nine capture the essence of the problem.

Producing this grid involves two steps. First, you must produce the joint probability distribution for the yield curve. That is, you need to produce the distribution of yield levels, which you would do by producing the yield distribution of a reference bond of your choosing. And then you need to produce the distribution of yield curve slopes. The resulting assumptions about yield distributions are displayed across the top and down the side.

EXHIBIT 4.3

Theoretical Delivery Option Value Equals Expected BNOC at Expiration

Basis Net of Carry at Expiration (Distribution)

Distributional Assumptions about Yields of Deliverable Issues			Yield Levels			
			Yields Down	Yields Unchanged	Yields Up	Distribution of Yield Levels
			bps(d) prob(d)	bps(0) prob(0)	bps(u) prob(u)	
Yield Curve	Steeper	bps(s) prob(s)	BNOC(s,d)	BNOC(s,0)	BNOC(s,u)	
	Expected	bps(e) prob(e)	BNOC(e,d)	BNOC(e,0)	BNOC(e,u)	
	Flatter	bps(f) prob (f)	BNOC(f,d)	BNOC(f,0)	BNOC(f,u)	

distribution of yield curve slopes

Basis Net of Carry at Expiration (Distribution)

Distributional Assumptions about Yields of Deliverable Issues			Yield Levels		
			Yields Down	Yields Unchanged	Yields Up
			-100 0.16	0 0.68	100 0.16
Yield Curve	Steeper	20 0.16	20	2	20
	Expected	Beta 0.68	25	1	15
	Flatter	-20 0.16	30	3	10

Second, you have to fill in the cells. That is, you need to provide the basis net of carry for the issue for each yield curve scenario. Doing this requires four additional steps. That is, you must identify the cheapest to deliver issue for each scenario. Then you must value the end-of-month options for that particular scenario. This allows you to reckon the futures price for each cell as the converted basis net of carry for the cheapest to deliver less the value of the end-of-month options. That is, for any given scenario

$$\text{Futures} = \frac{\text{CTD Price } - \text{ CTD Carry } - \text{ End-of-Month Option}}{\text{CTD Factor}}$$

And using this futures price, you can calculate the basis net of carry for each delivery issue for that scenario or cell.

Expected Basis Net of Carry

Once you have filled in the blanks in Exhibit 4.3 for any given deliverable note or bond, all that remains is to calculate the probability weighted average of the issue's basis net of carry values. This average is the expected value of the issue's basis net of carry and represents the expected gross payoff to buying this issue's basis.

Consider the hypothetical example shown in the lower panel of Exhibit 4.3. For this example, we suppose that the yield of our reference note or bond (for example, the on-the-run issue) can either rise or fall 100 basis points or remain unchanged. The most probable outcome is no change, and we have assigned equal probabilities to the increase and the decrease. We suppose, too, that the yield curve can either behave as our estimates of yield betas suggest it will, or that the curve between this issue and the reference issue will steepen or flatten 20 basis points more than expected. Here too we assume that the most likely outcome is what our yield betas suggest and the least likely outcomes are the unexpected or unusual steepening or flattening of the curve.

The hypothetical basis net of carry values might be those for a middling-duration issue—that is, an issue that will be cheapest to deliver if yields remain where they are but that will be an expensive issue if yields either rise or fall. The basis net of carry values shown in the center column represent hypothetical values for the end-of-month options in these three scenarios.

For such an issue, the effects of curve steepening and flattening depend on which way yields go. If yields fall, for example, the new cheapest to deliver will have a lower duration and most likely a shorter maturity than the current cheapest to deliver. If so, a steepening of the curve will tend to make the new cheapest to deliver less cheap relative to this particular issue and reduce its basis net of carry. A flattening of the curve, on the other hand, will make the new cheapest to deliver cheaper still and increase our issue's basis net of carry. If yields rise, these effects are just reversed, and the basis net of carry of our issue will tend to benefit from a curve steepening and to be hurt by an unusual flattening of the curve.

Given these values, we would calculate the expected basis net of carry for our issue as

$$
\begin{aligned}
& 0.16 \times [\, 0.16 \times 20 + 0.68 \times 2 + 0.16 \times 20 \,] && \text{(steeper curve)} \\
& + 0.68 \times [\, 0.16 \times 25 + 0.68 \times 1 + 0.16 \times 15 \,] && \text{(beta curve)} \\
& + 0.16 \times [\, 0.16 \times 30 + 0.68 \times 3 + 0.16 \times 10 \,] && \text{(flatter curve)} \\
& = 0.16 \times 7.76 + 0.68 \times 7.08 + 0.16 \times 8.44 \\
& = 7.41 \ (32\text{nds})
\end{aligned}
$$

If we are confident in our assumptions about the way the yield curve will play out, 7.41/32nds is the fair value of the basis net of carry for this particular deliverable issue.

This exercise is performed for each deliverable issue so that one determines the fair value of the basis net of carry for the entire deliverable set. If this work is done correctly, the relative richness or cheapness of the basis for each issue in the deliverable set should be consistent with the relative cheapness or richness of the futures contract.

A Word about the Value of Early Delivery

If you want to value the short's option to deliver early, you first need a rule for deciding when to deliver early. Consider the situation depicted in Exhibit 4.4, in which carry is negative and the cheapest to deliver's forward price is higher than its spot price. In a case like this, the short can avoid the consequences of negative carry by choosing to deliver early. Early delivery requires the short to surrender the value of any remaining switch and end-of-month options. Exhibit 4.4 also shows two possible futures prices—one for a low volatility setting and one for a high volatility setting.

If yields and yield spreads are not very volatile, the value of the short's remaining delivery options would be less than the negative carry. If we subtract the value of the short's remaining delivery options from the forward price, we find that the resulting futures

EXHIBIT 4.4

Negative Carry and Early Delivery

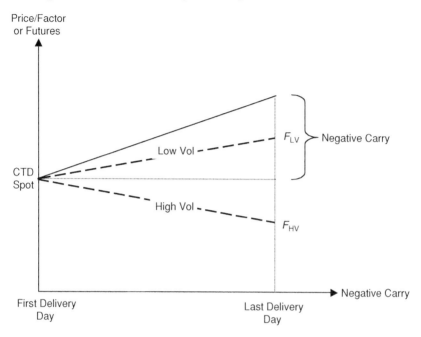

> **Rule of Thumb for Early Delivery**
> In a low-volatility setting, negative carry exceeds the value of the short's delivery options, and the best futures price for delivery on the last day would be F_{LV}. At this price, the CTD basis would be negative, and the short would choose to deliver on the first delivery day. Arbitrage would force the futures price down in this case to equal the converted spot price of the CTD. In a high-volatility setting, the short would wait until the last delivery day.

price, F_{LV}, is higher than the cheapest to deliver's converted price. If the short could actually deliver at this price, the CTD's basis would be negative. The CTD's spot price would be less than the futures invoice price for immediate delivery:

$$\text{CTD Factor} \times F_{LV} - \text{CTD Spot Price} > 0$$

and the short would realize an immediate profit.

Riskless profit is a rare thing, however, and one would expect arbitrage to force the futures price down in this instance until it equals the CTD's converted price. In other words, if early delivery is the short's best choice, then we would find that

$$\text{Futures Price} = \frac{\text{CTD Price}}{\text{CTD Factor}}$$

with allowance for a day's worth of carry and no remaining delivery options.

If yield and yield spread volatilities are high, on the other hand, the value of the remaining switch and end-of-month options would be greater than cost of negative carry. If so, the short will be willing to bear the costs of negative carry in exchange for the possibility of profiting from changes in the cheapest to deliver.

It is one thing to figure out whether the short should deliver early. If you are valuing the early delivery option, though, you need to combine the net payoff to this option with information about the probability distribution of negative carry, which in turn would depend on the probability distributions of term repo rates and the prices of deliverable issues. The expected futures price before the delivery month would then be reckoned as the sum of two values—the Probability of Early Delivery × Expected CTD Price / CTD Factor on Early Delivery Date and the Probability of Late Delivery × Expected Futures Price on Last Trading Day.

PRACTICAL CONSIDERATIONS

With this basic structure as a guide for valuing the switch and end-of-month options, you can tackle the actual problem of producing your yield distributions. Because everyone has different ideas about how to do this (including the authors), perhaps the best thing we can do is to offer you the following observations about the kinds of problems you will encounter and must wrestle with.

Volatility and Distribution of Yield Levels

We begin with implied volatility taken from the market for options on futures. As a first approximation, implied price volatility can be translated into an implied yield volatility as

$$\sigma_y = (\text{Yield} \times \text{Modified Duration}) \times \sigma_p$$

where σ_y is relative yield volatility and σ_p is relative price volatility, and the yield and modified duration are those of the cheapest to deliver. This is not ideal because, as we well know, the futures are driven by a basket of deliverable issues and the options expire roughly a month before the futures do. But the exchange-traded options provide us with a good starting point.

Yield Betas

The yield curve tends to flatten as yields rise and steepen as yields fall. A bond or note's yield beta is the amount by which its yield is expected to change for a 1-basis-point change in the yield of whichever issue you choose to use as your reference. Estimated yield betas provide an empirical way of capturing systematic change in the slope of the deliverable curve as yields rise and fall. Be aware, though, that estimated yield betas can vary greatly over time and that your assumptions about yield betas can have a big influence on your estimates of delivery option value.

Volatility and Distribution of Yield Spreads

Once you have determined the amount by which you expect the yield curve to flatten or steepen as yields rise or fall, you can deal with the random or unexpected changes in yield spreads. Estimates of the volatility of yield curve slopes are provided in Exhibit 4.5 for three key segments of the Treasury curve. Notice that because yield

EXHIBIT 4.5

Volatility of the Treasury Yield Curve Slope

30-year less 15-year

Change	Horizon				
	2 weeks	1 month	2 months	3 months	6 months
Largest decrease	-16.8	-12.3	-12.3	-15.5	-14.5
Largest increase	13.8	14.2	18.2	24.4	27.1
Standard deviation	3.7	4.9	6.0	7.3	9.3

10-year less 7-year

Change	Horizon				
	2 weeks	1 month	2 months	3 months	6 months
Largest decrease	-12.7	-15.0	-12.3	-16.2	-13.4
Largest increase	16.2	16.2	17.9	17.0	22.8
Standard deviation	3.5	4.6	5.9	7.0	10.3

5-year less 4-year

Change	Horizon				
	2 weeks	1 month	2 months	3 months	6 months
Largest decrease	-11.0	-10.8	-14.4	-8.4	-7.4
Largest increase	6.9	9.0	11.7	15.8	15.6
Standard deviation	2.5	3.3	4.5	5.1	4.2

changes on one part of the curve are positively correlated with yield changes on other parts of the curve, the usual square root of time rule does not apply to the volatility of yield spreads. The standard deviation of the distribution of the slope of the 15s/30s part of the curve will not double for a quadrupling of the pricing horizon.

Consistency between Forward Prices and Expected Forward Prices

However you produce your distributions of yields and yield spreads, you should make sure that each expected forward price (that is, the probability weighted average price of each issue's price at futures expiration) equals its actual market forward price, or cash price net of carry to futures expiration.

Consistency between Delivery Option Values and Futures Options Values

Once you have produced a distribution of yields and yield spreads and have determined the hypothetical futures price for each possible outcome, you can calculate the expected price of an at-the-money bond futures call. From this, you can back out an implied price volatility that can be compared with the structure of implied volatilities provided by actual exchange-traded options on futures. If you find that your model has mispriced this at-the-money call, you can compensate by increasing or decreasing your assumed yield volatility as needed. This consistency check works better with the bond and 10-year contracts, whose prices are more sensitive to changes in the level of yields than are the prices of 5-year and 2-year contracts.

Term Repo Specials

Occasionally, an issue that is on special in the term repo market will be cheapest to deliver. Not often, but sometimes. When this happens, you must make an appropriate allowance for specialness in the term repo market when reckoning forward prices.

Anticipated New Issues

The U.S. Treasury tends to be very predictable in the way it issues bonds and notes. With rare exceptions, the Treasury sticks to an auction cycle for notes and bonds at key maturities. You can, therefore, predict with considerable confidence when new issues at various maturities will be sold. Moreover, it is important that you do so, especially with the 2-year and 5-year note contracts, where anticipated new issues can make up the bulk of the deliverable set. The challenges you face in dealing with new issues are in knowing how to place them on the yield curve and in thinking about how an issue whose coupon you do not yet know will behave under different yield scenarios.

THE OPTION-ADJUSTED BASIS IN PRACTICE

Exhibit 4.6 compares the basis net of carry (BNOC) with theoretical values of the short's delivery options for issues that were deliverable into the June 2001 bond futures contract on April 4, 2001. This exhibit provides us with two key lessons, detailed in the next sections.

EXHIBIT 4.6

If the Basis Is Cheap, Futures Are Rich

Issue		Closing Price	Conversion Factor	Basis	Carry	BNOC	Theoretical Option Value	Option Adjusted BNOC
Coupon	Maturity							
						(32nds)		
5 3/8	2/15/31	98-08	0.9140	104.0	7.0	97.0	101.5	-4.5
6 1/4	5/15/30	109-14	1.0339	63.2	9.5	53.7	58.2	-4.5
6 1/8	8/15/29	107-02	1.0169	43.8	8.9	34.9	38.9	-4.0
5 1/4	2/15/29	94-18	0.8996	33.9	6.7	27.2	31.2	-4.0
5 1/4	11/15/28	94-15	0.8999	29.9	6.4	23.5	27.5	-4.0
5 1/2	8/15/28	97-30	0.9336	28.8	7.4	21.5	25.5	-4.0
6 1/8	11/15/27	106-14	1.0163	25.8	8.7	17.0	21.0	-4.0
6 3/8	8/15/27	109-25	1.0491	23.7	9.8	13.9	17.9	-4.0
6 5/8	2/15/27	113-03	1.0811	23.3	10.5	12.7	16.7	-4.0
6 1/2	11/15/26	111-10+	1.0645	22.0	9.8	12.1	16.1	-4.0
6 3/4	8/15/26	114-21+	1.0965	22.5	10.9	11.6	15.6	-4.0
6	2/15/26	104-18	1.0000	20.0	8.8	11.2	14.7	-3.5
6 7/8	8/15/25	116-01	1.1105	19.5	11.4	8.1	11.6	-3.5
7 5/8	2/15/25	125-22+	1.2033	20.3	13.7	6.7	10.7	-4.0
7 1/2	11/15/24	124-00	1.1866	21.4	12.9	8.5	12.5	-4.0
6 1/4	8/15/23	107-18	1.0303	15.2	9.7	5.6	8.6	-3.0
7 1/8	2/15/23	118-16	1.1349	17.3	12.4	4.9	8.4	-3.5
7 5/8	**11/15/22**	**124-20**	**1.1936**	**18.1**	**13.6**	**4.5**	**8.0**	**-3.5**
7 1/4	8/15/22	119-28	1.1481	17.4	12.9	4.6	8.1	-3.5
8	11/15/21	128-23+	1.2325	20.2	14.9	5.3	8.8	-3.5
8 1/8	8/15/21	130-04+	1.2456	21.6	15.8	5.8	9.3	-3.5
8 1/8	5/15/21	129-30	1.2438	21.1	15.4	5.7	9.2	-3.5
7 7/8	2/15/21	126-25+	1.2138	20.4	15.1	5.3	8.8	-3.5
8 3/4	8/15/20	136-28	1.3093	25.3	18.2	7.1	10.6	-3.5
8 3/4	5/15/20	136-22+	1.3069	27.8	17.7	10.1	13.6	-3.5
8 1/2	2/15/20	133-18+	1.2771	26.9	17.4	9.4	12.9	-3.5
8 1/8	8/15/19	128-28	1.2320	26.4	16.3	10.1	13.1	-3.0
8 7/8	2/15/19	137-02+	1.3089	33.1	19.0	14.1	17.6	-3.5
9	11/15/18	138-11	1.3195	38.3	19.0	19.4	22.9	-3.5
9 1/8	5/15/18	139-07	1.3272	40.7	19.6	21.1	24.6	-3.5
8 7/8	8/15/17	135-24+	1.2931	43.6	19.5	24.2	27.2	-3.0
8 3/4	5/15/17	134-06+	1.2775	45.5	18.5	27.0	30.0	-3.0
7 1/2	11/15/16	120-20	1.1484	40.4	14.0	26.4	29.4	-3.0

Source: *JPMorgan*

If the Basis Is Cheap, Futures Are Rich

Notice that basis net of carry is less than the theoretical option value for all issues in the deliverable set. The market price that shorts are paying for the embedded delivery options is less than we think the options are worth. As a result, the option-adjusted basis, which is the difference between BNOC and the theoretical value of the delivery options, is negative for each issue in the deliverable set.

The flip side of a cheap basis is a rich futures contract. If we use one of the two key relationships from the beginning of the chapter,

$$\text{Market Price} - \text{Theoretical Price} = -\frac{(\text{Actual Basis} - \text{Theoretical Basis})}{\text{Factor}}$$
$$= -\frac{\text{Option-Adjusted Basis}}{\text{Factor}}$$

for the cheapest to deliver, we find that the futures contract is about 3/32nds rich. That is,

$$\text{Market Price} - \text{Theoretical Price} = -\frac{-3.5 \text{ ticks}}{1.1936} = 2.93 \text{ ticks}$$

The fair futures price, as shown at the top of Exhibit 4.6, is 103-27, which is three ticks lower than the market price of 103-30.

The CTD's BNOC Is Pure Option Value

The only issue for which its basis net of carry is pure option value is the cheapest to deliver. For all other issues, basis net of carry represents a combination of this pure delivery option value and the amount by which the issue is expensive to deliver. Thus, BNOC for the 5-3/8% of 2/15/31 is 97/32nds, not because there is more true delivery option value for this issue, but because it would be a very expensive bond to deliver. One would lose nearly 3 price points by delivering this bond rather than the 7-5/8% of 11/15/22.

If you want an analogy with conventional options, you can think of the delivery options for the cheapest to deliver as "at the money" and the delivery options for all other issues as "in the money." Thus, the nature of the option play is the same for any issue in the deliverable set. Only the prices paid and received for the options are different.

CHAPTER 5

Approaches to Hedging

You can eliminate the risk in a long bond position simply by selling it. The question of hedging comes up only when a position cannot be liquidated in the spot market or if there is some good business reason for choosing not to sell the bond right away. Alternatives to selling the bond outright include

- Selling the bond forward
- Selling a different bond in the spot market
- Selling a different bond forward
- Selling a bond futures contract

Each of these alternatives may reduce the overall risk in your position, but each will suffer from some shortcoming or other and will produce hedge error or slippage.

The focus of this chapter is on the question of how best to hedge with Treasury futures and on the ways you can expect these hedges to work in practice. In doing so, we will cover the following:

- DV01 hedges and competing hedge objectives
- Standard industry rules of thumb
- Shortcomings of the rules of thumb
- Spot and repo DV01s
- Handling repo stub risk
- Creating synthetic bonds
- Option-adjusted DV01s

- Yield betas
- Reckoning the P/L of a hedge
- Evaluating the performance of a hedge
- Working with durations

DV01 HEDGE RATIOS AND COMPETING OBJECTIVES

Throughout this chapter, we approach the problem of reckoning hedge ratios as one of finding a futures position that has an equal but offsetting dollar value of a basis point. (Hedge algebra is illustrated in Exhibit 5.1.) This is a very common approach to hedging and makes good sense; however, it is not the only approach.

A hedger might choose, instead, to find a hedge ratio that minimizes the variance of the value of the combined position. Or the hedger might choose to use estimated regression coefficients to determine a hedge ratio for which expected changes in the value of the position are zero.

The differences between these competing objectives stem from imperfect correlations between changes in yields of the bonds the hedger holds and the bonds that drive the futures price. Considering the noise in these relationships, there are many times when the hedge actually makes things worse, either because the hedge makes money while the bond is making money or the hedge loses money while the bond is losing money. One of the ongoing costs of hedging, for that matter, is the ongoing aggravation of this kind of hedge slippage that is most likely to cause problems when nothing much is going on and yields are not changing very much.

We will take a closer look at the choices you have in dealing with imperfect correlations between yield changes when we tackle the problem of yield betas. Also, the appendix to this chapter provides a concise discussion of the calculations of yield betas and the differences between competing hedge objectives.

STANDARD INDUSTRY RULES OF THUMB

For several years, the industry has relied on two rules of thumb for determining hedge ratios. Both rules of thumb are based on the assumption that the futures price is driven by the price of the cheapest to deliver. The reasoning behind the rules of thumb is comparatively simple and straightforward, but as we will show in this

E X H I B I T   5.1

Futures Hedge Algebra

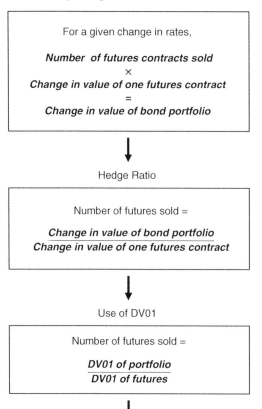

For a given change in rates,

Number of futures contracts sold
×
Change in value of one futures contract
=
Change in value of bond portfolio

Hedge Ratio

Number of futures sold =

Change in value of bond portfolio
Change in value of one futures contract

Use of DV01

Number of futures sold =

DV01 of portfolio
DV01 of futures

Use of modified duration

Number of futures sold =

Portfolio duration × Portfolio market value
Futures duration × (Futures price/100) × Contract par amount

section, the two thumb rules are not entirely consistent with one another and can produce what we think are highly inadequate hedge ratios in a number of important applications.

Rule of Thumb #1

The dollar value of a basis point for a futures contract is equal to the dollar value of a basis point for the cheapest to deliver *divided by* its conversion factor.

Rule of Thumb #2

The duration of a futures contract is equal to the duration of the cheapest to deliver bond.

The algebra that supports the first rule of thumb is based on the assumption that the futures price converges to the converted price of the cheapest to deliver issue at expiration. At expiration, then, we know that

$$\text{Futures Price} = \frac{\text{CTD Price}}{\text{CTD Factor}}$$

is almost exactly true except for a small amount of carry and the value of the remaining end-of-month options. From this relationship, the first rule of thumb follows immediately because

$$\text{Futures Price Change} = \frac{\text{CTD Price Change}}{\text{CTD Factor}}$$

almost by definition.

The second rule of thumb can be derived approximately from the first by dividing both sides by the futures price. The effect of dividing the left-hand side by the futures price is to produce a number equal to

$$\frac{\text{Futures Price Change}}{\text{Futures Price}}$$

which is the percent change in the futures price. On the right-hand side, we would have

$$\frac{\text{CTD Price Change}/\text{CTD Factor}}{\text{CTD Price}/\text{CTD Factor}}$$

which simplifies to

$$\frac{\text{CTD Price Change}}{\text{CTD Price}}$$

after the factors cancel. Thus, we know that the percent change in the futures price is equal to the percent change in the cheapest to deliver's price. Because a bond's duration is the percent change in its full price for a 1-percentage-point change in its yield, we can conclude that the duration of the futures contract at expiration is nearly the same as the duration of the cheapest to deliver bond.

The Rules of Thumb in Practice

To see how these rules of thumb might be used in practice, suppose we want to hedge $10 million face or par amount of the 5% of 2/15/11, the on-the-run 10-year note. As shown in Exhibit 5.2, its market price on April 5, 2001, was 100-17/32nds. Its full price including accrued interest was 101.222. Its modified duration was 7.67, and its DV01 per $100,000 face amount was $77.624, or $7,762.40 for the full $10 million.

How many of the June 10-year Treasury note futures would you need to hedge the $10 million position in the 5%?

To use the rules of thumb, we need to identify the cheapest to deliver note. With an implied repo rate of 3.508%, the 5-1/2% of 2/15/08 were cheapest to deliver. The relevant data for this issue include

$$\text{Futures Price} = 106\text{-}08/32\text{nds}$$
$$\text{Factor} = 0.9734$$
$$\frac{\text{DV01}}{\$100,000} = \$59.14$$
$$\text{Modified Duration} = 5.65$$

Using the rules of thumb, we would reckon that

$$\text{Futures DV01} = \frac{\text{CTD DV01}}{\text{CTD Factor}}$$
$$= \frac{\$59.14}{0.9734}$$
$$= \$60.76$$
$$\text{Futures Duration} = \text{CTD Duration}$$
$$= 5.65$$

To calculate the hedge ratio using the first rule of thumb, we would divide the DV01 of the portfolio by the DV01 of the futures contract. That is,

$$\text{Hedge Ratio \#1} = \frac{\text{Portfolio DV01}}{\text{Futures DV01}}$$
$$= \frac{\$7,762.40}{\$60.76}$$
$$= 127.8$$

which would require you to short 128 10-year Treasury note futures contracts.

EXHIBIT 5.2

Price and Yield Sensitivity Measures
(Close 4/4/01, Trade 4/5/01, Settle 4/5/01)

	Coupon	Maturity	2:00 PM Price-32nd	Yield	Jun-02 Factor	DV01/ $100,000	Modified Duration	Market futures prices			
								2-year 103-04+	5-year 105-22	10-year 106-08	Bond 103-30
								Assumed Yield Beta	Full $ Price	Term Repo	Imp-RP
T02	4.25	3/31/03	100-08+	4.109	0.9713	18.898	1.88	1.0000	100.335	4.640	3.819
T	5.5	3/31/03	102-16+	4.165	0.9917	19.156	1.87	1.0004	102.606	4.490	4.351
T	5.75	4/30/03	103-03+	4.162	0.9956	20.000	1.89	0.9997	105.603	4.490	3.789
T	5.5	5/31/03	102-21	4.193	0.9910	20.722	1.98	0.9973	104.575	4.490	3.489
T	5.375	6/30/03	102-17	4.174	0.9884	21.480	2.07	0.9950	103.957	4.490	2.831
F05	5.75	11/15/05	105-02+	4.516	0.9904	42.426	3.95	1.0000	107.334	3.620	3.716
N	5.5	2/15/08	103-27	4.834	0.9734	59.139	5.65	1.0548	104.603	4.460	3.508
N	5.625	5/15/08	104-15+	4.870	0.9793	61.067	5.72	1.0529	106.691	4.610	3.504
N	4.75	11/15/08	98-31	4.913	0.9273	62.469	6.20	1.0401	100.832	4.460	2.796
N	5.5	5/15/09	103-21	4.946	0.9693	67.584	6.39	1.0349	105.814	4.460	2.452
N	6	8/15/09	106-28+	4.981	1.0000	70.518	6.55	1.0305	107.719	4.460	2.990
N	6.5	2/15/10	110-17+	5.010	1.0329	75.362	6.76	1.0247	111.445	4.460	2.719
N	5.75	8/15/10	105-12+	5.020	0.9828	76.392	7.19	1.0129	106.185	4.090	1.478
N10	5	2/15/11	100-17	4.931	0.9284	77.624	7.67	1.0000	101.222	2.660	-3.085
B	7.5	11/15/16	120-20	5.512	1.1484	117.777	9.53	1.1365	123.567	4.540	1.629
B	8.75	5/15/17	134-06+	5.517	1.2775	129.623	9.42	1.1396	137.635	4.540	1.868
B	8.875	8/15/17	135-24+	5.525	1.2931	131.998	9.64	1.1337	136.991	4.540	2.175
B	9.125	5/15/18	139-07	5.545	1.3272	138.199	9.68	1.1325	142.798	4.540	2.522
B	9	11/15/18	138-11	5.557	1.3195	140.006	9.87	1.1273	141.874	4.540	2.679

B	8.875	2/15/19	137-02+	5.570	1.3089	140.204	10.14	1.1200	138.304	4.540	3.176
B	8.125	8/15/19	128-28	5.589	1.2320	136.143	10.47	1.1109	129.997	4.540	3.499
B	8.5	2/15/20	133-18+	5.595	1.2771	142.020	10.54	1.1091	134.752	4.540	3.603
B	8.75	5/15/20	136-22+	5.597	1.3069	145.587	10.39	1.1132	140.135	4.540	3.563
B	8.75	8/15/20	136-28	5.604	1.3093	146.824	10.63	1.1065	138.084	4.540	3.851
B	7.875	2/15/21	126-25+	5.618	1.2138	140.689	11.00	1.0965	127.885	4.540	3.987
B	8.125	5/15/21	129-30	5.620	1.2438	144.259	10.84	1.1010	133.125	4.540	3.956
B	8.125	8/15/21	130-04+	5.626	1.2456	145.486	11.08	1.0943	131.263	4.540	3.948
B	8	11/15/21	128-23+	5.637	1.2325	145.241	11.01	1.0962	131.872	4.540	3.993
B	7.25	8/15/22	119-28	5.638	1.1481	140.459	11.62	1.0797	120.876	4.540	4.035
B	**7.625**	**11/15/22**	**124-20**	**5.639**	**1.1936**	**145.452**	**11.40**	**1.0857**	**127.616**	**4.540**	**4.057**
B	7.125	2/15/23	118-16	5.641	1.1349	140.989	11.80	1.0748	119.484	4.540	3.989
B	6.25	8/15/23	107-18	5.649	1.0303	132.847	12.25	1.0625	108.426	4.540	3.852
B	7.5	11/15/24	124-00	5.646	1.1866	151.824	11.96	1.0704	126.942	4.540	3.627
B	7.625	2/15/25	125-22+	5.650	1.2033	154.223	12.17	1.0648	126.756	4.540	3.835
B	6.875	8/15/25	116-01	5.654	1.1105	146.628	12.53	1.0548	116.981	4.540	3.615
B	6	2/15/26	104-18	5.655	1.0000	137.041	13.00	1.0421	105.391	4.540	3.120
B	6.75	8/15/26	114-21+	5.653	1.0965	148.219	12.82	1.0470	115.604	4.540	3.195
B	6.5	11/15/26	111-10+	5.657	1.0645	145.565	12.78	1.0481	113.878	4.540	3.090
B	6.625	2/15/27	113-03	5.655	1.0811	148.018	12.98	1.0426	114.009	4.540	3.046
B	6.375	8/15/27	109-25	5.656	1.0491	145.999	13.19	1.0369	110.662	4.540	2.861
B	6.125	11/15/27	106-14	5.654	1.0163	143.269	13.16	1.0377	108.840	4.540	2.411
B	5.5	8/15/28	97-30	5.648	0.9336	136.376	13.82	1.0199	98.697	4.540	1.627
B	5.25	11/15/28	94-15	5.647	0.8999	133.305	13.81	1.0201	96.528	4.540	1.226
B	5.25	2/15/29	94-18	5.639	0.8996	134.028	14.07	1.0132	95.288	4.540	0.710
B	6.125	8/15/29	107-02	5.623	1.0169	148.424	13.75	1.0216	107.908	4.540	0.210
B	6.25	5/15/30	109-14	5.589	1.0339	153.141	13.69	1.0235	111.889	4.430	-2.096
B30	5.375	2/15/31	98-08	5.494	0.9140	144.027	14.55	1.0000	98.992	4.450	-8.676

Source: JPMorgan

Important Note. This rule of thumb, by the way, is the working rule that Bloomberg uses when you request a hedge ratio. As shown in Exhibit 5.3, if you had asked Bloomberg on January 25, 2002 to hedge $10 million of the 7-7/8% Treasury bond of 2/21 using the March 2002 bond futures contract, it would have suggested shorting 121 contracts. It arrived at this answer by noting first that the cheapest to deliver bond was the 7-7/8% of 2/21 (see box labeled Proxy Issue in the bottom section of Exhibit 5.3) and that its dollar value of a basis point was $.1346 per $100 face value of the issue. Combining this DV01 with its March 2002 conversion factor of 1.2092, Bloomberg calculated the DV01 for the March 2002 futures contract as $.1113 [= $.1346/1.2092] per $100 face value of the contract or $111.30 per contract. Given a DV01 of $13,460 for a $10 million position in the issue, Bloomberg calculates a hedge of 120.9 [= $13,460/$111.30] contracts, which is rounded to 121. In this example, note that we chose the cheapest to deliver as the bond to hedge so that all of the relevant information (with the exception of the bond's March 2002 conversion factor) would be available in the same exhibit. As a result, the hedge ratio in this example proved to be the bond's conversion factor.

If we calculate the hedge ratio using the second rule of thumb, we would divide the product of the portfolio's market value and its duration by the product of the portfolio equivalent value of the

EXHIBIT 5.3

Bloomberg Illustration for Rule-of-Thumb Hedge Ratio

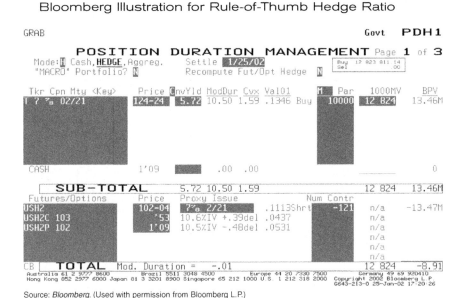

Source: *Bloomberg.* (Used with permission from Bloomberg L.P.)

futures contract and its duration. Given a full price including accrued interest of 101.222, the market value of $10 million face amount of the 5% would be $10,122,200. As shown at the top of Exhibit 5.2, the 10-year Treasury note futures price was 106-08/32nds (or 106.250). Because the nominal face value of the futures contract is $100,000, the futures contract can be treated as if it has a market value of $106,250. Thus, the hedge ratio calculation would look like

$$\text{Hedge Ratio } \#2 = \frac{(\$10,122,200 \times 7.67)}{(\$106,250 \times 5.65)}$$
$$= 126.9$$

which would require you to short 127 10-year Treasury note futures contracts, which is one less than the hedge produced by the first rule of thumb.

Why Are the Answers Different?   The second rule of thumb can be counted on to produce a slightly smaller hedge ratio because it misapplies the modified duration of the cheapest to deliver. Used correctly, modified duration is applied to a bond's full price, while the futures price at expiration would be the bond's converted market or net price (i.e., net of accrued interest). To produce the same answer as the first rule of thumb, we would have to scale up the portfolio equivalent value of the futures contract to reflect the cheapest to deliver's accrued interest.

Shortcomings of the Rules of Thumb

Rules of thumb survive only because they do a good enough job to get by. These rules of thumb suffer from two key shortcomings, however, and can be improved upon with the proper tools. From Chapter 4, we know that the relationship between the futures price and the cheapest to deliver is

$$\text{Futures Price} = \frac{\text{CTD Price} - \text{Carry} - \text{Delivery Option Value}}{\text{CTD Factor}}$$

which makes it clear that the rules of thumb ignore both changes in carry and the value of the short's delivery option value as yields rise and fall. For what follows, it helps if we rewrite this relationship as

$$\text{Futures Price} = \frac{\text{CTD Forward Price} - \text{Delivery Option Value}}{\text{CTD Factor}}$$

so that we can focus first on the key interest rate relationships between spot and forward prices and then on the importance of the delivery option values.

SPOT AND REPO DV01s

The main point of this section is that when using futures to hedge a bond or to create a synthetic bond, you must isolate two almost completely independent sources of interest rate risk. One is the change in bond forward prices given changes in spot bond yields with term repo or financing rates held constant. The second is the change in bond forward prices given changes in term repo rates holding spot bond yields constant. And because these are largely independent sources of risk, a complete hedge for a spot bond will include both futures (to cover changes in spot yields holding repo fixed) and a term money market position (to cover changes in repo rates holding spot bond yields fixed).

Forward Prices as a Function of Spot Yields and Repo Rates

We are accustomed to thinking of the forward price as the spot price less carry where carry is the difference between coupon income and repo or financing expense. To isolate the effects of the two key interest rates, however, it may be more helpful to write out the financing and coupon relationships directly. For the cheapest to deliver bond on April 5 (for settlement on April 6), the forward price can be written as

$$F = (S + \text{AI})_{4/6}\left[1 + R\left(\frac{39}{360}\right)\right]\left[1 + R\left(\frac{45}{360}\right)\right]$$
$$- \left(\frac{C}{2}\right)\left[1 + R\left(\frac{45}{360}\right) + \left(\frac{45}{184}\right)\right]$$

where F is the forward price, S is the spot price, AI is accrued interest, R is the term repo rate, and C is the annual coupon. This particular example is as complicated as it is because of the semi-annual coupon that falls on May 15. This relationship between the bond's spot price and its forward price is illustrated in Exhibit 5.4, which tracks the course of the bond's full price from 127.6160 on April 5 to 124.4312 on May 15 to 125.1373 on June 29. Thus, beginning

EXHIBIT 5.4

Getting from the Current Spot Price
to the Forward Price

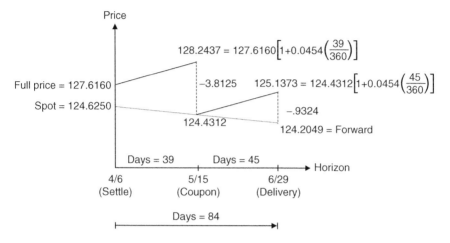

with the bond's spot price of 124-20/32nds (or 124.6125) on April 5, we arrive at a forward price for delivery on June 29 of 124.2049 [= 125.1373 − (7.625/2)(45/183)].

From this expression, we can see that the forward price is related to two interest rates: the bond's spot yield, which is derived from its spot price, and the term repo rate. A change in the bond's spot yield will produce a change in the forward price equal to

$$\frac{dF}{dy_s} = \left(\frac{dF}{dS}\right)\left(\frac{dS}{dy_s}\right) = \left[1 + R\left(\frac{84}{360}\right) + R^2\left(\frac{39}{360}\right)\left(\frac{45}{360}\right)\right]\left(\frac{dS}{dy_s}\right)$$

where dS/dy_s is the bond's spot price value of a basis point and which would simplify to

$$\frac{dF}{dy_s} = \left[1 + R\left(\frac{84}{360}\right)\right]\left(\frac{dS}{dy_s}\right)$$

if there were no intervening coupon. An increase in the bond's spot yield will be accompanied by a decrease in its spot price, and the forward price will decrease by more than the spot price because of the amplifying effect of financing.

A change in the term repo rate will produce a change in the forward price equal to

$$\frac{dF}{dR} = (S + AI)\left[\left(\frac{84}{360}\right) + R\left(\frac{39}{360}\right)\left(\frac{45}{360}\right)\right] - \left[\left(\frac{C}{2}\right)\left(\frac{45}{360}\right)\right]$$

which in turn would simplify to

$$\frac{dF}{dR} = (S + AI)\left(\frac{84}{360}\right)$$

if there were no intervening coupon. (In both cases, if the unit of change in the repo rate is 1 basis point, these values would be divided by 10 to produce a DV01 per \$100,000 par amount.) Unlike an increase in the spot yield, which would cause the forward price to fall, an increase in the term repo rate will cause the forward price to rise. Thus, if interest rates are rising, the forward price will tend to fall because the spot price is falling; however, it will fall less because of the offsetting effect of the increased cost of financing. For those who are more comfortable thinking about carry relationships, the effect of the increase in the repo rate is to increase financing expenses and thus to reduce carry. Thus, even if the spot price is falling, the forward price will fall less because of the decrease in the spread between the two prices produced by carry.

The Short-Term Independence of Spot Yields and Term Repo Rates

For the hedger, the importance of these two relationships stems from the fact that changes in spot yields and term repo rates, while both translate directly into gains or losses on the forward price (which produce corresponding cash gains and losses on futures), are largely independent of one of another, especially over the kinds of horizons that most hedgers contemplate. Even though repo rates and spot bond and note yields will tend to rise and fall together in the broad sweep of things, the two rates respond to different forces in the short term. Term repo rates respond to the Fed funds market and very short-term expectations about Fed policy; spot yields to longer-term expectations about macroeconomic forces.

This point is made clearly enough in Exhibits 5.5 and 5.6, which compare the relationships between Treasury yields and one-month term repo rates. The three panels of Exhibit 5.5 show the relationships between the levels of 5-year, 10-year, and 30-year Treasury yields and the level of one-month repo rates for January 1998 through October

EXHIBIT 5.5

Treasury Yield Levels versus One-Month Repo Rates
(January 1988 through October 2003)

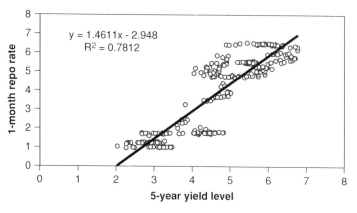

$y = 1.4611x - 2.948$
$R^2 = 0.7812$

5-year yield level

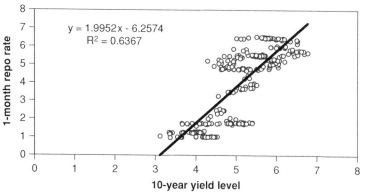

$y = 1.9952x - 6.2574$
$R^2 = 0.6367$

10-year yield level

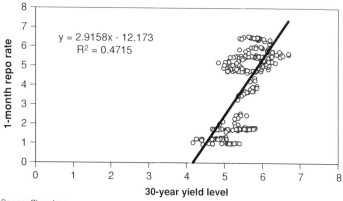

$y = 2.9158x - 12.173$
$R^2 = 0.4715$

30-year yield level

Source: *Bloomberg*

EXHIBIT 5.6

Weekly Changes in Treasury Yields and
Repo Rates
(January 1988 through October 2003)

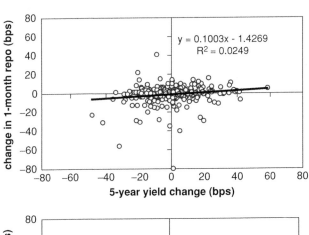

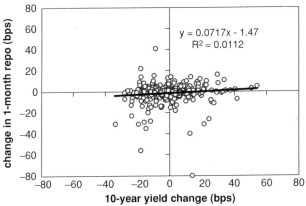

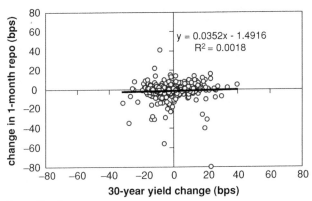

Source: *Bloomberg*

2003. This was a period during which the Fed was cutting rates in big chunks and sometimes unexpectedly. And, in a large sense, the Fed's rate cuts were accompanied by declines in the level of Treasury note and bond yields.

For a hedger, though, the more relevant relationships are those shown in Exhibit 5.6, which plots weekly changes in Treasury note and bond yields against weekly changes in the term repo rate. Here it is apparent that for a one-week horizon, there is no useful relationship at all between changes in the yield on a Treasury note or bond and the change in a term repo rate.

As a result, the hedger faces two independent sources of interest rate risk when hedging with futures: first, risks associated with changes in spot yields and, second, risks associated with changes in term repo rates.

To put these two sources of risk in perspective, consider their respective influences on the forward price of the 7-5/8% for June 29 delivery. With a term repo rate of 0.0454 and a spot DV01 of 145.45, the DV01 of the forward price with respect to a change in the issue's spot yield was

$$
\begin{aligned}
\frac{dF}{dy_s} &= \left[1 + 0.0454\left(\frac{84}{360}\right) + 0.0454^2\left(\frac{39}{360}\right)\left(\frac{45}{360}\right) \right] \times -145.45 \\
&= [1 + 0.01059 + 0.00003] \times -145.45 \\
&= 1.01062 \times -145.45 \\
&= -146.99
\end{aligned}
$$

per \$100,000 par amount, which is slightly more than one percent (or 1.54) higher than the spot DV01 of the 7-5/8%. With a full price of 127.616, the repo DV01 per \$100,000 was

$$
\begin{aligned}
\frac{dF}{dR} &= \frac{127{,}616\left[\left(\frac{84}{360}\right) + 0.0454\left(\frac{39}{360}\right)\left(\frac{45}{360}\right)\right] - \left[\left(\frac{7.625}{2}\right)\left(\frac{45}{360}\right)\right]}{10{,}000} \\
&= \frac{127{,}616[.233333 + .000143] - [3.8125 \times .125]}{10{,}000} \\
&= \frac{28.8398}{10} \\
&= 2.88398
\end{aligned}
$$

or \$2.88 per basis point per \$100,000 par amount.

Sign Conventions When reporting conventional DV01s for bonds or notes, we rarely if ever pay any attention to the sign. People just know that if the yield goes up, the price goes down. This practice means that we either take the same approach with repo DV01s and assume that people just know that the sign is positive or we can, if we show spot DV01s as positive numbers, show repo DV01s as negative numbers as a way of calling attention to the difference in the signs.

CREATING SYNTHETIC BONDS WITH FORWARDS AND FUTURES

An important application of our understanding of the effects of changes in spot yields and term repo rates on forward (and hence futures) prices is in the correct construction of a synthetic bond. A real bond in the spot market has two key features. First, its price rises and falls with changes in its spot yield. Second, it can be liquidated to produce a pot of cash equal to its full price. These two features of the real bond can be produced synthetically by combining a forward or futures position with a term money market instrument that matures on the forward or futures delivery date.

Using Forwards For example, to replicate $100,000 par amount of the 7-5/8% on April 5, we could combine $127,616 in a market investment at a money market rate of 4.54% for 84 days with a forward position on $100,000 par amount of the bond for delivery on June 29. The reason why this works is much easier to see if we can ignore the intervening coupon on the 7-5/8% and write the key relationships simply as

$$\frac{dF}{dy_s} = \left[1 + 0.0454\left(\frac{84}{360}\right)\right] \times -145.45 = \$146.99$$

and

$$\frac{dF}{dR} = \frac{127{,}616\left(\frac{84}{360}\right)}{10{,}000} = \$2.98$$

Because both of these effects on the forward price represent forward unrealized gains or losses, we have to determine the present values of both so they can be compared with changes in the value of our spot position. It is easy to see that the present value of the effect on the forward price equals the bond's spot DV01 if we use the same interest rate for discounting purposes. Thus, a forward position on $100,000 par amount of the bond is an exact match for $100,000 par amount of the bond in the spot market.

What then about changes in the term repo rate? If we invest $127,616 in a term investment for 84 days at a money market rate of 4.54%, the forward value of the investment is $128,967.88 {= $127,616 × [1 + .0454 (84/360)]}. The present value of this investment would be

$$\frac{\$127,967.88}{1 + R\left(\dfrac{84}{360}\right)}$$

where R is whatever the current money market rate happens to be. If the money market rate rises by 1 basis point, the present value of the investment would fall by $2.95, which would be just enough to offset the present value of the change in the forward price of $2.98. That is, $2.98/[1 + 0.0455 (84/360)] = $2.95. As a result, the rise in the value of the forward position produced by an increase in the term repo rate would be exactly offset by a decrease in the value of the term money market investment.

Using Futures. The big difference when using futures is in the size of the position. Changes in spot yields produce changes in forward prices that are translated directly into changes in futures prices and, as a result, directly into cash gains or losses today. As a result, you would need only 0.9895 [= $145.45/$146.99] futures to capture the effect of changes in spot yields on forward prices.

HANDLING REPO STUB RISK

Another way to think about the problem posed by the effect of changes in term repo rates on futures prices is from the hedger's perspective. If the term repo rate represents an independent source of risk in the hedge, then this source of risk must be hedged directly with the appropriate instrument. In particular, someone who wanted to hedge a spot position in the 7-5/8% would not only sell the appropriate number of futures contracts but would sell an 84-day money market instrument as well. The resulting position would look like

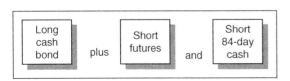

in which the short futures would capture the effects of changes in the level of spot yields, and the short position in an 84-day term cash instrument would offset the effect of changes in the term repo rate on the futures price.

The 84-day repo period is sometimes referred to as the "stub" period, and the risk associated with changes in the term money market rate is known as "stub risk." How a hedger chooses to handle stub risk depends on how much risk is involved and the costs of hedging the risk. In this example, the repo DV01 is just under $3/basis point, while the spot yield DV01 is $145/basis point. If money market conditions are stable, the hedger might be willing to live with the risk and do nothing about it.

On the other hand, if the hedger decides to do something about the risk, the most effective route is a term repo transaction in which the hedger is short the right amount of term cash. If there is a drawback to this approach, it is in the costs of the transaction because of the comparatively wide bid/asked spreads in the term repo market. Unwinding a term repo hedge can be costly.

The futures solutions to offsetting stub risk involve hedges constructed with Fed funds futures, 1-month LIBOR futures, or 3-month Eurodollar futures. Of these, the most effective would be a Fed funds futures hedge. [See *Hedging Stub Risk with Fed Funds Futures.*[1]]

OPTION-ADJUSTED DV01s

The next step in improving our hedge ratios is to incorporate what we know about the way the value of the short's delivery options change as yields rise and fall. Exhibit 5.7, which shows two competing deliverable bonds and a theoretical futures price schedule, illustrates why this is important.

First, when yields are below the crossover yield, the slope of the theoretical futures price curve is greater than the slope of the converted price curve for the low-duration bond, which is also the cheapest to deliver at these yields. As a result, the rule of thumb will produce hedge ratios that are too high because it imputes too low a DV01 to the futures contract.

---

[1] Galen Burghardt and Susan Kirshner, "Hedging Stub Risk with Fed Funds Futures," Carr Futures (now Calyon Financial), June 27, 1996. This article can be obtained from Galen Burghardt at galen.burghardt@calyonfinancial.com.

EXHIBIT 5.7

Option-Adjusted DV01s

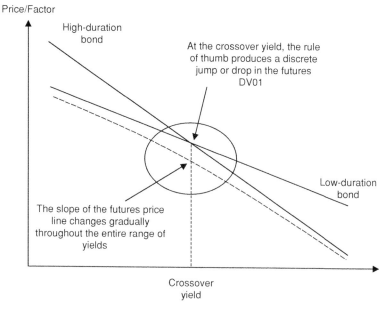

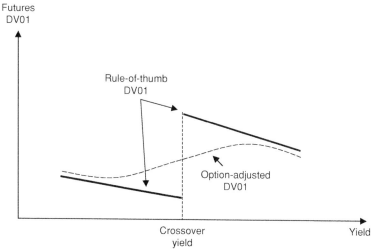

Then, when yields are above the crossover yield, the slope of the theoretical futures price curve is smaller than the slope of the converted price curve for the high-duration bond, which is cheapest to deliver at these higher yields. As a result, the rule of thumb produces hedge ratios that are too low.

Thus, the hedger is either overhedged at low yields or under-hedged at high yields. Further, the adjustment from one to the other is abrupt at the point where yields pass through the crossover point. Because of the knife-edge nature of the situation, a 1-basis-point change in interest rates can produce enormous changes in hedge ratios when the hedger relies on the rule of thumb.

In contrast, the theoretical futures price curve reflects the changing value of the short's delivery options and, as a result, produces a gradual change in the futures DV01. The lower panel of Exhibit 5.7 provides a useful comparison of the way the futures DV01 behaves under the two approaches. Consider the rule of thumb DV01 schedules first. When yields are low, the cheapest to deliver is the low-duration bond and the rule-of-thumb DV01 is low. We can see, too, that the rule-of-thumb DV01 gets lower as yields rise as a result of positive convexity in the price/yield relationship of a noncallable bond. But when yields pass through the crossover yield, the rule-of-thumb takes a discrete upward jump to equal the converted DV01 of the new cheapest to deliver, which is now a high-duration bond. As yields continue to rise, the rule-of-thumb DV01 again falls to reflect positive convexity in the high-duration bond's price/yield relationship.

Convexity of the Futures Price Curve. The behavior of what we call the option-adjusted DV01 is both smoother and more subtle than what we get with the rule of thumb. For example, if yields are either very high or very low, the futures price can exhibit the positive convexity of a firmly entrenched cheapest to deliver. When yields are around a crossover yield, however, the futures price can exhibit negative convexity, which is reflected in a DV01 that actually increases as yields rise.

Calculating Option-Adjusted DV01s. You find option-adjusted DV01s numerically. The first step is to produce a schedule or table of theoretical futures prices for a range of yields. The second step is simply to calculate the slope of the resulting curve at any given level of yields.

Exhibit 5.8 shows theoretical futures prices for different yield levels on April 5, 2001, together with option-adjusted DV01s at the different yield levels. To calculate these DV01s, we approximate the slope of the theoretical futures price curve by averaging the effect of equal-sized increases and decreases in yields. For example, we see that if yields fall 10 basis points from where they closed on April 4, the theoretical futures price would rise from 104.250 to 105.531, for

E X H I B I T   5.8

Calculating the Option-Adjusted DV01 for
the June 2001 Bond Futures Contract

On-the-run yield change (bps)	Theoretical futures price	DV01 per $100K
-60	111.844	
-50	110.563	128.13
-50	109.281	128.13
-30	108.000	126.56
-20	106.750	123.44
-10	105.531	125.00
0	104.250	126.56
10	103.000	126.56
20	101.719	126.56
30	100.469	128.13
40	99.156	129.69
50	97.875	131.25
60	96.531	

Source: *JPMorgan*

an increase of 1.281, or $1,281 per futures contract. In this direction, the value of a basis point would be $128.10. If yields were to rise 10 basis points, the theoretical futures price would fall from 104.25 to 103.00, for a decrease of 1.25, or $1,250 per contract. In this direction, the value of a basis point would be $125.00. The average of the two is (except for some background rounding) $126.55 [= ($128.10 + $125.00)/2], which is approximately the slope of the futures price curve at that point.

It is worth a minute to appreciate what happens to the option-adjusted futures DV01 as yields rise and fall. In the direction of falling yields, we see the DV01 fall over the first 30 basis point decrease in yields, after which we see the DV01 begin to rise again. This peculiar behavior can be explained first by a shift in emphasis from a relatively high-duration bond to a relatively low-duration bond as cheapest to deliver. Once the low-duration bond is secure as cheapest to deliver, however, the increase in the theoretical futures DV01 reflects the positive convexity of that low-duration bond. Going in the other direction, we find that the option-adjusted DV01 is either flat or is rising over the range of yield increases shown here. What we see in this direction is the effect of a shift in emphasis from low-duration to higher-duration bonds as cheapest to deliver. All that's missing from this pattern would be the fall in the option-adjusted DV01 that we would expect to see once yields have risen far enough to secure the highest-duration bond as the cheapest to deliver.

YIELD BETAS

Yields tend not to rise or fall in parallel. Rather, the yield curve tends to flatten as yields rise and steepen as yields fall. There are good theoretical reasons for this kind of thing (e.g., expected returns across the yield spectrum will be equal in a risk-neutral world) and plenty of evidence to back it up. As a result, the yield of shorter-maturity bonds will tend to rise or fall more than the yields of longer-maturity bonds.

If the hedger has a good idea of just how much the curve will tend to flatten or steepen as yields rise and fall, he or she can adjust the hedge ratios accordingly. To use yield betas correctly when reckoning hedge ratios, though, the hedger must pay close attention to the relationship between the bond or bonds he or she is trying to hedge and the reference bond that has been chosen to capture the price/yield behavior of the futures contract. In general, the yield beta hedge ratio for the i bond should be written as:

$$\text{Yield Beta Hedge Ratio} = \frac{(DV01_i \times \beta_i)}{(DV01_{\text{futures}} \times \beta_{\text{ctd}})}$$

$$= \left(\frac{DV01_i}{DV01_{\text{futures}}}\right)\left(\frac{\beta_i}{\beta_{\text{ctd}}}\right)$$

where β_i is the yield beta of the bond you want to hedge, β_{ctd} is the yield beta of the cheapest to deliver, and $DV01_{\text{futures}}$ is the value of the change in the futures price for a 1-basis-point change in the yield of the cheapest to deliver.

To see how this works in practice, consider Exhibit 5.9, which provides DV01 and yield beta information for three bonds, one of which was the cheapest to deliver on April 5 and one of which was the on-the-run bond. Also provided are two futures DV01s, one using the cheapest to deliver as the reference bond and one using the on-the-run as the reference bond. Notice that the futures DV01 with respect to a change in the on-the-run yield (132.92) equals the product of the futures DV01 with respect to a change in the cheapest to deliver yield and the ratio of the cheapest to deliver and on-the-run yield betas [= \$122.42 × (1.0857/1.000)].

EXHIBIT 5.9

Hedging a Portfolio of Bonds

Issue		DV01	Yield Beta	Memo
Coupon	Maturity			
7.5	11/15/16	117.78	1.1365	
7.625	11/15/22	145.45	1.0857	ctd
5.375	2/15/31	144.03	1.0000	otr
Futures (wrt ctd yield)		122.42		
Futures (wrt otr yield)		132.92		

In this setting, if you want to find the futures hedge ratio for the 7.5% of 11/15/16 using the on-the-run as the reference bond for the futures contract, the hedge ratio would be 1.007 [=($117.78 × 1.1365)/($132.92 × 1.0000)]. If you use the cheapest to deliver as the reference bond instead, the hedge ratio would still be 1.007 [=($117.78 × 1.1365)/($122.42 × 1.0857)], because the value of the denominator in both calculations is the same.

PUTTING IT ALL TOGETHER

Exhibit 5.10 provides a summary of the various risk measures you would need if using the June 2001 and September 2001 futures contracts. For the sake of information, we provide the standard rule-of-thumb DV01s that would be used by Bloomberg to calculate hedge ratios. Notice that these are very slightly different for the two contract months, because the September conversion factors are closer to 1.000 than are the June conversion factors. It is possible, too, for the cheapest to deliver to be different for different contract months.

We show option-adjusted DV01s for changes in the yields of two reference bonds—the cheapest to deliver and the on-the-run bond. The difference between the two is explained by their respective yield betas. The yield beta of the cheapest to deliver is 1.0857, while the yield beta of the on-the-run bond is 1.0000. If true, a 1-basis-point increase in the on-the-run bond's yield would produce a 1.0857-basis-point increase in the yield of the cheapest to deliver. Thus, if the DV01 with respect to a change in the cheapest to deliver bond's yield is 122.42, then by extension, the DV01 with respect to a change in the on-the-run yield should be 132.92 [≅ 1.0857 × 122.42].

E X H I B I T   5.10

Futures Risk Measures
(Close 4/4/01, Trade 4/5/01, Settle 4/6/01)

(Contract Jun-01)

	2-year	5-year	10-year	Bond
Market Price	103–04+	105–22	106–08	103–30
Theoretical Price	103–05+	105–21	106–09+	103–-25
Rule-of-Thumb DV01	38.63	42.84	60.76	121.86
Option-Adjusted DV01 wrt				
CTD yield	39.06	43.20	66.13	122.42
OTR yield	39.07	43.20	69.75	132.92
Option-Adjusted Duration wrt				
CTD yield	1.89	4.09	6.22	11.80
OTR yield	1.89	4.09	6.56	12.81
Repo DV01	-5.06	-2.50	-2.53	-2.46

(Contract Sep-01)

	2-year	5-year	10-year	Bond
Market Price	103–06+	105–08	105–25+	103–14
Theoretical Price	103–06+	105–06+	105–28+	103–08+
Rule-of-Thumb DV01	43.57	42.82	62.31	121.96
Option-Adjusted DV01 wrt				
CTD yield	45.25	44.23	69.06	124.20
OTR yield	44.99	44.23	72.71	134.85
Option-Adjusted Duration wrt				
CTD yield	2.19	4.20	6.52	12.03
OTR yield	2.18	4.20	6.87	13.06
Repo DV01	-10.43	-5.24	-5.27	-5.10

For the contracts, the option-adjusted DV01s are not very different from those provided by the simple rule of thumb. For the 10-year note contract, however, the difference is pronounced. In this particular example, the cheapest to deliver note was the lowest-duration note in the deliverable set. Competing bonds with higher durations were exerting an influence on the 10-year futures contract's price, and taking their presence into account produced an option-adjusted DV01 of $66.13 as opposed to $60.76. By this reckoning, the rule-of-thumb approach would yield hedge ratios about 10% larger than they should be.

We also show option-adjusted durations, which are calculated as the percent change in the portfolio equivalent value of the futures contract. For example, the option-adjusted duration of the June 10-year contract is shown as 6.22% [= $66.13 per bp × 100 bps/$106,250]%.

By the same token, you can calculate an option-adjusted DV01 for a contract as the product of its duration and portfolio equivalent value divided by 100 basis points.

The repo DV01s are shown with negative signs as a way of emphasizing the different directions in which changes in bond yields and term repo rates cause the futures price to go. That is, while an increase in spot yields will cause futures prices to fall, an increase in term repo rates will cause the futures price to rise.

Perhaps the most important thing to notice about repo DV01s is that they are, for the 5-year, 10-year, and bond contracts, all roughly the same size for a given contract month. This is because the repo effect is tied to the amount of money involved in purchasing the underlying cheapest to deliver. (The repo DV01 of the 2-year contract is roughly twice as large as it is for the other three contracts because this is a $200,000 par amount contract.) Because the repo effect is about the same size for contracts with different underlying maturities, the hedger will find that repo stub risk becomes a relatively larger problem, the shorter is the maturity of the contract. A repo DV01 of $2.46 for the Jun 01 bond contract is only 2% of the contract's spot DV01 of $122.42. For the 10-year contract, its repo DV01 of $2.53 represents 3.8% of its spot DV01 of $66.13. And for the 2-year contract, its repo DV01 of $5.06 is 13% of its spot DV01. So, as a practical matter, repo stub risk is relatively more important for anyone hedging with the shorter-term contracts.

RECKONING THE P/L OF A HEDGE

The P/L on a cash bond has three parts: price change, coupon income, and financing expense. If you own a real bond, you make or lose money as the price rises or falls, and with the passing of time, you earn an increasingly large claim on coupon income. From the sum of these two, you might subtract the explicit cost of financing the bond if you have borrowed to buy the bond. Or, if you have bought the bond outright, you might subtract the forgone earnings on the cash you would have if you had not bought the bond. Either way, the all-in return on the bond should reflect all three things.

In contrast, the P/L on a futures contract has only one part: price change. A futures contract is a fully leveraged position in bonds; it spins off no coupon income and entails no financing cost.

For a hedger who wants to know how his or her hedge is performing, therefore, the net P/L of the hedged position should reflect all four elements: price changes for both the bond and the futures, coupon income, and financing expense. This is especially important because a long bond/short futures position will tend over time to lose money on the convergence between the spot and futures prices. Some of this convergence is due to nothing more than carry, and if carry is not added to the hedge P/L, the hedge will look worse than it actually is.

EVALUATING HEDGE PERFORMANCE

There comes a time for every hedger to explain why a hedge did not perform according to plan. This time rarely comes when a hedged position has done really well, although perhaps it should. Instead, the time more often comes when a hedge is losing money and the boss wants to know why. We now have the tools that the hedger needs to explain why a hedge with futures does what it does. To evaluate the performance of a hedge, the key things that matter include

- Changes in the value of the short's delivery options
- Changes in yield spreads between bonds
- Changes in the stub repo rate (perhaps)

Let's consider each in turn.

Delivery Option Values.   As shown in Exhibit 5.11, a hedger who is long bonds or notes and short futures has a position that, if truly DV01-neutral, resembles a long straddle. By selling futures, the hedger gives up basis net of carry in exchange for a futures convexity that is less than that of the bonds he or she is hedging. In options parlance, the hedger is long yield volatility and will do well or badly depending on whether yields change more or less than the market expects. The simple passing of time will cost the hedger money. The basis net of carry that the hedger pays when selling futures will slowly decay as the futures price converges up to meet the converted price of the cheapest to deliver. If yields rise or fall enough, however, the benefits of actual or promised changes in the cheapest to deliver can more than offset the costs of convergence.

Also, the value of the delivery options can rise or fall simply because the market's expectations about yield volatility rise or fall. As a result, changes in expectations about yield volatility will produce gains or losses that simply add to or subtract from whatever

EXHIBIT 5.11

A Futures Hedge Is Like a Long Straddle

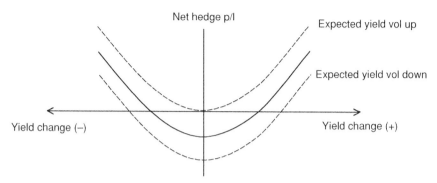

else the hedge is doing because rates are rising, falling, or not doing much.

Changes in Yield Spreads. If the hedger is long anything other than the cheapest to deliver, unexpected changes in yield spreads can produce gains or losses. In particular, if the yield on the bond you are hedging falls relative to the yield on the cheapest to deliver, or falls more than the bonds' yield betas would suggest, you will make more on the bond or lose less on the futures than expected.

Changes in the Stub Repo Rate. We know that changes in term repo rates will produce changes in the futures price that are unrelated to changes in spot yields. Whether this is a problem for the hedger really depends on whether the stub repo exposure has been hedged separately. If it has not—that is, if the hedger is simply long the bond and has done nothing to offset stub repo exposure—changes in term repo rates will be a source of extra gain or loss on the hedge. Increases in term repo rates will tend to hurt someone who is short futures, while decreases in term repo rates will tend to help.

WORKING WITH DURATIONS

Duration, as defined by Macaulay, is a weighted average of the times remaining to various cash flows where the weights are the relative present values of those cash flows. That is,

$$\text{Macaulay Duration} = \sum \frac{t P_t C_t}{P} \qquad \text{(for } t = 1 \text{ to maturity)}$$

where t is the time between now and a cash flow (measured in years), $P_t = 1/(1 + r_t)^t$ is the price of a \$1 zero-coupon bond that matures t periods from now, C_t is the amount of cash flow to be paid or received t years from now, and P is the market price of the entire instrument. Measured this way, the units are years. For example, a 10-year Treasury note might have a duration of 7 years.

Measured in years, Macaulay's duration is of no particular use to anyone. Transformed, however, duration has several useful properties including

- Its use as a risk measure
- Its additivity
- Its use in calculating hedge ratios.

It is used widely in managing bond portfolios.

Risk Measure   To get a useful measure of the sensitivity of a bond's price to a change in its yield, we define "modified duration" as

$$\text{Modified Duration} = \frac{\text{Macaulay Duration}}{1 + \left(\dfrac{r}{f} \right)}$$

where r is the annualized yield on the instrument and f is the payment frequency (e.g., $f = 2$ for a Treasury instrument to reflect semi-annual coupon payments). In this form, duration is the link between yield changes and price changes. In particular,

Percent Price Change $\approx -$ Modified Duration $\times$ Yield Change

where the yield change is expressed in percentage points. Hence, modified duration tells us the percentage point change in the price of a bond for a 1-percentage-point (100-basis-point) change in the bond's yield.

For example, on April 5, 2001, the 7-5/8% coupon Treasury bond maturing 11/15/22 had a modified duration of 11.40. At 2 p.m. (Chicago time) its price was 124-20/32nds (or 124.625) to yield 6.39% to maturity. Its full price including accrued interest was 127.616. A modified duration of 11.40 indicates that a 1-percentage-point increase in the bond's yield would cause its price to fall by 11.40% of its full price, or 14.55 [= 0.1140 × 127.616] points. If the yield on this bond increased 10 basis points to 6.49%, the bond's modified duration indicates that the bond's price would fall by 1.455 points, or slightly less than 47/32nds.

Additivity A second helpful property is that the duration of a cash bond portfolio is simply a weighted average of the durations of the component bonds. The weights are the relative holdings, at market prices, of the bonds in the portfolio. For example, a portfolio containing $50 million of a bond with a duration of 10 and $100 million of a bond with a duration of 6 has a duration of

$$7.3 = \frac{\$50 \times 10 + \$100 \times 6}{\$50 + \$100}$$

Hedge Ratio Because of the relationship between a bond or note's duration and its dollar value of a basis point, durations can be used in quick and easy hedge calculations. If the purpose of a hedge is to offset the price exposure in a portfolio, then the number of futures contracts that the hedger holds, when multiplied by the change in the value of one futures contract, should equal the negative of the change in the value of the portfolio to be hedged. If this condition is met, then the hedger will make as much on the hedge as is lost on the portfolio, or will lose as much on the hedge as is made on the portfolio.

Either way, as shown in Exhibit 5.1, for someone whose portfolio is net long so that a rise in interest rates produces a loss, the appropriate number of futures to sell is found for any given change in yields simply by dividing the change in the value of the portfolio by the change in the value of one futures contract. This can be done in either of two ways.

One way is to calculate the hedge ratio directly by dividing the dollar value of a basis point of the portfolio by the dollar value of a basis point for one futures contract. The other is to use the durations of the portfolio and the futures contract together with their market or market equivalent values. What allows you to do this is that an issue's or portfolio's DV01 is proportional to the product of its duration and market value divided by 100. In particular,

$$DV01 = \frac{Duration \times Market\ Value}{100}$$

where the dividing through by 100 reflects the convention of stating duration as the percent change in value for a 100-basis-point change in the yield. For example, with a full price including accrued interest of 128.9361 and a modified duration of 10.25%, the dollar value of a basis point for $1 million face or par amount of the 9-7/8% of 11/15/15 would be

$$DV01 = \left[\frac{\text{Duration} \times \text{Market Value}}{100}\right]$$

$$= \left[\frac{0.1025 \times 1.289361 \times \$1,000,000}{100}\right]$$

$$= \frac{\$1,321.60}{\text{per basis point}}$$

or \$132,160 for a 100-basis point change.

Armed with this relationship, we find that we can calculate the same hedge ratio by dividing the product of the portfolio's duration and market value by the product of the futures contract's duration and its market equivalent value. Or, if we were hedging one cash instrument with another, we would use the product of the duration and market value of the hedge instrument. Consider the problem of hedging \$100 million market value of an issue that has a duration of 5 using an instrument that has a duration of 10. The number of millions of the hedge instrument that would have to be sold or shorted would be calculated as

$$\text{Amount to Sell} = \frac{5 \times \$100 \text{ million}}{10 \times \$1 \text{ million}}$$

$$= \frac{\$500}{\$10}$$

$$= 50$$

That is, the hedger would sell \$50 million of the hedge instrument to offset the interest rate exposure in the portfolio. A check on this hedge can be made by calculating the duration of the hedged portfolio, which would be

$$\text{Hedged Portfolio Duration} = \frac{(5 \times \$100) + (10 \times -\$50)}{\$100 - \$50}$$

$$= 0$$

DURATION OF A FUTURES CONTRACT

Fitting bond futures into this hedging framework poses two challenges, both stemming from the fact that bond futures have neither periodic cash payments nor a yield to maturity. This means that bond futures have no market value in the same sense that a bond or note has a market value. Also, it means that we cannot calculate the duration of a futures contract as we do for a cash bond.

E X H I B I T   5.12

Measuring Duration with Futures in a Bond Portfolio

For calculating price exposure, a futures contract is treated as if it has a portfolio equivalent value of $100,000 par value of bonds. Thus, a futures price of 93 would produce a portfolio equivalent market value for one futures contract of $93,000. If the duration of the futures contract were 8, a 100-basis-point increase in the yield of the underlying bond would cause the futures price to fall 8 percent, or 7.44 [= 93 × 0.08] points. Under the terms of the contract, this would be a loss of $7,440 to the long and would have to be paid through the clearing house in the form of variation margin to the short.

When calculating the duration of a portfolio, however, you must remember that a futures contract ties up no cash and has no net liquidating value. That is, no money changes hands when a long or short position in a futures contract is established, and no money is either required or released when a futures position is unwound or offset. In practice, this means that the duration of a portfolio that contains bond futures (or note futures) is calculated as

Bond Duration *times* Bond Market Value

plus

Futures Duration *times* Futures Market Equivalent Value

the sum of which is divided by

Bond Market Value

In other words, the hypothetical market value of the futures position is used in reckoning price exposure, which is used in the numerator of the duration calculation. Only the actual net liquidating value or cashing out value of the portfolio, however, is used in the denominator.

For example, consider a portfolio that contains $100 million market value of bonds and notes and 200 *short* futures at a market price of 90. For the purpose of calculating exposure to yield changes, the futures would be treated as if they have a market value of $18 million [= 200 × $90,000]. If the duration of the cash bond and note portfolio were 5 and the duration of the futures contract 8, the duration of this particular portfolio would be

Portfolio Duration   = [($100 × 5) + (−$18 × 8)] / $100

                      = [$500 − $144] / $100

                      = 3.56

We meet the first challenge simply by treating a bond or note futures contract for the purpose of measuring price risk as if it has the portfolio equivalent value of $100,000 face value of an actual bond or note ($200,000 for the 2-year note contract). Thus, if the futures price were 105, the portfolio equivalent value of the futures contract would be $105,000. That is, the price risk in one futures contract would be the same as the price risk of $105,000 market value of a bond or note with the same duration. You must still be careful in reckoning the duration of a portfolio that contains bond and note futures, however. As we show at the end of this chapter, bond and note futures contribute price risk to a portfolio but no market value. As a result, their portfolio equivalent values appear in the numerator of the duration calculation but not in the denominator. See Exhibit 5.12 for an example.

We meet the duration challenge by linking the price sensitivity of the futures contract to a change in the yield of an underlying bond. In particular, once we have established the relationship between the price of the futures contract and the yield of an underlying bond, we can tie *changes* in the futures price directly to *changes* in the underlying bond's yield. Thus, we can calculate the duration of a futures contract directly by dividing the percent change in the futures price by the change in the yield of the underlying bond.

APPENDIX TO CHAPTER 5

Better Hedges
with Yield Betas?[1]

Galen Burghardt and Scott Lyden

The yield curve tends to flatten when yields rise and to steepen when yields fall, as illustrated in Exhibit A5.-1. Thus, the yield on a short-maturity or low-duration bond will tend to change more than the yield on a long-maturity or high-duration bond.

The systematic tendency of the yield curve to flatten and steepen as yields rise and fall poses an interesting challenge for hedgers who must use a bond that lies at one point along the curve to offset the exposure in a bond that lies at a different point along the curve. This is particularly true for anyone who uses Treasury bond or note futures to hedge cash bonds. The current 30-year Treasury bond, for example, matures in November 2027, while the current cheapest to deliver for the Treasury bond futures contract matures in February 2015. Thus, anyone hedging the current long

---

1 Originally published January 28, 1998, as a Carr Futures (now Calyon Financial) research note.

EXHIBIT A5.1

Shifts in the Yield Curve

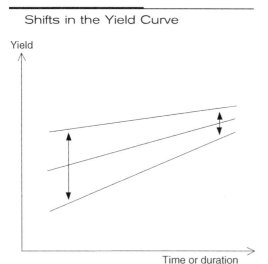

bond with Treasury futures would, in effect, be hedging a 30-year bond with an 18-year bond.

The usual approach to such a hedging problem is to find how much of the 18-year bond you would have to sell to produce an equal but offsetting dollar value of a basis point for the 30-year bond. This is, for example, the hedge solution that you get from Bloomberg if you ask it to hedge one bond with another. For instance, if you were to punch in GT30 <GOVT> PDH1 <GO>, you would be shown a hedge for the current long bond that has equal but offsetting DV01s.

The obvious drawback to this approach is that if you are hedging a 30-year bond with an 18-year bond, the resulting hedge has too much of the 18-year bond. Its yield changes more than basis-point-for-basis-point with the change in the yield on the 30-year bond, so you need less of the 18-year bond than the standard hedge solution suggests.

USING YIELD BETAS TO IMPROVE HEDGES

The standard solution to this problem is to use a *yield beta* to scale down the amount of the 18-year bond to compensate for its greater yield variability. In this example, the yield beta would be

$$\text{Yield Beta}_{18,30} = \frac{\Delta y_{18}}{\Delta y_{30}}$$

which is the change in the yield on the 18-year bond for a change in the yield on the 30-year bond. Armed with an estimate of the value of this yield beta, a better hedge ratio would be

$$\text{Hedge Ratio}_{18,30} = \frac{\text{DV01}_{30}}{\text{Yield Beta}_{18,30} \times \text{DV01}_{18}}$$

which would be smaller than the conventional hedge ratio. How much smaller depends, of course, on the value of the yield beta.

Estimating Yield Betas for Treasury Bonds and Notes

To estimate a set of yield betas for Treasury issues, you must choose something to measure distance along the x-axis in Exhibit A5.1. In practice, you can choose between duration and maturity. Of these two, the measure that offers the greatest promise is duration. Given this measure, and using Treasury yield data for the period from 1990 to date, we calculated standard deviations of yield changes at each duration. A scatter plot of these results, together with a least squares regression of standard deviations of yield changes against duration, is shown in Exhibit A5.2. In this exhibit, the lowest modified duration is 2, while highest modified duration is 12.5. (The relationship in Exhibit A5.2 tends to break down inside the two-year mark. For this reason, the empirical results presented in this note apply only to bonds of duration two years or more.)

E X H I B I T   A5.2

The Relationship between Yield Changes and Duration

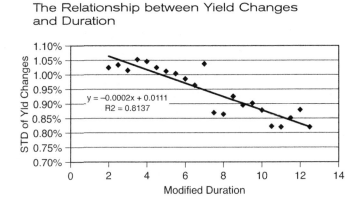

If we are willing to work with these regression results, and if we are willing to assume that yield changes at one duration are perfectly correlated with yield changes at another duration, a yield beta is simply the ratio of the standard deviation of yield changes at one duration to the standard deviation of yield changes at the other. In our work, we calculate all yield betas relative to the standard deviation of yield changes of whatever the current on-the-run long bond happens to be. Thus, the yield beta of the current long bond in our reports is always 1.000.

Suppose, for example, that the current long bond has a duration of 12.5. From Exhibit A5.3 we find that the estimated standard deviation of yield changes for a bond with this duration is 81.64

E X H I B I T   A5.3

Estimated Yield Betas

| Duration | Standard deviation of weekly yield changes | | Yield betas |
| | Estimated | Fitted | |
	(annualized)		
2	1.0246	1.0721	1.313
2.5	1.0335	1.0599	1.298
3	1.0154	1.0477	1.283
3.5	1.052	1.0355	1.268
4	1.0456	1.0234	1.254
4.5	1.025	1.0112	1.239
5	1.0122	0.999	1.224
5.5	1.0041	0.9868	1.209
6	0.9861	0.9474	1.16
6.5	0.9638	0.9625	1.179
7	1.0375	0.9503	1.164
7.5	0.8692	0.9381	1.149
8	0.8639	0.926	1.134
8.5	0.9259	0.9138	1.119
9	0.8949	0.9016	1.104
9.5	0.9021	0.8894	1.089
10	0.8776	0.8773	1.075
10.5	0.8221	0.8651	1.06
11	0.8199	0.8529	1.045
11.5	0.8509	0.8407	1.03
12	0.879	0.8286	1.015
12.5	0.8199	0.8164	1

basis points annualized. Suppose further that the bond that is currently cheapest to deliver for the Treasury bond futures contract has a duration of nine years. From Exhibit A5.3 we see that the estimated standard deviation of yield changes for a bond with this duration is 90.16 basis points annualized.

Given these estimates, then, the yield beta of the current cheapest to deliver relative to the current long bond would be 1.104 [= 90.16/81.64], which is the ratio of "fitted" standard deviations in Exhibit A5.3. In other words, for each basis point change in the yield of the current long bond, the yield of cheapest to deliver would be expected to change by 1.104 basis points. As a result, anyone hedging the long bond with bond futures needs about 10% fewer contracts than indicated by the standard hedge ratio.

USING YIELD BETAS TO IMPROVE HEDGES

To make all this more concrete, suppose we were to hedge a long position of $100 million par amount of the 6-1/8% of 11/15/27, which was the on-the-run 30-year Treasury on January 12, 1998. In Exhibit A5.4 we see that its modified duration was 13.94, its DV01 was $149.07 per $100,000 face amount, and its yield beta using our convention was 1.000. Thus, the total DV01 for $100 million of this bond would be $149,070 [= $149.07 × ($100,000,000/$100,000)].

On the same day, the cheapest bond to deliver into the March '98 Treasury bond futures contract was the 11-1/4% of 2/15/15, which had a modified duration of 9.24, a DV01 of $152.81 per $100,000 par amount, and a yield beta of 1.128. Also note that this bond's factor

EXHIBIT A5.4

Yield Betas for Selected Deliverable Bonds
(March '98 Bond Futures Contract, 1/12/98 Trade Date*)

Issue		Modified duration	DV01	Yield beta
coupon	maturity			
11 1/4	2/15/15	9.24	152.81	1.128
7 1/2	11/15/16	10.7	129.69	1.105
8 7/8	2/15/19	10.83	152.74	1.085
7 7/8	2/15/21	11.6	150.13	1.064
7 5/8	11/15/22	12.27	153.45	1.045
6 7/8	8/15/25	12.93	152.05	1.027
6 1/8	11/15/27	13.94	149.07	1

*using 1/09/98 closing prices

E X H I B I T   A5.5

Futures DV01s and Yield Betas
(March '98 Bond Futures Contract,
1/12/98 Trade Date*)

Futures contract	DV01**	CTD yield beta
Bond	117.84	1.128
10-year	61.81	1.234
5-year	42.89	1.274

*using 1/09/98 closing prices
**CTD DV01/CTD factor*

for the March '98 futures contract was 1.2968. Given this information, the standard rule of thumb for reckoning futures hedge ratios
would treat the futures contract as if it had a DV01 of $117.84 [=
$152.81/1.2968], which is simply the cheapest to deliver's DV01
divided by its factor. The standard rule of thumb would, as a result,
indicate that you should sell 1,265 [= $149,070/$117.84] of the March
'98 futures contract. (See Exhibit A5.5.)

This would, however, be too many contracts. For that matter, the
cheapest to deliver's yield beta of 1.128 suggests that the standard
hedge ratio would be about 12.8% too high. If the yield on the on-the-
run bond were to rise 100 basis points, the yield on the cheapest to
deliver would be expected to rise 112.8 basis points, and you would
end up making money on the hedge. On the other hand, if the yield
on the long bond were to fall 100 basis points, the yield on the
cheapest to deliver would be expected to fall by 112.8 basis points,
and you would lose money on the hedge.

A better hedge would be to sell 1,121 [= $149,070/(1.128 ×
$117.84)] of the March lows for the relatively greater variability of the
yield on the cheapest to deliver. As a result, the hedger can expect
the change in the value of his or her position in the on-the-run
bond to be just offset by changes in the value of his or her position
in Treasury futures.

HEDGING SOMETHING OTHER
THAN THE CURRENT LONG BOND

To hedge a bond other than the long bond, you must remember to
adjust the DV01 of the bond you are hedging by its yield beta as well
as the DV01 of whatever bond you are using as a hedge. For example,
if you wanted to hedge a position in the 7-7/8% of 2/15/21, whose

yield beta on January 12 was 1.064, you would simply scale up its DV01. The futures hedge for $100 million of this bond would be 1,202 = [(1.064 × $150,130)/(1.128 × $117.84)] of the March '98 bond futures contracts. Notice that the DV01s in both the numerator and denominator have been adjusted for the bonds' respective yield betas.

WHEN YIELD BETAS CAN GET YOU INTO TROUBLE

Yield betas have two kinds of problems that can get you into trouble. One is that they are not especially stable over time. Another is that yield changes for bonds with different durations are not perfectly correlated with one another.

Unstable Yield Betas

The idea that the yield curve tends to flatten as yields rise and steepen as yield fall is a more or less firmly embedded piece of conventional market wisdom. It is a statistical regularity for which there is considerable evidence. The only problem is that the regularity is actually somewhat irregular, and there are some times when it isn't even close to true.

On January 12, 1998, the on-the-run 10-year Treasury had an estimated yield beta of 1.186. From Exhibit A5.6, though, we find that its yield beta could have been as high as 2.88 (which is our estimate for 1991) or as low as 0.46 (which is what it was in 1993, when the yield curve flattened rather than steepened as yields fell). Thus,

E X H I B I T   A5.6

Yield Betas by Year*

Year	\multicolumn{4}{c}{On-the-run maturity}
	3	5	10	30
1990	1	1.17	1.49	1
1991	1.55	2.38	2.88	1
1992	1.64	2.19	2.41	1
1993	0.75	0.64	0.46	1
1994	1.26	1.52	1.78	1
1995	1.15	1.23	1.23	1
1996	1.28	1.4	1.4	1
1997	1.02	0.94	0.82	1

*ratios of standard deviations of weekly yield changes

yield betas will work better in some years and situations than in others. And in some years, such as 1993 and 1997, they might actually work against you.

Competing Hedge Ratios When Correlations Are Less Than 1.0

If correlations between yield changes are very much less than 1.00, you face an interesting set of choices about what you want your hedge to accomplish. In fact, as shown in Exhibit A5.7, the correlations between yield changes for issues that are fairly close to one another on the yield curve are quite high. Notice, for example, that the estimated correlation between changes in 30-year and 10-year yields is 0.97. The correlations between changes in 10-year and 5-year yields and between changes in 5-year and 3-year yields are also quite high. In these cases, satisfactory hedge ratios can be calculated without adjusting for imperfectly correlated yield changes.

COMPETING HEDGE RATIOS

But suppose, for some reason, that you want to hedge a long position in the on-the-run 30-year Treasury with a short position in the 5-year Treasury where the correlation between yield changes is only 0.88. In a case such as this, you can choose among four competing hedge ratios, each of which achieves some particular purpose.

These competing hedge ratios are summarized in Exhibit A5.8. Shown at the top is the *conventional hedge ratio*, which is simply the ratio of the DV01s of the two issues. This hedge ratio is designed to

EXHIBIT A5.7

Correlations and Standard Deviations of
Weekly Yield Changes
(On-the-Run Treasury Issues, 1990 through 1997)

Maturity	Correlations by maturity				Annualized standard deviations (basis points)
	30	10	5	3	
30	1	0.97	0.88	0.74	81.7
10		1	0.96	0.87	94.3
5			1	0.97	101.9
3				1	104.1

E X H I B I T   A5.8

Competing Hedge Ratios

Conventional

$$\frac{DV01_{30}}{DV01_{5}}$$

Yield Beta

$$\frac{DV01_{30}}{DV01_{5}} \times \frac{\sigma_{30}}{\sigma_{5}} = \frac{DV01_{30}}{DV01_{5}(\sigma_{5} / \sigma_{30})}$$

Yield Delta

$$\frac{DV01_{30}}{DV01_{5}} \times \frac{\sigma_{30}}{\sigma_{5}\rho_{5,30}} = \frac{DV01_{30}}{DV01_{5}(\sigma_{5} / \sigma_{30})\rho_{5,30}}$$

Minimum Variance

$$\frac{DV01_{30}}{DV01_{5}} \times \frac{\sigma_{30}\rho_{5,30}}{\sigma_{5}} = \frac{DV01_{30}\rho_{5,30}}{DV01_{5}(\sigma_{5} / \sigma_{30})}$$

give you equal and offsetting DV01s and is well suited for trading the yield spread between the two issues.

The *yield beta hedge ratio* looks like the conventional hedge ratio except that the DV01s have been weighted by the standard deviations of their respective yield changes. Because we have defined yield betas relative to changes in the yield of the on-the-run 30-year bond, we have rewritten this hedge ratio to show the DV01 of the 5-year note weighted by its yield beta.

The *yield delta hedge ratio* looks like the yield beta hedge ratio except that an allowance has been made for the correlation between changes in the two issue's yields. Since we are beginning with a position in the 30-year bond, the expected change in the 5-year yield in response to a change in the 30-year yield would be found by regressing changes in 5-year yields against changes in 30-year yields. If we were to do this, the 5-year's yield delta would be equal to the yield beta multiplied by the correlation between changes in the issues' yields.

An altogether different approach is to find the hedge ratio that minimizes the variance or standard deviation of day-to-day changes in the value of the portfolio. This *minimum variance hedge ratio*, if we start with a position in the 30-year bond and find the right amount of the 5-year note, looks like the yield beta hedge ratio except that the correlation between yield changes appears in the numerator.

Sample Calculations

Given the correlations and standard deviations shown in Exhibit A5.7, examples of these four hedge ratios are shown in Exhibit A5.9. With a correlation as low as 0.88, the sizes of the competing hedge ratios can be quite different. For example, the conventional hedge for $100 million of the 30-year bond would be $341.2 million of the 5-year note. Notice that this hedge ratio provides a zero net DV01 for the position but that the expected net DV01 (calculated using the estimated coefficient from a regression of 5-year yield changes on 30-year yield changes) would be $-$14,600.

The effect of allowing for the 5-year's yield beta would be to reduce the hedge to $273.6 million. When the correlation between two yield changes is less than 1.0, however, the yield beta adjustments overcorrects for the greater volatility of the 5-year note and produces a hedged position whose net expected DV01 is a positive $17,900.

If we increase the hedge ratio to $310.9 million of the 5-year, which is what we get if we divide the yield beta hedge ratio by a

EXHIBIT A5.9

Different Hedges for $100 Million of the OTR 30-Year Treasury (January 12, 1998)

| | | Hedge characteristics | | |
Hedge ratio	Short position in the OTR 5-year Treasury	Daily standard deviation*	Net DV01	Net expected DV01*
	($ mill)		($ thds)	
unhedged	0	770.3	149.1	149.1
	200	383.4	61.7	53.2
min. variance	240.7	365.9	43.9	33.6
yield beta	273.6	377.4	29.5	17.9
yield delta	310.9	415.8	13.2	0
conventional	341.2	462.5	0	-14.6

based on standard deviations and correlations for 1990-1997

correlation value of 0.88, we can reduce the expected change in the value of the portfolio to zero.

If the hedger wants to minimize the day-to-day variance of the value of the portfolio, the appropriate hedge would be $240.7 million of the 5-year. This is, however, the most bullish of the four hedged positions.

For the sake of comparison, we have included the unhedged position (to show how effective the various hedges are in reducing the position's DV01 or the day-to-day standard deviation of changes in its net value) and a hedge of $200 million (to show that the hedge of $240.7 million is a minimum variance hedge).

Authors' note: We would like to thank William Hoskins for his helpful comments.

Trading the Basis

Once you have a solid understanding of how Treasury bond and note futures are priced and how the relationship between futures and cash prices should behave, you are ready to undertake basis trading. The basic mechanics of buying and selling the basis were explained in Chapter 1. In this chapter, we examine the basic menu of basis trades, which includes

- Selling expensive bases
- Buying cheap bases
- Buying or selling "hot-run" bases
- Trading the calendar spread
- Trading RP special effects
- Basis trading when the CTD is in short supply

We close the chapter with a section on a number of practical considerations, including the difference between term and overnight financing, short squeezes, taking basis trades into a delivery month, and the importance of having the bonds in the box before making delivery.

SELLING THE BASIS WHEN IT IS EXPENSIVE

For several years in the 1980s, bond futures were chronically cheap, and it was possible to make money consistently by selling the bond basis. This was a time when portfolio managers could add a few hundred basis points to the yield on a portfolio doing nothing more than selling Treasury bonds out of portfolio and replacing them with their risk equivalent in Treasury bond futures. By the end of the 1980s, however, bond futures had become more or less fairly priced most of the time, and one could no longer profit from a naive short basis strategy.

Although Treasury bond futures are no longer chronically cheap, there have still been regular opportunities to profit from selling the 10-year basis. Because 10-year futures are widely used as a hedge by mortgage investors and other portfolio managers, the contract trades below fair value more often than not. This seems especially true when the "on-the run" 10-year Treasury note trades special in the repo market and hedgers find 10-year cash Treasuries expensive to short.

In selling the basis, you can choose between selling the basis of the cheapest to deliver and selling the basis of a non-cheap bond. As long as the basis is rich, you can expect to make money either way. Each approach has its own risk and return characteristics, however, and requires a separate analysis.

Selling the CTD Basis

Selling the basis of the cheapest to deliver note can be likened to selling out of the money strategic delivery options. If the note remains cheapest to deliver throughout the life of the contract all the way to expiration, the strategic delivery options will expire out of the money and be worthless. If this happens, its basis converges to zero, and your profit will be the difference between the change in the basis from the level at which you sold it and any costs of carrying the short position. In other words, all you stand to make by selling the basis of the cheapest to deliver is its basis net of carry.

If the note whose basis you have sold is replaced by another as cheapest to deliver, the strategic delivery options that are embedded in the basis you have sold go in the money. This can happen either because of a change in the general level of yields or because of a change in yield spreads among the notes in the deliverable set. Either way, the basis widens out and you lose money, and there is no limit to the amount of money you stand to lose.

Thus, a short basis position in the cheapest to deliver note has profit-and-loss characteristics very much like those in any short position in an out of the money option. The most you can make is the option's premium, and this you tend to earn slowly in the form of time decay as the option ages and approaches expiration. The option premium that you stand to earn from selling the cheapest to deliver's basis is its basis net of carry, and this you earn slowly as the basis converges to zero as the position approaches expiration of the futures contract. At the same time, the potential losses are unlimited.

Basis Net of Carry   By tracking the basis net of carry for the cheapest to deliver note or bond, we can see how much the basis market has been charging for the strategic delivery options embedded in the futures contracts. The top panel of Exhibit 6.1 chronicles the behavior of the net basis for the 5-year Treasury note contract from January 2000 through March 2002. The middle and bottom panels of Exhibit 6.1 track basis net of carry of the cheapest to deliver issues for the 10-year Treasury note contract and the Treasury bond over the same period. In all three cases, the basis net of carry is measured in ticks or 32nds on the vertical axis, and in all three exhibits, the powerful tendency for convergence corresponds neatly to the quarterly expiration cycle.

By themselves, the three panels in Exhibit 6.1 paint a rosier picture of selling the basis than is warranted because they do not account for changes in the cheapest to deliver that may have occurred. Rather, they track the net basis of whichever note or bond is cheapest to deliver on any given day. Any changes in the cheapest to deliver that took place will have reduced the amount that anyone selling the cheapest to deliver basis made over these periods.

The success of selling the basis of the cheapest to deliver issue depends on whether the issue remains cheapest to deliver. If it does, then the basis seller who carries the position to final delivery gets to keep the entire basis net of carry. If the original cheapest to deliver issue is replaced by another, then the basis seller loses some of, all of, or more than the original basis net of carry.

Experience with the Trade   A more realistic picture of the gains and losses from selling the cheapest to deliver basis is provided by Exhibit 6.2, which shows how a naive approach to selling the basis in the 10-year Treasury note contract might have performed from June 1998 through June 2004.

The first three columns of the exhibit identify the issue that was cheapest to deliver three months before the expiration of the futures contract. For example, the 7-1/2% of 2/05 was the cheapest to deliver 10-year note for the June 1998 futures contract. Three months before the expiration of the June contract, the issue's basis was 13.4/32nds. Carry amounted to 11.2/32nds, so the issue's basis net of carry was 2.1/32nds [= 13.4/32nds − 11.2/32nds]. At futures expiration, the issue's basis was 1.3/32nds and carry was also 1.3/32nds; therefore, the issue's basis net of carry was 0/32nds.

EXHIBIT 6.1

Basis Net of Carry of the Cheapest to Deliver

5-year note futures

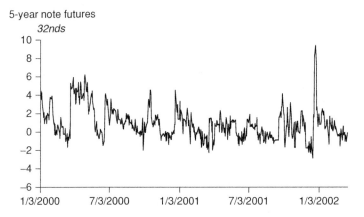

10-year note futures

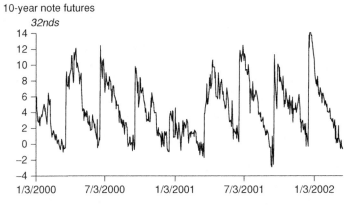

Bond futures

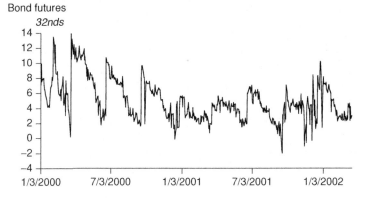

Source: JPMorgan

E X H I B I T 6.2

Cheapest to Deliver 10-Year Basis
(June 1998 to June 2004; 32nds)

Cheapest to Deliver			3 Months to Expiration			At Expiration			Change in
Contract	Coupon	Maturity	Basis	Carry	BNOC	Basis	Carry	BNOC	BNOC
Jun-98	7.5	Feb-05	13.4	11.2	2.1	1.3	1.3	0.0	-2.1
Sep-98	6.5	May-05	11.0	4.1	6.9	-0.7	0.2	-0.9	-7.8
Dec-98	6.5	Aug-05	7.0	3.8	3.2	2.2	0.8	1.4	-1.8
Mar-99	5.875	Nov-05	6.2	6.3	-0.1	2.2	0.7	1.5	1.6
Jun-99	6.875	May-06	18.4	13.0	5.3	2.5	1.5	1.0	-4.3
Sep-99	6.875	May-06	17.1	12.9	4.2	0.4	1.1	-0.7	-4.9
Dec-99	7	Jul-06	14.1	13.0	1.0	0.4	0.9	-0.6	-1.6
Mar-00	4.75	Nov-08	7.9	0.6	7.4	-0.2	-0.2	0.0	-7.3
Jun-00	4.75	Nov-08	5.3	-4.0	9.3	3.0	-0.8	3.8	-5.5
Sep-00	4.75	Nov-08	2.0	-9.0	11.0	-0.5	-0.9	0.4	-10.6
Dec-00	5.5	Feb-08	1.9	-7.0	9.0	7.7	-0.9	8.7	-0.3
Mar-01	5.5	Feb-08	-2.5	-6.6	4.1	-1.3	0.4	-1.7	-5.8
Jun-01	5.5	Feb-08	10.8	6.9	3.8	8.5	1.5	7.0	3.2
Sep-01	6	Aug-09	32.3	20.4	11.9	5.3	1.9	3.5	-8.5
Dec-01	6.5	Feb-10	46.9	36.8	10.1	4.7	5.0	-0.3	-10.4
Mar-02	6.5	Feb-10	45.8	27.4	18.4	15.7	2.7	13.0	-5.4
Jun-02	5.75	Aug-10	47.4	35.7	11.7	5.9	3.2	2.7	-9.0
Sep-02	6.5	Feb-10	51.0	41.4	9.7	8.9	4.4	4.5	-5.2
Dec-02	6	Aug-09	40.0	36.5	3.5	7.0	4.9	2.1	-1.5
Mar-03	6.5	Feb-10	49.6	44.9	4.7	4.6	4.9	-0.3	-5.0
Jun-03	6.5	Feb-10	50.1	44.8	5.3	4.2	5.1	-0.8	-6.1
Sep-03	5.75	Aug-10	44.7	42.4	2.2	4.9	4.9	0.1	-2.2
Dec-03	5.75	Aug-10	56.2	42.8	13.4	5.1	5.6	-0.5	-13.9
Mar-04	5	Feb-11	43.1	36.7	6.4	3.0	3.2	-0.2	-6.6
Jun-04	5	Feb-11	39.2	35.5	3.7	4.8	3.2	1.6	-2.1

All told, then, the trader who shorted the basis of the 7-1/2% of 2/05 three months before futures expiration netted 2.1/32nds on the trade. This net was the result of gaining 12.1/32nds on the gross basis, which decreased from 13.4/32nds to 1.3/32nds, but losing 10/32nds in carry. Note that the basis trader's net gain from selling the cheapest to deliver basis corresponds exactly to the change in the issue's basis net of carry. If this change is negative, the trader who sells the basis makes money. If this change is positive, the trader who sells the basis loses money.

The right-hand column of Exhibit 6.2 shows how much success one might have had selling the cheapest to deliver basis of the 10-year Treasury note contract. In 23 of the 25 cases shown, the basis net of carry fell. Even allowing for the two times the net basis rose, the average drop in the basis net of carry of what was the cheapest to deliver issue three months before expiration was 4.9/32nds.

If we compare the basis net of carry at the outset with its subsequent value at expiration, we find that the basis net of carry in the 10-year contract was sold on average at 6.7/32nds, of which the basis seller was able to keep 4.9/32nds.

Why Were the Trades Successful? When you sell out of the money options, you can expect to make money most of the time. Thus, the high ratios of gains to losses in Exhibit 6.2 are not enough by themselves to prove that the delivery options were overpriced, that the futures were cheap, and that the bases were rich. To determine richness or cheapness, you must have a way of analyzing the potential value in a basis position.

Consider the basis of the 6-1/2% of 2/15/10, which was cheapest to deliver into the December 10-year Treasury note contract. The note's price was 112-12+/32nds, the December 2001 futures price was 107-17+/32nds, and the note's basis was 46.9/32nds. Carry to delivery was 36.8/32nds, so that the basis net of carry for the 6-1/2% was 10.1/32nds.

How much of the 10.1/32nds should you have expected to keep? The answer depends on how likely it was that the 6-1/2% of 2/10 would become expensive to deliver, and if they did become expensive, on what its basis could become. A look at the situation suggests that the risks were low relative to the potential gains from selling the basis.

Parallel shifts in yields, for example, posed little or no threat to the trade. As shown in Exhibit 6.3, the 6-1/2% would remain close to being cheapest to deliver even if yields changed 30 basis points in either direction. For that matter, its projected basis at expiration was projected to be less than or equal to 6/32nds even with yield changes as large as 60 basis points in either direction.

Nonparallel yield changes, or changes in yield spreads between deliverable issues, posed some risks to the trade. In principle, a steepening of the yield curve for the deliverable issues could cause a shift in the cheapest to deliver to a longer-duration issue; a flattening of the yield curve could cause a shift in the cheapest to deliver to a shorter-duration issue. In practice, however, the 6-1/2% of 2/10 was likely to remain close to cheapest to deliver over a wide range of yield curve scenarios.

The largest risk to the trade was yield curve steepening in a selloff. For example, if yields rose 60 bp and the 7s/10s curve steepened 1.5 standard deviations, the projected net basis of the 6-1/2% of 2/10 would be 17/32nds. Because the curve typically steepens in a rally, this was a relatively low probability event. In this light, the 10.1/32nds basis net of carry looked like a lot to pay for delivery options that were so far out of the money and that promised to pay so little even if they did go in the money. In other words, the strategic delivery options seemed to be overpriced, which means that the futures were cheap and the basis was rich.

EXHIBIT 6.3

Projected Basis of 6-1/2% of 2/10
at December 2001* Expiration
(Projections as of 9/20/01)

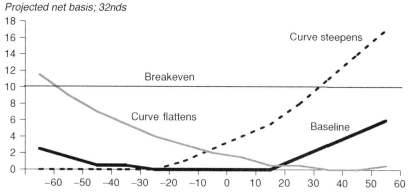

Projected net basis; 32nds

* Curve steepens assumes 7s/10s curve steepens 1.5 standard deviations; curve flattens assumes 7s/10s curve flattens 1.5 standard deviations.

As it happened, the 6-1/2% remained cheapest to deliver, and anyone who sold the basis was able to keep the entire basis net of carry.

Selling the Basis of Non-Cheap Bonds

Selling the basis of a non-cheap bond differs from selling the cheapest to deliver basis in two major respects. First, the basis net of carry for a non-cheap bond is expected to converge to a positive number rather than to zero at unchanged yields. Second, the basis of a non-cheap bond depends much more on the spread between its yield and the yield of the cheapest to deliver.

There are several reasons why a trader might prefer selling bases of non-cheap bonds rather than the cheapest to deliver when futures are cheap. First, selling a basket of deliverable issues rather than selling only the current cheapest to deliver issue can diversify risk and reduce exposure to flattening or steepening of the yield curve.

Second, traders often sell the basis of non-cheap bonds, rather than the cheapest to deliver basis, to take advantage of mispricings on the Treasury yield curve. By selling the basis of issues that are expensive on the yield curve, the trader expects to profit both from the cheapness of futures relative to the cheapest to deliver and from the richness of a particular issue relative to the cheapest to deliver.

BUYING THE BASIS WHEN IT IS CHEAP

A long basis position has risk characteristics like those of a long option position. The downside is limited to basis net of carry, and the upside is unlimited. As we showed in Chapter 2, the options embedded in long bases positions can increase in value both as yields change and as the slope of the yield curve changes. Any trader who wants to buy a bond call, a bond put, or a bond straddle can do it synthetically in the basis market. Similarly, any trader who wants to buy a call or put or straddle on the slope of the deliverable yield curve can do it synthetically in the basis market.

In contrast to Treasury note futures, which have tended to trade cheap, Treasury bond futures have consistently traded rich over the past few years (see Exhibit 6.4). This means that the options embedded in bond futures have been consistently undervalued by the market. On average, from January 2000 to January 2002, bond futures have averaged 2/32nds rich during the period two months before expiration.

Two factors account for the expensiveness of bond futures during this period. First, the Chicago Board of Trade changed the notional coupon of Treasury futures from 8% to 6% beginning with the March 2000 expiration. This change, which has moved the notional coupon closer to actual Treasury yields, has increased the uncertainty around the cheapest to deliver bond and substantially raised the delivery option value in Treasury bond futures. To date,

EXHIBIT 6.4

Mispricing of Treasury Bond Futures
(Futures Price–Fair Value; 32nds)

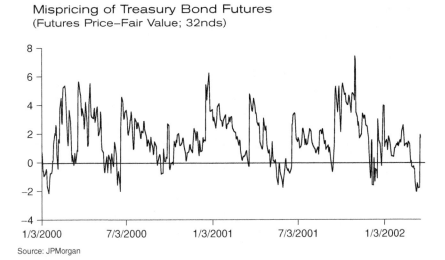

Source: JPMorgan

this higher delivery option value has not been fully reflected in Treasury bond futures prices.

Second, starting in late 1999, reductions in long-end Treasury supply have increased volatility in the slope of the long end of the Treasury yield curve, resulting in more frequent switches in the CTD bond (see Exhibit 6.5). For example, in early 2000, the Treasury announced a buyback program and reduced 30-year Treasury issuance, resulting in a significant flattening of the 10s/30s Treasury yield curve. Similarly, in October 2001, the Treasury's surprise announcement suspending 30-year Treasury bond issuance flattened the yield curve and caused bases at the long end of the deliverable bond curve to widen significantly.

The high yield curve volatility at the long end of the Treasury curve has made it especially attractive to own bond bases at the wings of the deliverable bond curve whenever they have become close to being cheapest to deliver. As Exhibit 6.6 highlights, the net basis of the 6% of 2/26, which was cheapest to deliver in early October 2001, widened from 9/32nds to 50/32nds after the Treasury announced the suspension of 30-year Treasury bond issuance. The announcement caused the 10s/30s Treasury curve to flatten significantly and highlighted the fact that high-duration-bond bases are valuable options on yield curve flattening.

The richness of bond futures has created opportunities for option traders as well as basis traders. For example, because yield driven options have recently been cheaper in the basis market than in the real options market, option traders who want to buy interest rate volatility

EXHIBIT 6.5

Treasury Bond CTD Switches

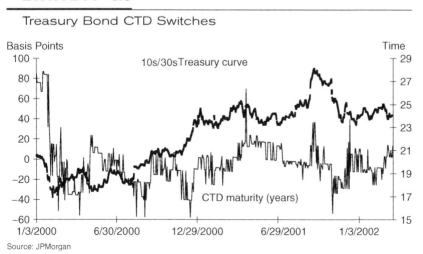

Source: JPMorgan

E X H I B I T   6.6

High-Duration Bond Bases Widen When the Curve Flattens

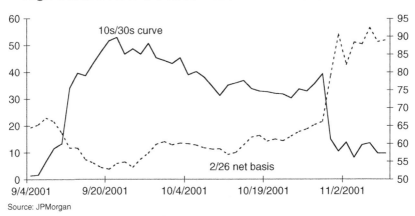

Source: JPMorgan

can get a better deal in the basis market. Alternatively, for those who do not want to take an outright long volatility position in the basis market, it is possible to spread cheap volatility in the basis market against rich volatility in the bond options market. In this approach, which we explain in Chapter 7, the trader buys the options embedded in bond futures by buying the bond basis and selling real or explicit options against this position. If done correctly, such a volatility spread trade will profit from a narrowing in the implied volatility spread.

TRADING THE BASIS OF "HOT-RUN" BONDS

Basis traders often trade the basis of "on-the-run" (OTR) or "hot-run" Treasuries, which are the most recently auctioned benchmark issues, are the most actively traded, and typically trade at a premium to issues that have been auctioned earlier. The OTR basis holds two advantages for someone trading the basis. One is that the market for its basis is very liquid and typically is more liquid than that for the cheapest to deliver's basis. The other is the new issue effect, which is a richening of the note after it is auctioned and a cheapening of the note when it is replaced at the next auction by a new on-the-run issue.

Exhibit 6.7 illustrates the new issue effect for 5-year Treasury notes averaged over the four semiannual auction cycles running from May 2000 to May 2002. During this period, new 5-year Treasury notes were auctioned every six months in May and November, with

EXHIBIT 6.7

Yield Spread Patterns around 5-Year Treasury Auctions

5-year Treasury yield – old 5-year Treasury yield; May 2000 - May 2002 bp

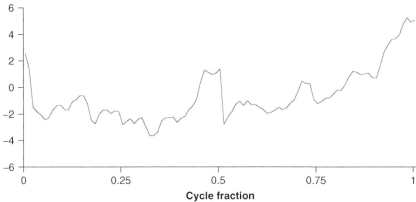

Source: JPMorgan

scheduled reopenings in February and August. As the chart high-lights, the yield spread between the OTR 5-year and old 5-year declined (i.e., became more negative) following an auction, meaning the newly auctioned issue richened on the yield curve. One reason for this richening is that recently auctioned Treasuries are actively used as hedging vehicles in the market. As these short hedges grow early in the quarter, the issue often becomes scarce in the repo market, causing it to richen. As a result, the OTR yield declines relative to the yield on surrounding issues.

Typically, this richening is reversed as time passes and the market prepares for the new supply that will come with the next auction. On average, over the last four cycles, the OTR issue cheapened relative to the old 5-year Treasury about 5 bp in the 1-1/2 month period before a new issue was auctioned.

Because the cheapest to deliver 5-year is usually the old 5-year, trading the OTR basis is a liquid way to position for a change in the yield spread between the OTR and old 5-year Treasury. In the early part of the quarter, when the new issue is likely to richen, basis traders can profit by buying the OTR 5-year basis. This position will benefit as the yield spread between the current and old 5-year narrows. In the latter part of the quarter, when the OTR issue is likely to cheapen, basis traders can profit by selling the OTR 5-year basis. This position will benefit as the yield spread between the OTR and old 5-year increases.

Of course, these trades are not without risks. For one thing, yield spreads between OTR and off-the-run issues can be volatile and can produce fairly large P/L swings in basis positions. For another, some of the anticipated change in yield spreads, especially the cheapening of the OTR issue that occurs toward the end of the quarter, is usually priced into the forward market. This is because OTR issues usually trade special in the repo market, meaning that the reverse repo rate on the OTR is significantly lower than the repo rate on off-the-run issues. As a result, selling the OTR basis is a negative carry trade, and the position will require a large enough move in yield spreads to offset this negative carry in order to be profitable.

BASIS TRADING WHEN THE CTD IS IN SHORT SUPPLY

In most market environments, the use of deliverable baskets in Treasury futures combined with a large and liquid U.S. government securities market, has resulted in a well-functioning delivery process for Treasury futures. On rare occasions, however, the lack of available supply in the cheapest to deliver issue has produced delivery squeezes that have distorted the behavior of futures prices relative to the prices of cash Treasuries. These distortions have created both risks and opportunities for basis traders.

The risk of CTD delivery shortages has been an increasingly important theme during 2005 for the 5-year and especially 10-year Treasury futures contracts. The shortage is a byproduct of two events that have increased the risk of delivery squeezes. First, the size of the Treasury futures market has exploded; open interest in 10-year futures reached 2.1 mm contracts in May 2005 representing a 50% increase from May 2004. The growth partly reflects the declining costs of trading in Treasury futures as electronic trading has grown. Second, the shortage is a byproduct of a prolonged period of bull flattening in the Treasury yield curve. The combination of the Fed raising rates at the short end of the yield curve, and declining intermediate yields has flattened the deliverable yield curves and firmly entrenched the CTD issue as the shortest maturity issue in the basket.

A key result of the bull flattening of the deliverable yield curves is that it has richened non-CTD issues relative to the CTD making delivery of non-CTD issues prohibitively expensive. For example, at this writing (May 2005) the net basis of the CTD into June 2005 10-year futures, which is the 4-7/8% of 2/12, is a full point below the net basis of the 2nd cheapest to deliver issue which is the 4-3/8% of 8/12. The richening of the non-CTD issues has effectively reduced deliverable supply. With only one issue in serious contention for CTD status, deliverable supply has, for all intents and purposes, declined to the available float in the current CTD. Moreover, any short unable to obtain the CTD 4-7/8% of 2/12 to meet June 10-year delivery either must face exchange fines for late delivery (which are severe) or must deliver the next CTD 4-3/8% of 8/12. In this case, the short loses the net basis of the 4-3/8% of 8/12 or roughly 1 point.

The unusual combination of events that have raised the risk of delivery failure in 2005 has caused significant distortions in the behavior of deliverable bond bases. June 2005 CTD net bases in both 5-year and 10-year futures have traded negative for most of the delivery cycle; for example, during the first 2 weeks of May 2005, the net basis of the June 10-year CTD averaged *negative* 2/32nds. Although this may appear to violate a basic arbitrage condition for futures, it actually reflects the potential cost of a delivery failure. Any arbitrageur that buys the CTD basis at a price below carry (negative net basis) locks in a riskless profit only if it can deliver the CTD. If it cannot, it must deliver the next CTD in which case it incurs a loss equal to the net basis of the second CTD. This intuition produces a simple fair value equation for the CTD net basis in cases where the outstanding amount of the CTD is insufficient to meet all delivery obligations.

At delivery,

$$\text{Fair value(CTD BNOC)} = \text{prob. of delivery failure} \times \\ \text{(CTD BNOC} - \text{2nd CTD BNOC)}$$

where delivery failures means the short is unable to deliver the CTD and must deliver the next cheapest to deliver bond.

For example, assuming the available supply of the CTD is enough to meet only 90% of deliveries, and the difference in the BNOC of the cheapest and next cheapest equals 1 point, the fair value of the CTD net basis is equal to negative 3.2/32nds, or

$$-3.2/32\text{nds} = .10 \times 32/32\text{nds}$$

Note that in cases where the CTD net basis is negative, this relationship can be used to imply the market's probability of a delivery failure. That is, for cases where the CTD BNOC is negative,

$$\text{Implied probability of delivery failure} = \frac{\text{CTD BNOC}}{\text{CTD BNOC} - \text{2nd CTD BNOC}}$$

Delivery shortages and negative net CTD bases create both risks and opportunities for basis traders. Three common ways for traders to position for or hedge against a shortage of the CTD are selling the basis of an expensive to deliver bond, buying the CTD or buying futures versus non-deliverable bonds or swaps (asset swapping the bond), or buying the calendar spread. All three take advantage of an expected richening of the CTD and futures relative to other issues or derivative contracts as delivery approaches. In the first case, the trade benefits from the fact that, as the CTD richens and pulls futures along with it, the basis of non-CTD bonds should fall. This decline in the basis of a non-CTD bond also serves the purpose of effectively increasing deliverable supply. This is because, as the basis of non-CTD bonds narrow towards zero, the cost of a delivery failure from delivering the second CTD goes away.

Bond calendar spreads usually widen in cases where available supply in the front month CTD is low relative to anticipated deliveries. In these cases, shorts that are unwilling to go to delivery are likely to roll their position by buying front month futures and selling back month futures causing the calendar spread to widen. Stated differently, as the costs of a delivery failure increases (either because the probability of failure increases or the BNOC of the next CTD increases), the price at which shorts are willing to roll their position should rise as well.

One important caveat on basis trading in cases where the CTD is in scarce supply is worth highlighting. Exchange rules explicitly prohibit market manipulation including trades that are designed to create shortages or squeezes in deliverable issues. Because penalties for violating exchange rules are at the discretion of the exchange and can be severe, basis traders need to understand exchange rules and should not be involved in trades with the intention of exacerbating shortages in CTD supply.

TRADING THE CALENDAR SPREAD

Once you determine fair values for the bases in each contract month, estimating the fair values of bond and note calendar spreads is easy and provides another opportunity for traders and hedgers. The fair value of a Treasury note or bond futures contract is found by turning the standard basis equation on its head to get

$$\text{Futures Fair Value} = \frac{\text{CTD Price} - \text{CTD Basis Fair Value}}{\text{CTD Factor}}$$

Examples of this calculation are shown for the 5-year and 10-year note contracts and for the Treasury bond contract in Exhibit 6.8. For example, on April 5th 2001, the cheapest to deliver note into the 5-year contract was the 5-3/4% of 11/05. Given its price of 105-2.5/32nds and the theoretical value of its June basis of 13.8/32nds, we find the fair value of the June futures contract to be 105-21.2/32nds [= (105-2.5/32nds – 13.8/32nds)/0.9904].

As Exhibit 6.8 shows, the June 5-year Treasury contract was trading a mere 0.8/32nds above fair value, which is about as close to being fairly priced as possible. The September 5-year note contract also was almost fairly priced in the market.

The June bond and 10-year note contracts, however, were both trading about 2/32nds to 3/32nds above their theoretical fair values. The mispricings for the September bond and 10-year contracts were larger still at nearly 5/32nds.

Notice that the size of the mispricing of the futures contracts is roughly the same as the option-adjusted basis. The sign, however, is different. A bond or note's option-adjusted basis is simply the difference between the market or actual value of its basis *less* the theoretical value of its basis. Saying that a bond or note future contract is underpriced is simply another way of saying that its basis is rich.

Fair Values for Treasury Note Calendar Spreads

Once we have the fair values of the futures contracts for any two contract months, we can use fair values to determine the fair value of the calendar spread between those contract months. Consider the actual and theoretical June/September calendar spreads for April 4, 2001 that are shown in Exhibit 6.9. Given the closing prices for the 10-year note contract, the actual spread between the June and September futures was 14.5/32nds. By our reckoning, the theoretical of "fair" value of the spread should have been 16.9/32nds.

In other words, the June/September calendar spread in the 10-year Treasury note futures was underpriced by about 2.4/32nds. The calendar spread in bond futures was underpriced by nearly 2/32nds. Similarly, the calendar spread for 5-year futures, on the other hand, appears to have been about 1/32nd cheap.

Profiting from Mispricings in Calendar Spreads

Mispricings in the calendar spread can have important implications for spread traders, basis traders, and hedgers.

EXHIBIT 6.8

Basis and Futures Mispricings
(April 4, 2001, Closing Prices)

Contract (1)	Cheapest to Deliver (2)	Price* (3)	Factor (4)	Basis** (5)=(3)-(4x11)	Carry** (6)	Theoretical Option Value** (7)	Theoretical Basis** (8)=(6+7)	Option-Adjusted Basis (9)=(5-8)	Theoretical Futures Price** (10)=(3-8)/(4)	Actual Futures Price** (11)	Futures Mispricing** (12)=(11-10)
					June Contract						
5-Year	5-3/4% of 11/05	105-02+	0.9904	13.0	13.7	0.1	13.8	-0.8	105-21.2	105-22	0.8
10-Year	5-1/2% of 2/08	103-27	0.9734	13.4	6.0	9.5	15.5	-2.1	106-05.9	106-08	2.1
Bond	7-5/8% of 11/22	124-20	1.1936	18.1	13.6	8.2	21.7	-3.7	103-26.9	103-30	3.1
					September Contract						
5-Year	5-3/4% of 11/05	105-02+	0.9908	25.5	26.9	0.5	27.4	-1.9	105-06.1	105-08	1.9
10-Year	5-5/8% of 5/08	104-15+	0.9801	25.4	15.1	14.7	29.8	-4.4	105-21.1	105-25+	4.5
Bond	7-5/8% of 11/22	124-20	1.1926	40.5	31.9	14.2	46.1	-5.6	103-09.3	103-14	4.7

* Prices are in points and 32nds of a point
** In 32nds

Source: JPMorgan

E X H I B I T   6.9

Calendar Spread Mispricing
(April 4, 2001, Closing Prices)

	Actual			Theoretical			
Contract	June Futures Price*	Sep Futures Price*	Spread**	June Futures Price*	Sep Futures Price*	Spread**	Spread Mispricing**
(1)	(2)	(3)	(4)=(2-3)	(5)	(6)	(7)=(5-6)	(8)=(4-7)
5-Year	105-22	105-08	14	105-212	105-061	15.1	−1.1
10-Year	106-08	105-25+	14.5	106-059	105-211	16.9	−2.4
Bond	103-30	103-14	16	103-269	103-093	17.7	−1.7

Spread Trades   The first and most obvious way to take advantage of a mispricing of the calendar spreads in note futures is to trade the spreads outright. On April 4, for instance, one might have bought June and sold September 10-year note futures at a spread that was 2.4/32nds under fair value. This strategy may well be more risky than the expected profits warrant, however. For one thing, the calendar spread is subject to considerable yield curve risk and is, as a result, highly variable for reasons other than changes in mispricings. For another, unlike basis relationships, there is nothing that forces a calendar spread to converge to fair value at expiration.

Enhanced Basis Trades   A second and potentially more fruitful approach would be to use mispriced calendar spreads to establish richer or cheaper basis positions in deferred contract months. For example, if the calendar spread is rich, a basis trader can sell the spread (that is, sell the lead contract and buy the deferred contract) and deliver into the lead contract at expiration. The trader now has a short position in the note and a long position in the deferred futures contract. The return from selling the basis this way is higher by the amount of the calendar spread mispricing than it would have been if the basis trader had simply sold the note and bought the deferred contract at the outset.

If the calendar spread is cheap, of course, basis traders could establish cheap long basis positions in the deferred contract by buying the spread and taking delivery at the expiration of the lead or nearby contract. Given the mispricings shown in Exhibits 6.8 and 6.9, for example, this could have been an especially attractive way to buy the September cheapest to deliver 10-year note basis, which was trading about 4/32nds below fair value. Buying the September 10-year basis, by first buying the June/September calendar spread in 10-year futures, would add 2/32nds to 3/32nds to the expected gain on this position.

Lower-Cost Hedging   A third approach is valuable for hedgers who find it necessary to roll futures positions from one contract month to the next. For this group, the decision about when to roll can have a substantial effect on the cost of running a hedge. If the spread is cheap, as shown in Exhibit 6.9, buying the spread is a good way to roll a short position from a nearby contract month to a more distant contract month. If the spread is trading above fair value, on the other hand, selling the spread can be an effective way to roll a long position into a more distant contract month.

Patterns in Calendar Spreads

In addition to analyzing fair values for calendar spreads, we have also found it helpful for hedgers and spread traders to be aware of the historical behavior of calendar spreads. Exhibit 6.10 shows the average value of Treasury bond calendar spreads from June 1997 through March 2001. The average value of the spread generally has fallen going into first notice day. This pattern likely reflects the roll activity of longs that are unwilling to risk taking early delivery and therefore must roll before first notice day. As a result of this pattern, institutions that have to roll a short position in the lead contract to a short position in the next contract month have fared well by buying the calendar spread just before first notice day (that is, the last business day in the month before the delivery month); institutions

EXHIBIT 6.10

Average Treasury Bond Calendar Spreads

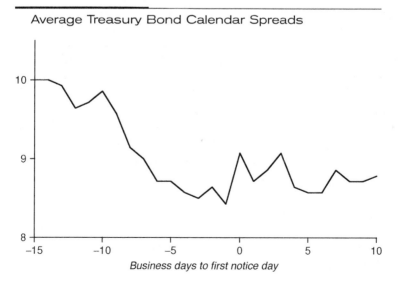

Business days to first notice day

that have had to roll long positions have done well by rolling early and selling the spread well before first notice day.

PRACTICAL CONSIDERATIONS IN TRADING THE BASIS

Anyone who trades the basis comes face to face with a wide range of real-world problems. Some of these we have mentioned in passing already or dealt with explicitly. Four important issues come up regularly:

- RP specials
- Term financing versus overnight financing
- Short squeezes
- Delivery month

The problems raised by RP specials and the question about term versus overnight financing involve the cost of financing a long bond position or the return to invested funds that one can earn on the proceeds of a bond sale. The profit margins in a basis trade are not necessarily large, and what may seem to be the mundane problem of daily financing can make the difference between profitable and unprofitable trades.

Minor short squeezes occur frequently in issues that have small public supplies or that have been salted away in portfolios for years. Major short squeezes occur rarely, but when they do, the results can be staggering. In the section on short squeezes coming up in the chapter, we recount what happened during perhaps the worst squeeze in the history of U.S. basis trading: the well-remembered squeeze of the 9-1/4% of 2/16 that occurred in the spring of 1986.

All of the timing and delivery options become eligible for exercise during the delivery month. Delivery becomes a real possibility, and the basis trader must weigh the alternatives of closing out the trade, rolling the futures leg of the trade into the next contract month, or going through to delivery.

RP Specials

In our example in Chapter 1 of selling the basis of the 7-5/8% of 2/25, we showed that the profit from the sale was sensitive to the rate that could be earned on the proceeds of the sale of the bond. For example, if the reverse RP rate was 4.50, the profit on the trade was $3,630.90. If the reverse RP rate was only 1.00%, however, the trade produced a loss of $13,622.04.

In practice, uncertainty about financing rates is a source of both risk and opportunity in basis trading. Part of the uncertainty about financing rates stems from a bond's status in the RP market. To understand the RP market, it is important to distinguish between general collateral and specials:

> **General collateral**. General collateral, or "stock," comprises whatever Treasury issues are readily available to be lent or borrowed, typically somewhat below that day's Federal funds rate.
>
> **Specials**. An RP special is a request to borrow a specific Treasury issue. Specials can trade at RP rates substantially lower than the rate for general collateral. If the reverse RP rate for a particular bond is below the general collateral RP rate, the bond is said to be "on special."

When you sell a bond short against futures, you kill two birds with one stone by "reversing in" the particular bond you are short. The first is that you get a bond that allows you to make good on your short sale. The second is that you invest the proceeds of your short sale.

In a reverse RP transaction, you buy the issue with an agreement to sell the issue back at a predetermined price at a later date. What you earn on the transaction is called the *reverse repo rate*. If the specific issue that you are looking for is not readily available, the reverse RP rate on the specific issue may be several percentage points below the general collateral reverse RP rate. At times, an issue cannot be found at all, and the short must fail to deliver. In such a case, the short pays the coupon interest on the issue that he or she is short, and earns no RP interest at all.

Formally, whenever you specify a particular issue in a reverse RP transaction, you are requesting a "special." In practice, though, the particular bond is said to be "on special" only if the reverse RP rate is below the general collateral rate.

RP Special Example   The importance of a bond being "on special" is apparent in the behavior of the bases of newly issued "hot-run" Treasuries (see preceding section on trading "hot-run" bases). As an example, consider the performance of the basis of the newly issued 5-year Treasury (6-3/4% of 5/05) versus the old 5-year Treasury (5-7/8% of 11/04) during May to June of 2000 (trade dates May 16, 2000 to June 20, 2000). In mid-May, the overnight repo rate for both the 5/05 and 11/04 Treasuries was trading at around 5.40%, which was close to general collateral repo rates. As time passed, however, the 6-3/4% of 5/05 began to trade special in the repo market, while repo on the 5-7/8% of 11/04 continued to track general collateral repo rates. On average during this period, the reverse repo rate on the 6-3/4% of 5/05 equaled 5.48, compared to a rate of 6% on the 5-7/8% of 11/04.

The specialness of the 6-3/4% of 5/05 in repo caused its basis to increase from 6.3/32nds to 7.4/32nds, while the basis of the 5-7/8% of 11/04 fell from 4.4/32nds to 0/32nds over this period. At the same time, there was much more negative carry incurred by anyone who shorted the 6-3/4%. A summary of the P/L from shorting the two bases is as follows:

Short $10 mm 5-7/8% of 11/04 basis

Coupon interest paid	($55,876)
Reverse RP interest earned	$56,340
Cash/futures P/L	$13,750
Total	$14,211

Short $10mm 6-3/4% of 5/05 basis

Coupon interest paid	($64,198)
Reverse RP interest earned	$53,360
Cash/futures P/L	($3,438)
Total	($14,276)

Thus, selling the basis of the 5-7/8% proved profitable, while selling the basis of the 6-3/4% was not. Of the $14,276 loss on the sale of the basis of the 6-3/4%, nearly $11,000 was because of the lower reverse RP rate available on the 6-3/4% of 5/05.

A Source of Risk   In practice, issues can go on and off special as market conditions change. For basis traders, the uncertainty about a bond's status in the RP market is then a source of risk that deserves close attention. Anyone who is long the basis of a bond that is "on special," for example, faces the possibility that the bond will return to the general collateral pool. If it does, its RP rate will rise and the bond's basis will fall. Anyone who is short the basis of a bond that is in the general collateral pool faces that the possibility that the bond will go "on special." If it does, its reverse RP will fall, and the bond's basis will increase.

Either way, the basis trader should be careful to keep track of an issue's availability, how much can be borrowed, and how actively it trades.

Opportunities to Trade   A bond's status in the RP market may also provide an opportunity to trade. For instance, a bond may be on special in the term RP market but general collateral in the overnight RP market. If it is, its basis will reflect the higher term RP rate, and the basis trader has an opportunity to sell the basis and finance the position at the overnight reverse RP rate.

RP Specials and the Cheapest to Deliver   The possibility of specials complicates somewhat the problem of identifying the cheapest to deliver. If all bonds were stock or general collateral, the bond with the highest implied repo rate would be the cheapest to deliver. To be more precise, you should compare a bond's implied repo rate with its own repo rate. The bond with the largest difference between its implied repo rate and its reverse repo rate is the cheapest to deliver.

Term Financing versus Overnight Financing

For a basis trade, the cash bond can be financed with either a term RP arrangement or a string of overnight RPs. Financing overnight offers two advantages. With a positively sloped yield curve, a string of overnight RPs can be cheaper than financing with a term RP. Also, a position financed overnight is easier to unwind than a position financed with a term RP.

The chief drawback to financing a position overnight is the exposure to a shift in the slope of the yield curve. For a long basis position, an increase in the overnight RP rate will increase the cost of carry and will reduce the profit on the trade. For a short basis position, a decrease in the overnight RP rate will reduce the reverse RP interest and will reduce the profit on the trade.

Short Squeezes

Trading the basis from the short side (selling bonds short and buying futures) involves several risks that must be considered. The proceeds from the short sale must be invested in a reverse RP and the particular issue must be "reversed in."

- The reverse RP rate for readily available collateral is generally 10 to 25 basis points lower than the RP rate. If the issue is not readily available to reverse in, you only earn the reverse RP "special" rate.
- There is no theoretical limit to how low the special rate can go. It can even be negative in extreme circumstances.

For example, in late May of 2005, the 4 7/8% of 2/12, which was CTD into June 2005 10-year futures, traded in overnight repo at a rate of negative 15%. The issue was in such scarce supply that investors were willing to earn a negative interest rate in order to get physical possession of the collateral for purposes of delivering it into the futures contract.

- The short seller of a cash bond must pay the coupon interest until the short sale is covered. This expense is most often greater than the interest earned on the reverse repo. In such a case, the short seller's carry is negative, and the risk is that a drop in the reverse repo rate can increase the already negative carry to the point where a short basis trade becomes unprofitable.
- The short seller is obligated eventually to buy back the same issue that was sold short. This can become difficult with illiquid issues, or with any issue that is involved in a "short squeeze."

A *short squeeze* develops when the obligations of short sellers to cover their sales exceeds the amount of an issue that is readily available. The most obviously attractive basis short sales often pose the greatest danger of being hurt by a short squeeze. This is due to the increased demand to reverse in the issue and to buy it back when many other basis traders are trying to do the same thing.

The Short Squeeze of 1986

Although it happened a number of years ago, the most dramatic basis short squeeze in U.S. basis markets was that of the 9-1/4% of 2/15/2016 in May 1986. In April, the 9-1/4% was trading at a yield spread of between 25 to 40 basis points below the 12% of 8/15/2013-08, which was one of the cheapest bonds to deliver. During May, the yield spread rose to over 100 basis points. This caused the 9-1/4 basis to widen by about 6 points, or $60,000 per $1 million face value. Meanwhile, the basis of the high-coupon, shorter-maturity bonds such as the 12% of 8/15/2013-08 continued to narrow and approach convergence. Exhibit 6.11 shows the contrast between the move in the 9-1/4% basis and the move in the 12% basis during this period.

What Caused the Short Squeeze? This dramatic short squeeze was caused by the following factors:

- It seemed like an obvious spread play to short the outstanding current long bond (the 9-1/4%) against a long position in the new when-issued long bond, the bond futures contract, or the 10-year note contract. During several earlier cycles, the current bond had traded at a premium to other bonds and

E X H I B I T   6.11

September 1986 Bond Basis

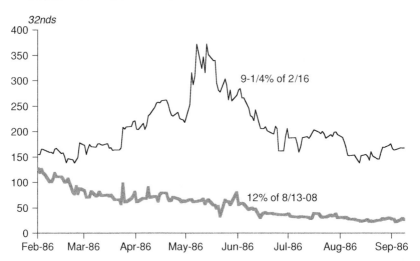

had given up the premium after the refunding when it was replaced by a new current bond. Expecting a similar pattern, spreaders built up a massive short position in the 9-1/4%.

- Most of the 9-1/4% issue was owned by Japanese institutions that did not make the issue available to borrow in the repo market. There was no theoretical problem here. Rather, Japanese institutions were unaccustomed to RP transactions and were unwilling to set what for them would have been a precedent. Nevertheless, the effect was staggering. The reverse RP rate on the 9-1/4% approached 0%, and finally the issue couldn't be borrowed at all. There were rumors that some small dealers had traded the issue at a negative reverse RP rate. This meant that they actually paid interest to lend money for the privilege of reversing in the 9-1/4% as collateral.

- The problem was compounded by funds selling old issues that were approaching historical cost because of the decline in yields. Many of these older issues were cheap to deliver, and having them sold out of portfolio only caused the basis of the 9-1/4% to widen further.

The short squeeze of the 9-1/4% resulted from a rare combination of events. The market was unusually disorderly, and it seems unlikely that things could ever be that bad again. But then again, there are many basis traders whose feelings about shorting the basis are highly colored by their memories of that event.

Controlling the Risk of a Short Squeeze   To minimize the risk of a short squeeze in a basis short sale, the trader should choose an issue that is available both to borrow and to buy back to cover the short sale. Check both the overnight and term reverse RP rates. Determine the issue size and the amount that remains unstripped. Monitor carefully for signs of the possible development of a short squeeze. Three common signs of a short squeeze are a declining RP special rate, a large amount of short sales in an issue, and changes in its yield spread to similar issues. Finally, consider using a stop-loss point to establish a maximum risk level. Theoretically, there is no maximum limit to a potential loss on a basis short sale when the bond you are short is being squeezed.

Basis Short Sales versus Selling the Basis out of Portfolio In principle, the risks of a short squeeze are the same whether the basis sale is accomplished by selling the bond short or by selling the bonds out of a portfolio. In the first case, however, any losses from a short squeeze take the form of hard cash payments. In the second, the loss takes the form of a forgone capital gain. The first is a *realized* loss, while the second is an *opportunity* loss. Both are equally real; however, the practical consequences of the realized loss, which takes the form of cash paid out, are more dire than those of the missed opportunity, which takes the form of a reduction in long-term performance.

The portfolio manager's comfort comes from not needing to recognize the loss. When it comes time to unwind the basis trade and put bonds back into the portfolio, the portfolio manager is not constrained to buy back the same bond that was sold in the first place. In the spring of 1986, for example, the 9-1/4% easily could have been replaced by a bond of similar maturity and coupon but with a substantially higher yield. Many active portfolio managers were swapping out of the 9-1/4% of 2/15/2016 at the time anyway.

The good news is that the depressing effect of a short squeeze on the performance of a portfolio manager who sells the basis is offset at least in part by the gains from the basis sale. In fact, the portfolio manager who regularly sold the basis through the mid-1980s using a diversified portfolio of bonds would have outperformed the cash portfolio even with the dramatic short squeeze of 1986.

Taking a Basis Trade into the Delivery Month

As the delivery month approaches, the prospect of either making or taking delivery becomes a real consideration. The first notice day falls on the second business day before the beginning of the contract month.

Some basis traders are better suited than others to make or take delivery. Those who would find delivery a costly undertaking have two main alternatives:

- Unwinding the trade with offsetting transactions
- Rolling the futures leg of the trade into the next contract month

Those who are short the basis have a third alternative: "refresh" the long futures position. This is done by buying and selling futures in the same contract month. While this may seem a strange thing to do, the transactions get rid of old long positions and put new long positions in their place. Because deliveries are assigned to the oldest longs, the transactions allow the trader to forestall the possibility of taking delivery on a long futures position, at least until the last trading day. All open long positions after the last trading day must, of course, stand for delivery.

Even those for whom delivery is not especially costly must think about delivery as the last trading day approaches. The value of the basis of the cheapest to deliver at this point reflects the combined value of remaining carry and the value of the end-of-month option. If the trader thinks the end-of-month option is mispriced, the most attractive alternative may be to set up the position for delivery, buying or selling futures so that there is exactly one futures contract for each $100,000 par value of the bonds in the position.

Altogether, then, there are three main alternatives, not counting the refreshing trade. That is, the basis trader can unwind the trade, roll the futures leg of the position, or set up for delivery.

Unwinding the Trade   Unwinding a trade involves taking offsetting positions in both the cash and futures markets. Chapter 1 provides examples of how this is done for both long and short basis positions.

Rolling the Futures   Rolling the futures involves replacing the futures in the position with futures from the next contract month. For example, if you are long the basis and therefore short futures, rolling the futures means buying futures in the lead or current contract month and selling futures in the next contract month. The effect of these transactions, which can be accomplished by "buying the futures calendar spread," is the same as simultaneously selling the basis in the current month and buying the basis in the next contract month.

If you are short the basis, rolling the futures requires selling futures in the lead contract month and buying futures in the next contract month. In this case, rolling the futures means that you simultaneously buy the current month basis and sell the basis in the next contract month.

When you roll the futures position, therefore, you eliminate any concerns about deliveries in the current month. For example, if you were short the basis, you no longer need be concerned about wild card deliveries. At the same time, you are taking a new position on the deferred contract's basis. Whether this is a reasonable thing to do depends largely on how you view the futures calendar spread.

For the most part, the spread between futures prices for the lead month and any deferred month changes very little. When trading activity begins to switch from the lead contract in the next contract, however, the futures price spread sometimes changes and briefly opens a window during which rolling the basis trade forward by rolling the futures makes sense.

In practice, rolling the futures position entails nothing more than buying the futures calendar spread or selling the futures calendar spread. Buying the futures calendar spread means buying the front-month contract and selling the back-month contract. Selling the spread is just the opposite. To roll over long basis positions, one buys the futures spread. One sells the spread to roll over short basis positions.

Recall that a bond's conversion factor is the approximate price at which the bond would yield 6% to maturity as of the first delivery day of the contract month. The only thing that can complicate an otherwise simple trade is that the conversion factors are different for each contract month. Because the bond will have three fewer months to maturity by the time the first day of the next contract month rolls around, the conversion factor will be closer to 1.

As a practical matter, however, the difference is quite small and matters only for very large basis positions, usually over $100 million. For example, the June 2002 conversion factor for the 8-1/8% of 8/21 is 1.2390, while the September 2002 conversion factor is 1.2371. In a basis trade involving $10 million face amount of the 8-1/8%, the number of futures contracts would be 124 for either contract month. In a basis trade involving $100 million face amount of the issue, a September basis position would require 1,239 contracts, while a December basis position would require 1,237 contracts. The difference is small but gets larger with the size of the trade and the number of times the trade is rolled.

Setting Up for Delivery   Carrying the trade through delivery means simply accepting delivery for short basis positions, or making delivery for long basis positions.

The key to setting up for delivery is "covering the tail." Each futures contract calls for the delivery of $100,000 par value of an eligible bond. A correctly constructed basis trade, however, requires holding futures in a conversion factor ratio to cash. In the case of the 8-1/8% of 8/21, for example, the ratio of futures to bonds in the position would be about 1.24 futures for each $100,000 par value of the bonds if they were the cheapest to deliver. This would be 124 futures for each $10 million face value of the bonds.

If you make delivery on a long basis position, and the bond's conversion factor is greater than 1, you have to cover the tail by either buying additional bonds or buying back the extra futures contracts. If you do not cover the tail and you are assigned on all the futures in your short basis position, you will find yourself taking delivery of more bonds than you are short.

Once trading in the expiring futures contract stops on the last day of trading, the correct ratio of futures to bonds for a well-hedged position is one-to-one. The extra 24 futures in the basis trade with the 8-1/8% represent unwanted price risk. For example, if you are long $10 million of the 8-1/8% and short 100 futures contracts, you are completely hedged. You know the invoice price at which you can sell each of the bonds.

If you keep the extra 24 short futures after the expiration of trading in the futures, however, you are exposed to an increase in bond prices. You must make delivery on the 24 futures, and if bond prices rise, you will lose the difference between the converted futures price, which is fixed when trading expires, and the higher cash price of the bond.

Once again, if the conversion factor is greater than 1, you can cover the tail in the trade either by reducing the short futures position or by adding to the size of the cash position. In either case, the trick to covering the tail is to do it as near as possible to the termination of futures trading. Any mismatch in timing exposes you to price risk. At the same time, trading at the closing bell can be tumultuous and takes place within a range of prices. The best time to cover the tail in a basis trade, therefore, is just before the close of trading. The timing mismatch that results is small, and the market typically is liquid.

CHAPTER 7

Volatility Arbitrage in the Treasury Bond Basis[1]

Sometime in the middle of 1989, the golden age of yield enhancement with Treasury bond futures came to a close. Bond futures, which had been chronically cheap for several years, seemed to become more or less fairly priced. As a result, bond fund managers could no longer outperform the market simply by replacing physical bonds with their duration equivalent alternative in the form of Treasury bond futures and cash.

Sophistication in the pricing of Treasury bond and note futures clearly has stepped up a notch. Key to this new understanding has been a heightened appreciation for the strategic delivery options that are embedded in bond futures. The short's rights to decide what bond to deliver and when to deliver it represent a valuable collection of options whose value plays a large role in shaping the behavior of Treasury bond futures prices.

As a result, we have two arenas for trading the volatility of bond yields—the Treasury bond basis market and the Treasury bond options market. Our research suggests that, on most days, the two markets pay about the same price for yield volatility. From time to time, however, the prices are different enough to warrant the trouble of constructing arbitrage trades to take advantage of the difference.

In this chapter we provide a thumbnail sketch of how we value the strategic delivery options that are embedded in Treasury bond

---

1 This is a reprint of a *Journal of Portfolio Management* article. © 1993 by *The Journal of Portfolio Management*, Spring 1993. Reprinted with permission.

futures, and how we put together volatility arbitrage trades when futures seem to be mispriced.

OVERVIEW

The short's rights in a Treasury bond futures contract to decide what bond to deliver and when exert an important influence on the relationship between the futures price and the prices of bonds that are eligible for delivery. The short pays for these options in the form of a futures price that is lower than it would be if carry were the only consideration.

The value of these strategic delivery options depends on how volatile the futures market expects bond prices to be. This is the same volatility, of course, that drives the prices of bond options. As a result, there are two markets in which one can trade bond price volatility—the Treasury bond basis market and the bond options market. Because the options in both arenas are driven by the same underlying economic forces, the prices paid for volatility in both places should conform to one another.

As it is, we find that the two markets do not always agree. When they do not, one can buy cheap volatility in one market while selling rich volatility in the other.

THE OPTIONS EMBEDDED
IN BOND FUTURES

The short gets to decide what bond to deliver, and it is this right that tends to dominate the behavior of the Treasury bond futures price. The short's relentless search for the cheapest bond to deliver produces the cash/futures price relationship shown in Exhibit 7.1.

At expiration, the futures price converges to the lowest of the converted cash prices of bonds in the eligible delivery set. As Exhibit 7.1 shows, the cheapest to deliver tends to be a high-duration bond when yields are high, a lower-duration bond when yields are low, and the middling-duration bond when yields are around 7.6%.

Partly for the sake of simplicity, we have chosen three bonds that tend to appear in actual deliveries under these circumstances. The 10-3/8% of '12-07 exhibit the lowest duration of the three and tend to be cheap to deliver when bond yields are low. The 8-1/8% of '19, in contrast, exhibit a high duration and tend to be cheap to

EXHIBIT 7.1

Cash/Futures Price Relationships

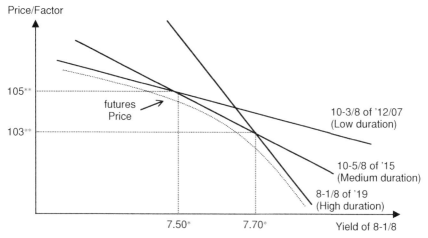

*Approximate crossover yields as of 1/5/92
**Approximate crossover futures prices as of 1/5/92

deliver when bond yields are high. In the range of yields around 7.6%, the 10-5/8% of '15, which exhibit a middling duration, tend to dominate deliveries.

Before expiration, the relationship between the futures price and the converted cash prices resembles the dashed line in Exhibit 7.1. The distance at any point along the line between the futures price and the lowest converted cash price represents the sum of two things:

- Carry
- Value of strategic delivery options

Notice that the gap between the converted cash prices tends to widen in the neighborhood of the switch points. It is at these points that uncertainty about what bond will be cheapest to deliver is greatest. As a result, it is at these points that the value of the strategic delivery options is greatest.

CALLS, PUTS, AND STRADDLES

Given the cash/futures price relationships sketched out in Exhibit 7.1, we can see easily how the bases of the three issues resemble familiar option positions. Consider, for example, the basis of the 8-1/8% of

'19. By definition, a bond's basis is the difference between its own price and the futures price multiplied by its conversion factor, or

Basis = Cash Price −(Conversion Factor × Futures Price)

In Exhibit 7.2, we see that the basis of the 8-1/8% is smallest when yields are high and it is the cheapest to deliver. Its basis tends to widen, however, as yields fall and lower-duration bonds become cheap to deliver.

The basis of the 8-1/8%, then, rises as bond yields fall and bond prices rise. A call option on bond futures behaves the same way. As bond yields fall, bond and bond futures prices rise, thereby lifting the value of calls on bond futures. In this sense, the basis of the 8-1/8% is like a call option on bond futures.

The basis of the 10-3/8% of '12-07, in contrast, is a lot like a put option on bond futures. As yields rise, bond and bond futures prices fall. Exhibit 7.3 shows that when this happens, the basis of the 10-3/8% tends to increase. So, of course, will the value of puts on bond futures.

Because of its position in the middle of the deliverable pack, the basis of the 10-5/8% of behaves much like a straddle, which is a combination of a call and a put. As shown in Exhibit 7.4, its basis is

E X H I B I T   7.2

Basis of 8-1/8% Is Like a Call Option on Bond Futures

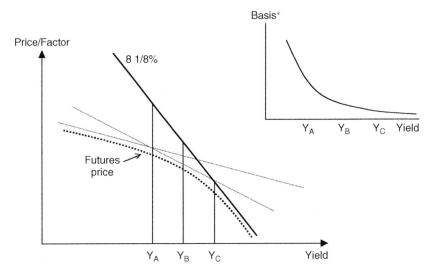

*Basis = Price − (Factor × Futures)

E X H I B I T   7.3

Basis of 10-3/8% Is Like a Put Option on Bond Futures

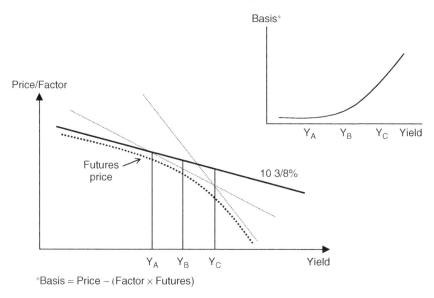

*Basis = Price − (Factor × Futures)

smallest when yields are around 7.60%, and it tends to increase as yields either rise or fall from this neighborhood. This, of course, is just how the value of a straddle behaves.

TWO ARENAS FOR TRADING VOLATILITY

The value of a bond's basis and the value of bond options both are driven by the level and volatility of bond prices. Because the unifying force behind bond prices is bond yields, we have two arenas for trading long-term yield volatility. The first is the market for conventional or real options on bonds and bond futures. Bond options are traded over the counter, and options on bond futures are traded on the floor of the Chicago Board of Trade. The other is the market for what we call synthetic options, which are constructed using bond basis positions.

Although the two kinds of options are driven by the same underlying bond yield volatility, the two instruments are not completely interchangeable and are not traded by exactly the same people. As a result, the prices paid for options on yield volatility in the two markets diverge from time to time.

EXHIBIT 7.4

Basis of 10-5/8% Is Like a Straddle on Bond Futures

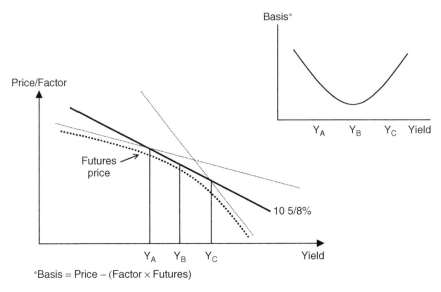

*Basis = Price − (Factor × Futures)

THE OPTION-ADJUSTED BOND BASIS

Our approach to determining whether yield volatility is trading at the same price in both the basis and the options markets is to value the strategic delivery options in bond futures directly. To do this, we begin with implied volatility in the market for options on bond futures. With this, we simulate possible interest rate paths, taking into account the systematic relationships that we observe between the level of bond yields and the yield spreads between the various deliverable issues.

For example, we find that the yields on callable Treasuries fall faster than noncallable Treasury yields when bond prices are rising and rise faster than noncallable Treasury yields when bond prices are falling. Once we have simulated the interest rate paths, we can assign values to each of the key strategic delivery options (i.e., the quality, switch, and timing options) along each of these paths and then work backward to calculate the expected present value of these options in bond basis terms.

Examples of these calculations are shown in Exhibit 7.5, which provides basis, carry, and delivery option information for the full set of deliverable bonds for April 23, 1992. The column labeled Theoretical Option Value represents our estimate of the portion

EXHIBIT 7.5

Option-Adjusted Basis
(Closing Price for Thursday, April 23, 1992,
in 32nds; June Futures Price = 98-02)

Coupon	Maturity	Actual Basis	Carry	Theoretical Option Value	Theoretical Basis	Option-Adjusted Basis
10.375	11/15/12-07	71.0	31.9	37.8	69.7	1.30
12.000	08/15/13-08	76.4	37.7	37.5	75.2	1.25
13.250	05/15/14-09	82.1	42.1	38.5	80.6	1.49
12.500	08/15/14-09	73.9	39.3	33.5	72.8	1.13
11.750	11/15/14-09	73.9	36.6	36.2	72.7	1.20
11.250	2/15/15	51.4	34.1	16.8	50.9	0.53
10.625	8/15/15	42.6	32.0	10.2	42.3	0.36
9.875	11/15/15	39.0	29.5	9.1	38.6	0.43
9.250	2/15/16	33.6	27.4	6.0	33.5	0.15
7.250	5/15/16	25.9	20.8	5.1	25.8	0.07
7.500	11/15/16	26.1	21.6	4.4	26.0	0.05
8.750	5/15/17	32.9	25.7	6.9	32.6	0.28
8.875	8/15/17	30.5	26.2	4.3	30.4	0.10
9.125	5/15/18	35.1	26.9	7.9	34.7	0.24
9.000	11/15/18	34.6	26.5	7.9	34.4	0.19
8.875	2/15/19	31.4	26.1	5.3	31.5	−0.02
8.125	8/15/19	27.5	23.7	3.9	27.6	−0.12
8.500	2/15/20	31.5	24.9	6.7	31.6	−0.11
8.750	5/15/20	35.1	25.7	9.4	35.1	0.06
8.750	8/15/20	33.6	25.7	8.1	33.7	−0.12
7.875	2/15/21	31.4	22.9	8.8	31.7	−0.21
8.125	5/15/21	35.5	23.6	11.9	35.5	−0.04
8.125	8/15/21	34.1	23.6	10.7	34.3	−0.22
8.000	11/15/21	39.9	23.2	16.7	39.9	−0.06

Notes:
1. Carry (in 32nds) is calculated for the period ending on the last delivery day and
assumes a 3.80 repo rate.
2. Theoretical option values are calculated from DCNYF Option-Adjusted Basis
Pricing Model. Estimates assume 10.1 percent yield volatility (9.0 percent price volatility).
3. Theoretical basis equals carry plus theoretical option value.
Source: JPMorgan

of each bond's basis that can be attributed to the bond contract's delivery mechanism.

For example, we estimate the theoretical option value in the basis of the 8-1/8% of 8/15/19, which was cheapest to deliver on April 23, as 3.9/32nds (i.e., 3.9 ticks). The theoretical option value in the basis of the 10-5/8% of '15 is 10.2 ticks.

Adding each bond's theoretical option value to its carry produces its theoretical basis, which we then compare with its actual basis. In particular, we subtract a bond's theoretical basis from its actual basis to determine its option-adjusted basis, or OAB, which is shown in the righthand column of Exhibit 7.5.

If delivery options embedded in the futures contract are trading at a level consistent with the level of implied volatility in the market for real options on Treasury bond futures, each bond's OAB should be zero. The OABs shown in Exhibit 7.5 are nearly all less than one tick, which is about as close to zero as this kind of modeling permits. Given the closing prices for Thursday, April 23, then, we would conclude that the March futures contract was fairly priced.

If a bond's OAB were greater than zero, however, we would conclude that the basis is rich, which means in turn that futures are cheap. If a bond's OAB were negative, on the other hand, we would conclude that the bond's basis is cheap, which means that futures are rich. A sufficiently large positive OAB indicates that one should sell the bond basis. A sufficiently large negative OAB suggests that one should buy the bond basis.

HISTORY OF MISPRICINGS

Our bond basis data allow us to get a reliable reading on the option-adjusted basis of both the lead and deferred bond futures contracts as far back as May 1989. The OAB history for these two series is shown in Exhibit 7.6.

As the history shows, the option-adjusted basis has spent much of the time trading within a range of five ticks on either side of zero. There have been, however, several episodes of substantial mispricings.

EXHIBIT 7.6

The Option-Adjusted Bond Basis
(May 1989 to May 1992)

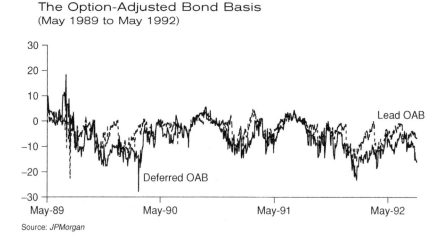

Source: *JPMorgan*

Throughout the summer of 1989, for example, the OAB for the deferred bond futures contract was exceptionally high, while the lead contract appears to have been more fairly priced. During this time, which corresponds roughly to the end of the golden age of yield enhancement with cheap bond futures, the deferred bond futures still appear to have been cheap. Replacing physical bonds with a duration equivalent position in deferred bond futures still promised to enhance the yield on a bond portfolio.

Since then, the largest mispricings in the bond basis have occurred just before year-end in 1990 and 1991. In both cases, the OAB of the of the deferred contract fell below –10 ticks, meaning that cash bonds were trading substantially cheap relative to bond futures.

VOLATILITY ARBITRAGE

Because we take implied volatility from the market for options on bond futures as our starting point for valuing the delivery option embedded in bond futures, any mispricings we find in the bond basis really are relative to what the market is paying for volatility in the real options market. As a practical matter, however, we have no way of knowing whether the market forecast of volatility that comes out of the bond options market is better or worse than the volatility forecast that comes out of the basis market. Rather, we prefer to look at the two markets as alternative places for trading bond yield volatility.

Looked at this way, any significant mispricing of bond futures that shows up in a large positive or negative OAB is really a signal that there may be an opportunity to improve the return on a volatility trade or to arbitrage the difference between the two. For example, a large negative OAB indicates that the bond basis market is paying a lower price for bond yield volatility than is the bond options market. If so, any trader looking to take a long position in bond volatility should give serious thought to buying the bond basis rather than real bond options. On the other hand, any trader looking to take a short position in volatility can get a better price in the real options market.

Also, if the mispricing is large enough, an arbitrageur could buy cheap bond volatility in the bond basis market and sell rich bond volatility in the options market. Done correctly, such a trade promises to take out the spread in implied volatilities between the two markets.

In practice, volatility arbitrage requires considerable care, because the vehicles for trading volatility are not the same. The classical notion of arbitrage is a set of offsetting transactions designed to profit from a price discrepancy but in which the arbitrageur has no risk. In volatility arbitrage, a goal of no risk is unattainable.

Even so, proper trade construction can keep the risk within bounds. The key to volatility arbitrage trading is in finding bond basis positions on the one hand and real option positions on the other that have profit/loss profiles that resemble each other as closely as possible. We do this through an optimizing routine that examines available exchange-traded options on bond futures and finds the best match for any given bond basis position.

Examples of what volatility arbitrage trades look like are shown in Exhibits 7.7 and 7.8. In all cases, OABs were at least five ticks (32nds) negative, so we recommended buying the basis and selling real options. Thus, all the trades that we recommended were long volatility in the basis market and short volatility in the real options market.

Consider, for example, the trade that we recommended on December 19, 1990. On that occasion, the OAB was −12.9 ticks. The

EXHIBIT 7.7

Report Card on Bond Basis Recommendations 1990

Date	Option Adjusted Basis	Basis Position	Hedge (CBOT Bond Options)	Net P/L before Commisions* (ticks)
01/24/90	−6.6	Buy $100mm Mar 10-3/8 of '12-07 and $50mm Mar 7-1/4 of '16	Sell 126 Mar 94 calls Sell 172 Mar 96 calls Sell 192 Mar 96 puts	3.4
05/16/90	−6.0	Buy $100mm Sep 11-1/4 of '15 or Buy $100mm Sep 10-5/8 of '15	Sell 229 Sep 92 calls Sell 86 Sep 90 puts Sell 218 Sep 92 calls Sell 100 Sep 96 puts	12.6
08/06/90	−5.7	Buy $100mm Sep 11-1/4 of '15 or Buy $100mm Sep 10-5/8 of '15	Sell 186 Sep 94 calls Sell 98 Sep 90 puts Sell 214 Sep 94 calls Sell 73 Sep 90 puts	10.5
11/19/90	−6.1	Buy $100mm Mar 7-1/2 of '16 or Buy $100mm Mar 7-1/4 of '16	Sell 239 Mar 94 calls Sell 235 Mar 94 calls	−0.6
12/19/90	−12.9	Buy $100mm Mar 10-3/8 of '11-07	Sell 128 Mar 96 puts	8.5
Average	−7.5			6.9

*Commissions can be expected to be less than one tick.

EXHIBIT 7.8

Report Card on Proprietary Basis Trades
(December 1990 to January 1992)

Trade date entry	Trade date exit	Basis position	Option hedge*	Net P/L after commissions (ticks)
12/4/90	1/14/91	Mar 7-1/4 of '16	Short 1.56 Mar 94 calls Short 1.47 Mar 98 calls	6.4
12/18/90	1/14/91	Mar 10-3/8 of '12-07	Short 2.0 Mar 96 puts Short 0.63 Mar 92 puts	7.8
1/18/91	1/30/91	Mar 10-3/8 of '12-07	Short 1.5 Mar 96 puts	3.3
2/19/91	3/5/91	Jun 10-3/8 of '12-07	Short 2.0 Jun 96 puts Short 0.5 Jun 100 calls	1
4/8/91	5/30/91	Sep 10-5/8 of '15	Short 2.9 Sep 98 calls Short 0.57 Sep 94 puts	1.8
12/10/91	1/15/92	Mar 8-1/8 of '19	Short 2.76 Mar 104 calls	-0.5
Average				3.3

*Hedge ratios shown are per $1 million basis position.

construction of the trade was fairly simple. A long March 1991 basis position in $100 million face value of the 10-3/8% could be well matched by a short position in 128 of the March 1991 96 puts.

Other trades could be more complex. Our first recommendation, based on January 24, 1990, prices, for example, combined two separate basis positions in the 10-3/8% and the 7-1/4%, and offset this position with short options in the March 1990 94 calls, 96 calls, and 96 puts.

REPORT CARD

We have two readings on how well these kinds of trades might have done. The first comes out of the complete set of trade recommendations that we made to our clients during 1990. For these, Exhibit 7.7 shows how a mechanical approach to trading our recommendations during 1990 would have done.

The net P/L shown there is the result of putting on the positions on the date shown, financing any bond position in the overnight RP market, and taking off the position when the options in the position expire. The prices used to determine these P/Ls were exchange settlement prices, and the net figures do not reflect transaction costs. One could, of course, have done better or worse than this by trading the positions actively.

In any case, we find that the average mispricing of the basis was just under 7.5 ticks, and the average profit, before trading costs, on the five different sets of trades was just under 7.0 ticks. The trades exhibit some variability in their profitability, which we discuss later.

The second reading, shown in Exhibit 7.8, is given by the performance of trades that we undertook on behalf of proprietary traders. The difference between these and the trades shown in Exhibit 7.7 is that these are real. As a result, the net P/L figures reflect actual trade prices, actual financing costs, and actual trading costs, including brokerage. To equalize the sizes of the trades, the option hedges shown in Exhibit 7.8 are the numbers of options required to hedge $1 million of a long basis position in the respective issues.

Although the average P/L was smaller in the actual trades, the size and range of outcomes is typical for this kind of work. Because this is as much like arbitrage as it can be, the gains and losses tend to be small. Also, because it is not arbitrage in the original sense of a riskless trade, the outcomes are variable.

A third reading on results comes from a methodical examination of historical data on the bond basis and option prices. Although we have been following volatility arbitrage trades actively only since January 1990, our database allows us to look as far back as May 1989 with considerable reliability and see how our approach would have fared.

In our simulations, which we carried through August 1990, we looked at both the lead and the deferred contracts. Whenever the option-adjusted basis was more than three ticks away from zero, we initiated a trade designed to take out the spread, financed the position term to option expiration, and lifted the trade at option expiration. The results of this exercise are shown in Exhibit 7.9.

In all, we found a total of 297 different cases in which either the lead or the first deferred futures contract was mispriced. These were not, of course, entirely independent events, because mispricings can last several days. Also, on a number of days, both the lead and deferred contracts were mispriced. The distribution of these cases across quarters is shown under Number of Trades.

Under P/L performance, we show the worst, best, and average profit from these trades. In the right-hand column, we also show the standard deviation of profits. Out of 297 separate trades, the worst was a loss of 16.7 ticks, and the best was a gain of 29.2 ticks,

EXHIBIT 7.9

Simulated Performances of Bond Basis Arbitrage
(Cheapest to Deliver Issues May 1989 to August 1990)

Contract	Number of trades	P/L performance (in ticks)			
		Worst	Best	Average	Standard deviation
All	297	-16.7	29.2	4.9	8.6
Sep-89	20	-10.0	18.4	1.3	6.9
Dec-89	77	-1.9	16.8	6.8	4.7
Mar-90	78	-13.4	18.7	-2.1	5.9
Jun-90	65	-16.7	23.5	5.3	9.2
Sep-90	57	-9.5	29.2	12.5	8.2
Memo: Unhedged Basis Trades	297	-12.4	53.8	6.8	13.4

with an average gain of 4.9 ticks. The standard deviation of profits around this average was 8.6 ticks.

The results of doing just the basis part of the trade are shown in the bottom row. Two things stand out. First, in some respects, the unhedged positions look better. The worst case was a smaller loss, the best case was a higher gain, and the average gain was nearly two ticks larger. On the other hand, the standard deviation of profits was considerably larger—13.4 ticks as opposed to 8.6 ticks. In light of these results, a trader could have traded just the basis and earned a higher expected return in exchange for a higher-risk strategy.

The second thing that stands out in the unhedged results is that the expected return from simply trading the basis was very significantly positive. Given our approach of taking implied volatility in the market for real options as our reference point for finding mispricings in the futures market (rather than the other way around), the real options market appears to be a better forecaster of volatility than is the bond basis market. Is anyone surprised?

EXAMPLES OF YIELD ENHANCEMENT

Even though the golden age of yield enhancement with cheap bond futures has gone by the boards, money managers should give serious consideration to what can be done with bond volatility arbitrage to improve risk/return profiles. To show what can be done, we used the results of our simulated trading exercise to create a synthetic bond portfolio.

To construct a synthetic portfolio, we assumed that all cash in the portfolio was invested in Treasury bills to return 6.5%. In light of our actual experience in 1990, we limited the number of trades to five per year. We took the average profit to be 5.0 ticks per trade, and for reckoning the risk, we used the historical standard deviation of 8.6 ticks.

As shown in Exhibit 7.10, the results appear promising. For example, using our recommended leverage ratio of 20 to 1, the average return on the portfolio would have been 22.1%. The worst case was a return of –1.9%, and the best case was a return of 46.2%.

For the sake of this comparison, we take the worst and best cases to be the results of trades that are two standard deviations above or below the average. Using this standard, roughly 95% of all investment outcomes would have been within the range shown.

These returns are attractive. It is the rare bond fund that could expect to outperform Treasury bills by 15.6 percentage points while exposing the investor to a possible loss of only 1.9% for the year.

LEVERAGE

Exhibit 7.10 makes it plain that the results depend largely on how much risk the investor is willing to take. For all practical purposes, the largest basis position that one can do is roughly 25 times one's cash position. Exchange margin requirements and one's cash requirements in the RP market really do not permit much more.

On the other hand, one can be as conservative as desired. For example, an investor could have increased the expected return by nearly four percentage points by stretching cash resources to the limit. The cost of doing this, of course, is a wider range of possible returns and a larger loss in the worst case.

An investor could also have limited the worst case to a *gain* of 2.3 percentage points by limiting the size of the basis position to 10 times the size of available funds. The cost of safety, of course, would have been a lower expected return.

WORDS OF CAUTION

The risk in volatility arbitrage trading stems from the differences between the bond basis and options on bond futures as vehicles for

EXHIBIT 7.10

Simulated Rates of Return on a Bond Basis
Arbitrage Fund

Leverage Ratio	Cash Needed for $100 mm Basis Position	Total return		
		Worst Case (-2sd)	Best Case (+2sd)	Average Return
25:1	$4mm	-4.00%	56.10%	26.00%
20:1*	$5mm	-1.90%	46.20%	22.10%
10:1	$10mm	2.30%	26.30%	14.30%

Note: Assumes Treasury bill yield of 6.5%

*Recommended leverage ratio

trading bond yield volatility. In particular, a bond's basis is subject to changes in yield spreads among deliverable bonds as well as to changes in carry, which can change either because of general changes in the slope of the yield curve or because of changes specific to the RP market. Much of the variability in the returns shown in Exhibits 7.7, 7.8, and 7.9 reflects this kind of risk.

Also, even with good engineering, the P/L profiles for bond basis and real option positions cannot be made to match each other perfectly. As a result, we find that the outcome of a trade can depend on where bond prices end up.

A third source of discrepancy is in the different horizons of the two kinds of options. Options on bond futures expire about a month before the last trading day for the underlying futures contract. As a result, the delivery options embedded in futures can have a higher vega than the real options. This means that the bond basis can be more sensitive to changes in implied volatility than the real options in the hedged position.

OTHER APPLICATIONS

Our approach to valuing the basis has applications outside of volatility arbitrage trading. In particular, an understanding of option-adjusted bases can be valuable both to hedgers and to futures spread traders.

Besides knowing how to calculate the correct hedge ratio for a hedge, a hedger should know whether futures are rich or cheap.

For example, negative OABs suggest that futures are expensive and that selling futures can be more profitable or less costly than doing the hedge by selling cash bonds. On the other hand, positive OABs suggest that futures are cheap and that shorting futures may be worse than shorting cash bonds for hedging.

Exhibit 7.6 shows that the option-adjusted basis for the lead and deferred contracts do not track each other perfectly. Frequently, for that matter, the lead contract exhibits a radically different OAB than that of the deferred contract. In such a case, an alternative approach to bond volatility arbitrage as outlined previously is a calendar spread in futures—selling the expensive contract and buying the cheap contract.

CHAPTER 8

Nine Eras of the Bond Basis

We have used this chapter as a place for recounting interesting developments in our understanding of the behavior of Treasury bond futures and of the forces that have shaped its pricing and the ways we have used the contract. In the 1994 edition, we had identified 7 "eras" of the bond basis. In this edition, we add two more: "the long dry spell" (1995 through 1999) and "6% factors and the rebirth of bond basis trading" (2000 to ?). We also include a brief discussion of what appears to be a fundamental shift away from the bond contract and toward the 10-year note contract as the trading and hedging vehicle of choice.

THE BIRTH AND MATURATION OF BOND FUTURES

Our understanding of what drives bond futures and of the options that are embedded in the contract terms did not emerge fully formed on the day the bond futures pit was first opened for trading. For that matter, when it was first introduced in 1977, the bond futures contract was thought to be too complicated, and there was some question about whether it would succeed. The "delivered basket" idea, which was old hat in conventional commodity futures, was new to financial futures, and the markets took some time to adjust.

As it turned out, the years since 1977 have been exceptionally fruitful for learning the ins and outs of the futures contract. The Treasury securities market has covered a lot of ground over the past

15 years. The market has grown at a breathtaking pace. Yields have gone from comparatively low levels in the 1970s, to phenomenally high levels in the early 1980s, to low levels in the early 1990s. The slope of the yield curve has gone from positive, to negative, and back to positive again. Yields have gone from being stable, to highly volatile, to comparatively stable, to comparatively volatile, and back to comparatively stable.

Each radical change in the interest rate environment, whether in the level of yields, the slope of the yield curve, or the overall volatility of yields, has brought to light a new facet of the relationship between the futures contract and the market for Treasury securities.

VOLATILITY OF YIELDS SINCE 1977

Paul Volcker arrived at the Fed when inflation in the United States was running out of control. By the fall of 1979, the situation had become intolerable, and Volcker's Fed embarked on a period of sharply tighter money. The effect of those policies and their aftermath is best characterized by the three panels of Exhibit 8.1. The top panel shows what has happened to the level of yields, as measured by yields on 30-year Treasury bonds. When Volcker began his term, long-term rates were around 8%. Soon after, long-term rates rose to about 14%, a level from which yields have been falling on and off ever since.

The second panel shows what happened to the slope of the yield curve, which we measure by the difference between the yields on 30-year Treasury bonds and 2-year Treasury notes. The initial impact of tight money was to force short-term yields well above long-term yields. This was followed by the "free fall" of short-term rates during the spring of 1980, which in turn was followed by a second sortie into negative yield-curve territory. Since late 1981, the slope of the yield curve has been either flat or positive.

The bottom panel shows the three-month historical volatility of long-term Treasury yields. The change in monetary policy regimes prompted a sharp increase in yield volatility. Since then, following a brief settling down in 1984, bond yields have been more volatile than they were in the 1970s, though not quite as volatile as they were during the early Volcker years.

NINE ERAS OF TRADING

Throughout these dramatic shifts in yield curve settings, the behavior of the bond futures contract has gone through nine more-or-less distinct eras:

Bond Yield, Yield Curve Slope, and Bond Yield Volatility

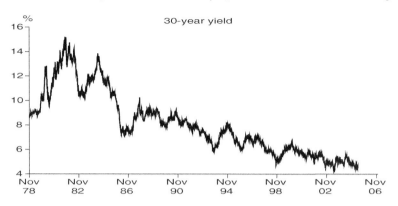

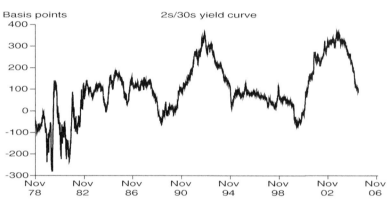

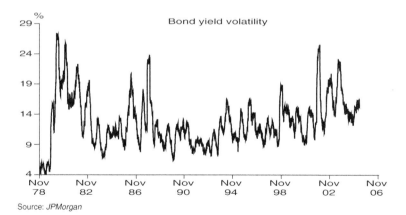

Source: *JPMorgan*

- Cash and carry—1977 and 1978
- Negative yield curve—1979 through 1981
- Positive yield curve—1982 through 1984
- Golden age of yield enhancement—1985 through 1989
- Volatility arbitrage—1990 through 1991

- Death of gamma—June 1991 through June 1993
- The callables' last hurrah—July 1993 through 1994
- The long dry spell of the 11-1/4%—1995 through 1999
- 6% factors and the rebirth of bond basis trading—2000 to ?

We discuss the characteristics of each of these periods in turn, tracking the record of actual bond deliveries at the Chicago Board of Trade as a guide to T-bond futures behavior.

FIRST ERA: CASH AND CARRY (1977 AND 1978)

This period is perhaps the easiest of the six eras to describe. Yields were low and stable, and the yield curve was positively sloped. These were the early days of the bond contract, and its trading was very similar to trading in other contracts (e.g., wheat, corn, and soybeans) at the Board of Trade. Bonds were bought in the cash market and sold in the futures market if the cost of financing those bonds before the period was less than the price differential between the bonds and the futures. Nothing could have been simpler.

With the positively sloped yield curve, it paid to buy bonds and deliver them against the futures. Moreover, it paid to deliver them on the last possible day. Exhibit 8.2 bears this out, showing in the form of an index the average delivery date of delivered bonds. The index is constructed so that a bond delivered on the first day of the delivery month has a delivery index reading of 1; a bond delivered on the last day has an index reading of 30 or 31. For most of this period, the

EXHIBIT 8.2

Average Delivery Dates of Delivered Bonds

delivery index is close to the top of the scale, which indicates that all or nearly all bonds were delivered on the last possible day.

By the end of 1978, deliveries began to come in early. It was at this time that the bond futures contract began to change character and that some of the richness of the contract began to come to light.

SECOND ERA: NEGATIVE YIELD CURVE (1979 THROUGH 1981)

This was the era when Paul Volcker was conducting his monetarist experiment. Its consequences for interest rates are demonstrated vividly in Exhibit 8.1. Yields rose from 8-1/2% to 14-1/2%. The slope of the yield curve swung back and forth between negative and positive; at times short-term rates were as much as 200 basis points higher than long-term rates. The period also was characterized by sharply rising yield volatility. Volatility rose from a sleepy 4% (annualized) to well over 16%.

The effect of this environment on the bond futures contract was fascinating. The most obvious consequence of a negatively sloped yield curve is that it costs money to hold bonds for a long time. Therefore, one would expect bond deliveries to take place early in the delivery month. This is borne out by Exhibit 8.2, which shows that most deliveries took place within the first week of the delivery month, at least during the first few delivery cycles.

Then a curious thing happened. The yield curve slope became even more negative, but deliveries started taking place later and later rather than earlier and earlier.

The explanation for this delivery behavior is rooted in the "wild card" option. A wild card play is the delivery of bonds into the futures contract in response to a sharp change in bond prices after futures trading has closed for the day. To take advantage of the wild card, at least three things are required:

- A short position in bond futures
- A delivery factor for the delivered bond significantly different from one
- Enough bond volatility to cause a big change in bond prices between the close of the futures market and the deadline for delivery notice

Of these three, the second two were ushered in with the new interest rate regime. The high level of yields brought with them high-coupon Treasury bonds, which in turn carried the

E X H I B I T   8.3

Government Securities Dealer Positions
in Bonds and Bond Futures

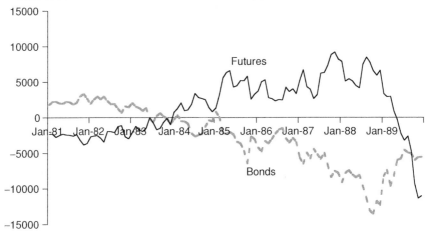

Face amount bonds and notional amount in futures; $ mm

Source: Federal Reserve Board

high conversion factors needed to make the wild card play profitable. Moreover, the high volatility of yields, especially in late-afternoon trading when the money supply figures were released, provided the necessary swings in bond prices.

Thus, the wild card option gained value. Exhibit 8.2 shows its effect on the timing of deliveries. Even though carry was negative during much of this period, traders held on to their short futures positions to take advantage of wild card opportunities. As they did, deliveries tended to fall later and later in the contract month.

At the beginning of 1981, the Federal Reserve began to require primary government securities dealers to report their positions in both cash bonds and futures. As shown in Exhibit 8.3, dealers were, on balance, long cash bonds and short a roughly equivalent number of bond futures. That is, they were "long the basis."

THIRD ERA: POSITIVE CARRY (1982 THROUGH 1984)

Starting in 1982, yields began to decline, and the yield curve resumed its "normal," or positive, slope. Volatility fell off somewhat from its highs in the early 1980s, and actually returned to its old levels briefly in 1984.

With the return of positive carry, there was no longer a clear cost incentive to deliver bonds early. Rather, the incentive was to deliver as late in the contract month as possible. The delivery evidence bears this out. As shown in Exhibit 8.2, most bonds were delivered near the end of the contract month after 1981.

The exceptions to this rule took place during the second half of 1982 and the first quarter of 1983, when the average delivery index was close to 20 days. A wild card option was at work. In this case, however, carry was positive, and the effect of the wild card was to accelerate rather than delay deliveries.

Dealers stayed long the basis until the middle of this period so that they too could take advantage of the shorts' wild card option. (See Exhibit 8.2.) From the middle of 1983, however, the primary dealers' positions began to shift to a short basis. As yields stabilized, the volatility needed for wild card plays disappeared.

FOURTH ERA: THE GOLDEN AGE OF YIELD ENHANCEMENT (1985 THROUGH 1989)

The fourth era in this chronicle runs from the beginning of 1985 through the end of 1988. During this period, yields were generally falling, the yield curve was comparatively flat but still positively sloped, and yields were fairly volatile. (See Exhibit 8.1.)

On the whole, this era does not appear much different from the preceding one. Exhibit 8.2 shows that most deliveries took place at the end of the delivery month. Some wild card options appear to have been exercised early in 1986, and a possible switch option was exercised in late 1987.

Even so, the positions of primary government securities dealers suggest that something about the period was different. Note that dealers throughout these years were short the basis in a positive carry environment.

Their behavior cannot be explained by the change in the yield curve as a whole. Rather, the shift in their basis position seems to have been prompted in the first instance by a change in the slope of the long end of the yield curve.

Around 1985, a number of events conspired to cause great demand for long-dated Treasury bonds:

- The bull market in bonds increased demand for long-dated zero-coupon bonds.

- The U.S. Treasury, in an effort to accommodate this demand, stopped issuing callable bonds and 20-year bonds, and concentrated on fixed maturity 30-year bonds.
- The reserve surplus of Japan began to be invested aggressively in long-dated Treasury bonds.

Exhibit 8.4, which shows the yield difference between 30-year and 20-year Treasuries, illustrates the effect of these events clearly. The slope of the long end of the yield curve became sharply negative. By the middle of 1985, the longest eligible bonds yielded 30 basis points less than the shortest eligible bonds. They became extremely expensive, and dealers shorted the cash bonds and hedged by buying futures contracts.

The short basis position of the primary dealers continued to grow through 1988, even though the relative expensiveness of long-dated Treasury bonds fell off for the most part. What accounted for the growth?

The explanation we find plausible is that the dealers discovered the profitability of being short the basis as a byproduct of their initial yield curve play with long-dated bonds. We believe dealers found that the premium in the basis was too large or, what is the same thing, that the embedded options in short futures positions were overpriced. As a result, a short basis position, with one impressive interruption during the short squeeze of 1986, was a profitable position to have maintained.

E X H I B I T   8.4

Average Yield Spread between 30-Year
and 20-Year Treasuries

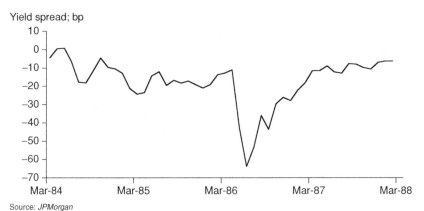

Source: *JPMorgan*

The end-of-month option, which comes into play during the week or so remaining in the delivery month after trading in the futures contract has expired, appeared during this era. As shown in Chapter 3, the basic ingredients for the end-of-month option to have value are

- Two or more close contenders for the cheapest to deliver
- Enough volatility in yields to create uncertainty in traders' minds about which bond might actually be cheapest to deliver

As yields passed through the 9% region, the first of these conditions was met. Further, there were enough episodes of high yield volatility during this year to supply the uncertainty. As a result, the end-of-month option had a noticeable influence on the bond basis during a number of futures expirations. The effect is not absolutely clear in the delivery index, however, because the end-of-month option, even if exercised, does not accelerate deliveries.

FIFTH ERA: VOLATILITY ARBITRAGE (1990 THROUGH 1991)

Sometime during the middle of 1989, the golden age of yield enhancement came to an end. During the first half of 1989, yields fell, the yield curve flattened, and volatility decreased substantially. Exhibit 8.5 shows that a radical shift in the pricing of bond futures took place as well. The positive option-adjusted basis of the bond futures contract before 1989 indicates that futures were cheap. During the early months of 1989, however, the option-adjusted basis of the bond contract passed through zero and, on at least three occasions, was noticeably negative so that futures on these occasions were as much as 10 ticks expensive. Then, by early 1990, it seems that the option-adjusted basis of bond futures settled in around zero and that the bond futures contract became more or less fairly priced.

The transition from bond futures that were cheap to bond futures that were rich and then, finally, to bond futures that were more or less fairly priced is reflected in the retreat of primary government securities dealers from the short basis position that they had maintained for the several years during the golden age of yield enhancement. By the middle of 1989, the combined bond futures position of primary dealers had fallen to almost zero.

Clearly, there was a new game in town. One could no longer enhance the yield on a bond portfolio simply by selling bonds, investing the proceeds in money market instruments, and establishing a

EXHIBIT 8.5

Option-Adjusted Bond Basis Lead Contract, 7/88 to 7/90

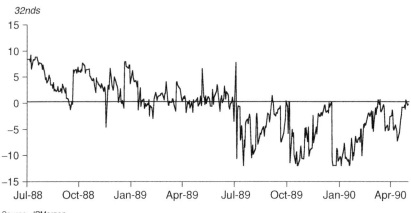

Source: *JPMorgan*

risk-equivalent long position in cheap bond futures. Instead, any-one interested in taking advantage of mispriced bond futures had to know how to value the options embedded in the contracts and how to construct trades that would allow one to arbitrage differences between the price paid for volatility in the bond basis market and the price paid for volatility in the market for options on bond futures. We were among those who knew how to do volatility arbi-trage, and we wrote about it as early as January 1990. During 1990 and 1991, as explained in Chapter 7, we put together a successful track record that involved five or six trades a year. (See Exhibits 7.7 and 7.8 for a summary of this track record.)

The comparatively small number of trades that we were able to do is a good indication of just how fairly priced bond futures had become.

SIXTH ERA: THE DEATH OF GAMMA (JUNE 1991 THROUGH JUNE 1993)

The sixth era began in June 1991, when the bond market in the United States was poised on the verge of a tremendous rally fueled in part by Federal Reserve monetary policy. The cheapest to deliver bond, which was the 7-1/2% of '16, was trading at a yield of about 8.5%. Over the next six months, bond yields fell about 100 basis points, and by the end of the year, the 7-1/2% of '16 were trading at a yield just under 7.5%.

Under what we had come to think of as normal circumstances, such a large drop in bond yields would have caused a shift in the cheapest to deliver from the 7-1/2% to one of the low-duration, callable bonds such as the 10-3/8% of '12-07. This time, however, the 7-1/2% remained cheapest to deliver, and the big question was why. The answer lay in what happened to yield spreads among bonds in the deliverable set.

Given the horizons of most people who trade the basis for a living, what happened to yield spreads during the 1991 rally could be likened to the 100-year flood. As shown in Exhibit 8.6, the yield spread between the 10-3/8% of '12-07 and the 7-1/4% of '16 had hovered around 15 basis points for years. Sometimes the spread was higher and sometimes lower, but always the spread was around 15 basis points. Then came the rally of 1991 and a radical steepening of the yield curve. The spread between the 10-3/8% and the 7-1/4% fell from 15 basis points to a negative spread of 20 basis points. The effect was to keep the 10-3/8% expensive in a rising market.

Yield spreads also became very directional during this period. A rise in bond prices would be accompanied by a steepening of the yield curve. A fall in bond prices would be accompanied by a flattening of the yield curve. The extreme regularity of this relationship between yield spreads and bond prices is shown in Exhibit 8.7, which shows

EXHIBIT 8.6

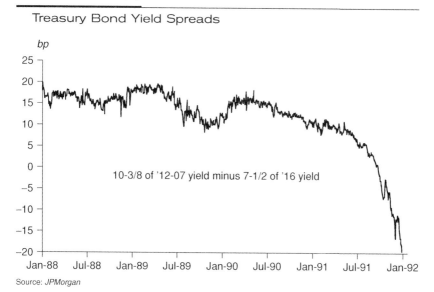

Treasury Bond Yield Spreads

10-3/8 of '12-07 yield minus 7-1/2 of '16 yield

Source: *JPMorgan*

the spread between the yield on the 7-1/2% of 11/16 and the yield on the 12% of '13-08. On average, this yield spread increased 3 basis points for every 10-basis-point drop in bond yields.

The consequences of this relationship between yield spreads and yield levels for the behavior of the bond basis were profound. Instead of the 7-1/2% becoming expensive to deliver as yields fell, the increase in the yield on the 7-1/2% relative to the yields of lower-duration bonds in the deliverable set was enough to keep it cheapest to deliver. Exhibit 8.8 shows that even though yields fell

EXHIBIT 8.7

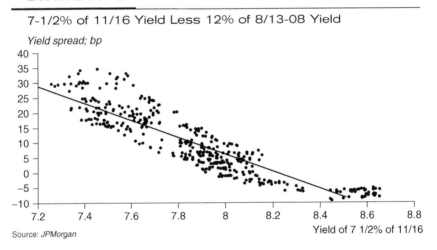

7-1/2% of 11/16 Yield Less 12% of 8/13-08 Yield

Source: *JPMorgan*

EXHIBIT 8.8

Delivery History, June 1991 to June 1993

Contract Month	Most Delivered Bond	Yield on Last Delivery Day
June 1991	7-1/2% of '16	8.53
September 1991	7-1/2% of '16	7.91
December 1991	7-1/2% of '16	7.48
March 1992	7-1/2% of '16	8.02
June 1992	7-1/2% of '16	7.84
September 1992	7-1/2% of '16	7.41
December 1992	9-1/4% of '16	7.44
March 1993	9-1/4% of '16	7.01
June 1993	9-1/4% of '16	6.65

Source: *JPMorgan*

EXHIBIT 8.9

Effect of Yield Spread Changes on 7-1/2% Basis

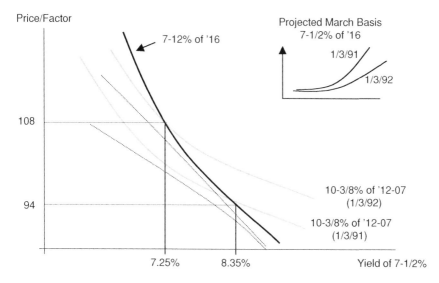

from 8.53% at the end of June 1991 to 7.41% at the end of September 1992, the 7-1/2% of '16 were the most delivered bond in every delivery month. Only in December 1992, when there was a slight flattening of the yield curve, were the 7-1/2% of '16 replaced by the 9-1/4% of '16 as the cheapest to deliver bond.

Because much of the value of the strategic delivery options in the bond contract stems from the switch option, the behavior of yield spreads during this period robbed the basis of much of its option value. For the basis of the 7-1/2%, for example, the effect was like that of raising the strike price on a call option. As shown in Exhibit 8.9, the effect of an increase in the yield spread between the 7-1/2% and the 10-3/8% was to lower the crossover yield. The insert shows that the drop in the crossover yield shifted the relationship between the basis of the 7-1/2% and the level of futures prices to the right. It was as if the implicit strike price of this embedded option were raised and the gamma in the position pushed out of reach. As a result, basis traders who expected the basis of the 7-1/2% to increase as yields fell below 8% were greatly disappointed. The effect of their disappointment on the value of the delivery option premium in the bond basis is shown in Exhibit 8.10.

EXHIBIT 8.10

Option Premium in the Bond Basis*

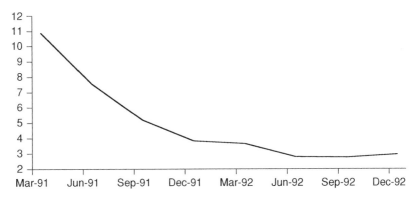

* Average BNOC of CTD Bond during the three months before expiration
Source: *JPMorgan*

SEVENTH ERA: THE CALLABLES' LAST HURRAH (JULY 1993 THROUGH 1994)

In July and August of 1993, the yield curve flattened during a bond market rally, thereby reversing its behavior of the previous two years. As a result, the last remaining callable bonds in the deliverable set became cheap to deliver, the option-adjusted duration of the bond futures contract dropped substantially, and the basis of the long bond increased about a point and a half.

The behavior of the yield curve can be seen in Exhibit 8.11, which tracks the price of the September 1993 bond futures contract and the yield spread between the 11-1/4% of 2/15 and the 12-1/2% of 8/14-09. In early July, the 11-1/4% were the cheapest of the non-callable bonds, and the 12-1/2% were the cheapest of the three remaining callable bonds. The rally in the market is illustrated by the increase in the bond futures price from 114 to around 122. The flattening of the yield curve from the beginning of July through mid-August is shown by the drop in the yield spread between the 11-1/4% and the 12-1/2%.

The relative cheapness of the two bonds is shown in Exhibit 8.12, which shows the difference between their bases net of carry. At the beginning of July, the basis net of carry for the 11-1/4% was between 1/32nds and 20/32nds below the basis net of carry for

EXHIBIT 8.11

September 1993 Bond Futures and Bond Yield Spreads

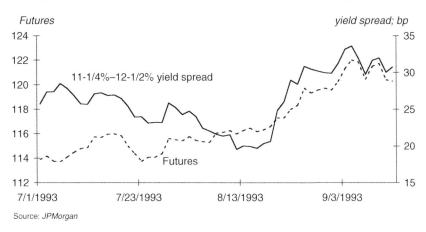

Source: *JPMorgan*

EXHIBIT 8.12

September 1993 Futures Duration and CTD Switches

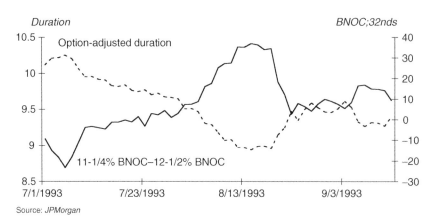

Source: *JPMorgan*

the 12-1/2%. By late July, they were roughly equal, and by August 12, the basis net of carry for the 12-1/2% was 35/32nds below that for the 11-1/4%. Even allowing for what appears to have been a squeeze of the callable issues in late August, the 12-1/2% remained cheapest to deliver.

The effect on the contract's effective duration was, as one might expect, dramatic. The option-adjusted duration of the September contract, which is shown in Exhibit 8.12, fell from slightly more than

EXHIBIT 8.13

The 7-1/8% of 2/23 Basis

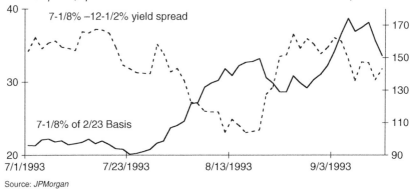

Source: *JPMorgan*

10 to around 9. In contrast, the durations of all bonds in the deliverable set were increasing because of the fall in yield levels.

The bond market rally, combined with the switch in the cheapest to deliver, also had a dramatic effect on the basis of the on-the-run bond (7-1/8% of 2/23), which increased from about 90/32nds in late July to nearly 170/32nds in early September. Much of the increase in the basis of the 7-1/8% can be attributed to the drop in its yield spread against the 12-1/2%, and you can see in Exhibit 8.13 how the increase in this spread in late August partly reversed the change. The bond market rally continued, however, and its effect on the expensiveness of the 7-1/8% was more than enough to offset the increase in the yield spread.

EIGHTH ERA: THE LONG DRY SPELL OF THE 11-1/4% (1995 THROUGH 1999)

When the last of the callable bonds disappeared from the deliverable set in December 1994, and with bond yields well below any of the usual crossover points, the 11-1/4% of '16, which were the lowest-duration bonds in the deliverable set, became firmly entrenched as the cheapest to deliver. And they remained so from early 1995 through the expiration of December 1999 contract. During these years, the contract exhibited no particular option value and could be treated as a forward on the 11-1/4%.

We think of these years as the long dry spell. As shown in Exhibit 8.14, because the 11-1/4% were so firmly established as

EXHIBIT 8.14

Bond CTD Maturity and Delivery Option Value

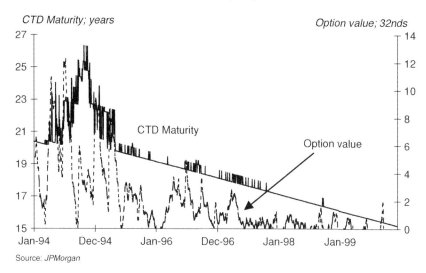

Source: *JPMorgan*

cheapest to deliver, the maturity of the cheapest to deliver, which had varied widely until early 1995, began to drift slowly down from slightly more than 19 years in early 1995 to 15 by the end of 1999. At the same time, the option value in the bond contract during these years rarely traded at more than a couple of 32nds.

One natural consequence of the shortening effective maturity of the bond contract was that it became less useful as a hedging tool for those trading the long end of the market. By the end of 1999, one would have been hedging 30-year yield exposure with the equivalent of a 15-year bond.

Another consequence was that basis traders had little to do and began to drift away from the market. There was just not enough optionality left for a basis trader to make a living. All that was really left were low-margin carry trades that required huge size to make enough money to make them worthwhile. Basis trading as an occupation nearly died out during these years.

NINTH ERA: 6% FACTORS AND THE REBIRTH OF BOND BASIS TRADING (2000 TO ?)

The Chicago Board of Trade's eventual response to this long dry spell was to reduce the hypothetical yield for calculating conversion factors from 8% to 6%. The first contracts for which the new conversion factors were used were those for March 2000, which were first listed for trading in April 1999. This was a momentous change for the CBOT, which had used 8% factors for its Treasury contracts since 1977.

The result was a rebirth of basis trading. The switch from 8% to 6% factors made it possible once again for changes in the cheapest to deliver to become not only a possibility but a working reality. Rather than reflecting the 11-1/4%, the bond contract came to reflect a fairly broad subset of the deliverable set, with maturities in the neighborhood of 20 years. Because these issues were fairly large and numerous, the contract became less susceptible to the squeezes or pressures that could have a pronounced effect on a single issue. And because the issues were more centrally located in the range of deliverable maturities, the bond contract came to reflect the behavior of a broader part of the yield curve.

Exhibits 8.15 and 8.16 provide vivid illustrations of the immediate effect that 6% factors had on the bond contract. Exhibit 8.15, for example, shows both how the cheapest to deliver maturity has varied since the introduction of the new factors and the increase in the value of the embedded delivery options. Exhibit 8.16 shows the basis net of carry for bonds in the deliverable set for the December 1999 contract on December 13, 1999, and for the December 2002

EXHIBIT 8.15

Bond CTD Maturity and Delivery Option Value

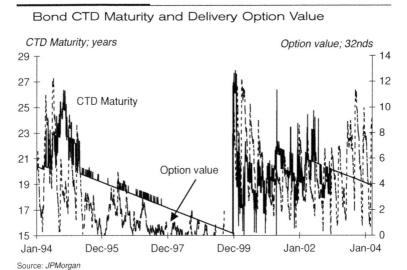

Source: *JPMorgan*

E X H I B I T   8.16

Net Bases for Deliverable Bonds

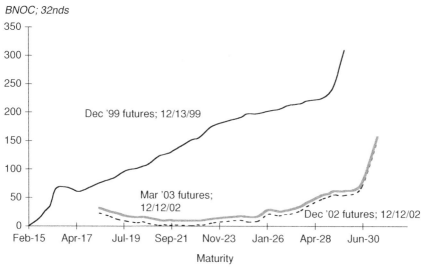

Source: *JPMorgan*

and March 2003 contracts on December 12, 2002. As the exhibit shows, in December 1999, basis net of carry was simply an increasing function of time to maturity. The shortest-maturity bond had a basis net of carry of zero, and every other bond was expensive to deliver. In December 2002, on the other hand, bonds a with wide range of maturities appeared to be almost equally cheap to deliver.

The first half of 2000 provided the market with a rich set of lessons in just how profitable basis trading could be. During the first quarter alone, 22 bonds were cheapest to deliver at one time or another. In addition, when the Treasury announced that it intended to start buying back long-term Treasury issues, the result was a drop in Treasury yields accompanied by a severe inversion of the long end of the yield curve. Exhibit 8.17 provides a useful chronicle of basis trading during these months. In the upper panel, you can trace the basis net of carry for three different bonds—the 9-7/8% of 11/15 (a low-duration bond), the 8% of 11/21 (a medium-duration bond), and the 6-1/8% of 11/27 (a high-duration bond). As the exhibit shows, bond yields rose during most of December 1999 through the middle of January 2000. During these weeks, as one would expect with rising yields, the basis net of carry of the 6-1/8% fell and by early January become cheapest to deliver. Basis net of carry for the

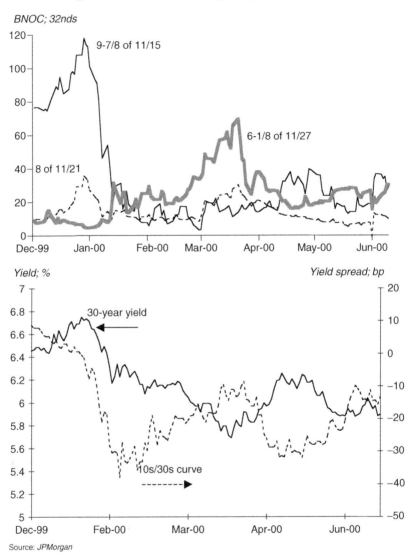

EXHIBIT 8.17

Reemergence of Basis Trading Opportunities

Source: *JPMorgan*

9-7/8% and the 8% both increased, and in the case of the 9-7/8% (the lowest-duration bond), increased quite a lot.

Then the Treasury announced its buyback program. What followed was a decrease in bond yields accompanied by a sharp inversion of the deliverable yield curve. The 10s/30s spread, which had been trading close to zero at the beginning of January, fell to almost –40 basis points. This was a highly improbable combination of events, and both changes—the drop in yields and the "flattening" of the deliverable yield curve—served to cheapen the 9-7/8% and the 8%, and to richen the 6-1/8%. For a brief span, all three bonds were almost equally cheap. Then the 9-7/8% became cheapest to deliver, while the basis net of carry of the 6-1/8% began to rise sharply. Thereafter, changes in bond yields and the slope of the curve behaved more along usual lines and produced further changes in the cheapest to deliver. During these months, the rather dramatic changes in the richness and cheapness of these three bonds provided ample opportunity to trade the basis.

CHANGING OF THE GUARD–THE RISE OF NOTES AND FALL OF BONDS

Until recently, Treasury bond futures were the dominant Treasury contract both in terms of trading volume and open interest. But the Treasury bond contract peaked sometime between October 1997, when trading volume reached its highest rate (Exhibit 8.18), and June 1998, when open interest reached is highest level (Exhibit 8.19). By 2002, both trading volume and open interest in the 10-year note futures were nearly twice as high as they were for Treasury bond futures.

EXHIBIT 8.18

Average Daily Trading Volume in Bond and Note Futures

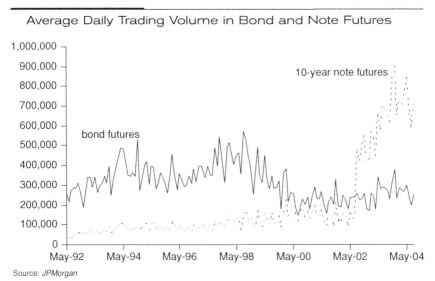

Source: *JPMorgan*

EXHIBIT 8.19

Open Interest in Bond and Note Futures

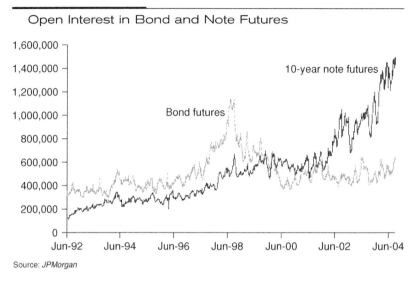

Source: *JPMorgan*

This may well be a permanent shift in the market's demand for Treasury futures. On the one hand, the 30-year Treasury market that has flourished in the United States for so long is very unusual by world standards. Moreover, it is not entirely clear that it contributes much to the efficiency of U.S. capital markets. Only a very small fraction of the present value of outstanding cash flows is accounted for by cash flows with scheduled payment dates past 10 years. Moreover, the U.S. Treasury has reduced long bond issuance. In January 2000, it announced its intention to actually buy back outstanding Treasury bonds and began its buybacks in March 2000. In October 2001, it discontinued the sale of 30-year Treasury bonds. And although the Treasury has recently (May 2005) indicated it may begin reissuing long bonds in 2006, bond issuance is likely to remain small relative to issuance of Treasury notes.

In contrast, the 10-year part of the market has flourished. This maturity is the more common issuance point for the European and Japanese government markets and is a focal point for cross-border interest rate spread trades. Moreover, this is the part of the yield curve that U.S. mortgage hedgers gravitate to. Because the U.S. mortgage market represents one of the largest debt markets in the world, and interest rate risk is actively managed, hedging activity from this sector of the market has substantially increased trading volume in 10-year note futures.

If the shift from bond to note futures is permanent, this may work to the long-term benefit of the Treasury futures market. One characteristic of the 10-year note futures is that they behave much more like a hedger's contract than do Treasury bond futures. The ratio of open interest to trading volume has, over its life, been about 2.5 times higher for the 10-year note contract than for the bond contract. Put differently, it takes 2.5 times longer for the open interest in notes to turn over than it does for bonds. This larger open interest creates depth and liquidity in the 10-year Treasury futures market that makes it an extremely effective and low-cost risk management tool for both traders and hedgers.

WHERE DO WE GO FROM HERE?

The chief lesson that we draw from this chronicle is that anyone trading Treasury futures must be flexible and perhaps a bit humble. The need for flexibility is clear from the changes the contract has gone through over the past 25 years. The need for humility stems from the difficulty in predicting just how the contract should best be used in a new interest rate setting. For example, at the outset of trading in bond futures, no one could have anticipated that dealers would be short the basis in a negative yield-curve environment. Even so, this came about because of the relative pricing of short- and long-maturity deliverable bonds.

In the future, unexpected changes in the pricing of bonds relative to one another and relative to futures will produce changes in the optimal use of bond futures. To be sure, we have learned a great deal about the behavior of the bond futures contract, but it would be presumptuous to suppose that we have seen and know it all. New and sophisticated players are coming into the Treasury market all the time. The economic and policy forces at play now are quite different from those in place several years ago. Our own prognosis is that the bond contract in particular will continue its intriguing behavior throughout this decade.

CHAPTER 9

Non-Dollar Government Bond Futures

Government bond futures have done a lot to change the face of global interest rate trading. The success of the Treasury bond contract in the United States inspired exchanges around the world to list futures on their own (and other) government's bonds. In some cases, as with the German government bond (Bund) contract listed first at London International Financial Futures Exchange (LIFFE), futures were the only vehicle for shorting a country's bonds. Futures trading has improved the liquidity of their related markets and has encouraged the development of repo markets where there were none before. Futures greatly reduced the barriers to trading for foreigners by eliminating the need for delivery and custodial facilities, and helped to reduce the drag associated with withholding taxes.

By far and away the most actively traded non-dollar contracts are those on German government debt. If one uses numbers of contracts as the standard, trading in Eurobund, Eurobobl, and Euroschatz futures dwarfs everything else. Following the completion of monetary union in Europe, the German contracts have more or less elbowed out the other European government bond contracts, including those of France, Italy, and Spain. If one uses portfolio equivalent value, then Tokyo's Japanese government bond (JGB) contracts hold a respectable second place. There are active but smaller markets for futures on the bonds of Australia, Canada, Korea, and the United Kingdom. And there are much smaller futures markets for the government bonds of several other countries, including Switzerland.

The purpose of this chapter is to provide an introduction to the key non-dollar futures contracts—how they are structured, how they relate to their respective cash markets, and key trading themes in the European markets. In particular, we take a look at

- Market shares for active government bond futures
- Key contract specifications
- Cash/futures relationships
- Histories of optionality and mispricings
- Trading themes in the European markets

ACTIVE NON-DOLLAR GOVERNMENT BOND AND NOTE FUTURES

Once it was clear that the Treasury bond futures contract was a success, several futures exchanges abroad followed with contracts of their own. The London futures exchange, LIFFE (now Euronext/LIFFE), listed a contract on U.K. Gilts in 1982. The Tokyo Stock Exchange (TSE) listed its JGB contract in 1985, and LIFFE listed the German Bund contract in 1988, although trading in this contract has migrated to Eurex in Frankfurt.

At this writing (in 2005), if one uses futures trading volume as a guide, there are really only two actively traded government bond futures markets: Germany and the United States. As shown in Exhibit 9.1, for the year ending 30 September 2002, combined trading in Eurobund, Eurobobl, and Euroschatz futures accounted for 61% of global bond futures trading. U.S. Treasury futures came in

EXHIBIT 9.1

Global Bond Futures Trading
(Year Ending September 30, 2002)

Country	Contract	Market Share	
		Volume	Open Interest
Australia	3-year	3	7
	10-year	1	3
Canada	10-year	trace	2
Germany	2-year	16	12
	5-year	17	13
	10-year	28	15
Japan	JGB	1	1
Korea	3-year	2	2
UK	Long gilt	1	2
US	5-year	8	13
	10-year	14	20
	Bond	9	10

Germany = 61% of volume and 40% of open interest

U.S. = 31% of volume and 43% of open interest

second with 31% of global volume, which left 8% of the market to be shared by Australia, Japan, Korea, and the United Kingdom.

Germany's market share is a little less skewed if one uses open interest as the standard. As of the end of September 2002, open interest in the Germany government contracts was 40% of the global bond futures market. Treasury futures accounted for 43% of the market, which left 17% to be shared among the remaining markets.

Exhibit 9.2, which compares aggregate Treasury and German government futures, shows how quickly the German market caught

E X H I B I T   9.2

Growth of U.S. Treasury and German
Government Futures Market

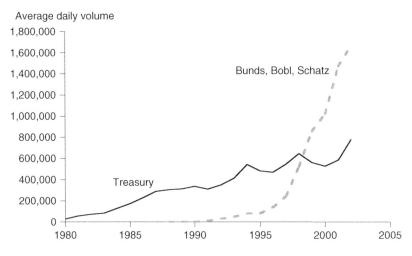

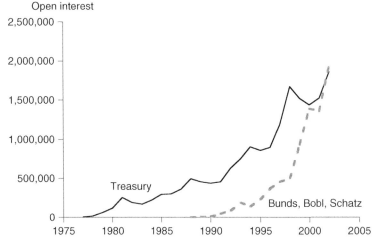

up to and passed the U.S. Treasury market. The contract was listed first in 1988 at LIFFE, which was a pioneer in non-dollar government futures. In the late 1990s, Eurex succeeded in drawing the business to Frankfurt through an aggressive marketing program for its electronic trading platform. Today, in part because of the low cost of trading futures electronically and in part because the German debt market has become a major proxy for trading European interest rates, the Eurobund, Eurobobl, and Euroschatz complex has grown to be the largest government bond futures market in the world.

The Transition to Electronic Trading

The remarkable success of the Eurobund, Bobl, and Schätz complex at Eurex underscores the growing importance of electronic trading in futures. The futures industry's transition to electronic trading was really pioneered by exchanges abroad. Financial futures trading in Japan was electronic from the very outset.

But the first real evidence that electronic trading would be a major force in the futures business came in 1998, when Eurex (then the DTB) finally, after several years trying, claimed most of the market share in the Bund contract. Until that time, all of the trading and liquidity in Bund futures resided at LIFFE, where the contract was first introduced nearly 10 years earlier and where open outcry pit trading was employed. The impact of this lesson was so grave for LIFFE that it chose to close its trading floor and to commit itself to developing a highly effective electronic platform with which to stave off further competitive threats from Eurex.

The importance of electronic trading also can be seen in the volume of trading in Eurobunds, -Bobls, and -Schätze at Eurex relative to the level of activity in Treasury futures at the Chicago Board of Trade. Even though the U.S. Treasury market is significantly larger than the German government bond market, open interest in German government futures at Eurex was, at the end of September 2002, roughly the same as it was in Treasury futures at the CBOT. And, more telling, the volume of trading was twice as great at Eurex as at the CBOT. That is, each of these two complexes held about 40% of the world's open interest in government futures, but Eurex had 61% of the market share in trading, while the CBOT had only 31%. (See Exhibit 9.1.)

In time, we believe that the CBOT will heed the lessons learned in Europe and that most, if not all, Treasury futures trading will be electronic.

EXHIBIT 9.3

Non-Dollar Government Bond Futures Activity

Contract	Exchange	Contract Value		Portfolio value ($billions)	
		Local	U.S. $s	Trading Volume	Open Interest
3-year CGB	SFE (Australia)	102,838.11	55,799.30	3.7	19.9
10-year CGB	SFE (Australia)	105,379.69	57,178.35	1.2	7.9
Euro-Bund	Eurex (Germany)	112,750.00	114,235.06	86.49	82.27
Euro Bobl	Eurex (Germany)	109,950.00	111,398.18	50.07	67.99
Euro-Schatz	Eurex (Germany)	105,180.00	106,656.35	46.04	61.27
10-year JGB	TSE (Japan)	140,400,000.00	1,152,614.73	29.73	55.43
3-year KGB	KSE (Korea)	106,990,000.00	87,517.38	5.08	6.51
10-year	Bourse de Montreal (Canada)	107,330.00	68,900.49	0.50	5.15
Long Gilt	Euronext/Liffe (UK)	120,810.00	189,476.16	5.78	17.21
Total				228.58	323.73

Portfolio Equivalent Value

The number of contracts traded is only one measure of a market's size. From a trader's perspective, the contracts vary greatly in size. Exhibit 9.3 translates contract trading volume and open interest into portfolio equivalent values in U.S. dollars, using closing contract prices and exchange rates as of September 30, 2002. For example, Sydney's Commonwealth Government Bond (CGB) contracts were worth just under US$60,000, while LIFFE's long Gilt contract was worth almost US$190,000, and Tokyo's JGB contract was worth more than US$1 million. As a result, the portfolio equivalent value of trading in JGB futures averaged $29.7 billion a day, which compared favorably with the size of the Eurobund, Eurobobl, and Euroschatz markets.

CONTRACT SPECIFICATIONS

Exhibit 9.4 provides thumbnail contract specifications for the most active non-dollar contracts. All of these contracts have taken some lessons from the design of the Chicago Board of Trade's Treasury futures contracts. Although two of these markets use cash settlement rather than physical delivery, all of them use the idea of a hypothetical coupon for translating market prices or yields into a contract value. Those markets that use physical delivery employ conversion factors like those developed by the CBOT. And, through a set of forces that have greatly narrowed the range of hypothetical coupons, most of these markets have gravitated to a 6% coupon; although, the Gilt contract uses a 7% coupon, and the Korean Treasury bond contract uses an 8% coupon.

EXHIBIT 9.4

Key Contract Specifications
(As of September 1, 2004)

Contract	Exchange	Contract Size	Hypothetical Coupon	Contract Standard	Last Trading Day	Settlement Method	Delivery or Settlement Day
3-year Australian Government Bond	Sydney Futures Exchange	A$100,000	6%	3-year Commonwealth government Treasury bonds declared by the exchange for a specific contract month	15th day of the contract month	Cash; based on mean of quotes from 10 randomly selected dealers	The business day following last trading day
10-year Australian Government Bond	Sydney Futures Exchange	A$100,000	6%	10-year Commonwealth government Treasury bonds declared by the Exchange for a specific contract month	15th day of the contract month	Cash; based on mean of quotes from 10 randomly selected dealers	The business day following last trading day
Euro-Bund	Eurex	€100,000	6%	German Federal bonds (Bundesanleihen) with a remaining term upon delivery of 8½ to 10½ years.	2 exchange trading days before the delivery day of the contract month	Delivery	The 10th calendar day of the respective delivery month
Euro Bobl	Eurex	€100,000	6%	German Federal Debt Obligations (Bundesobligationen) and Bunds with a remaining term upon delivery of 4½ to 5½ years.	2 exchange trading days before the delivery day of the contract month	Delivery	The 10th calendar day of the respective delivery month
Euro-Schatz	Eurex	€100000	6%	German Federal Treasury notes (Bundesschatzanweisungen), Bobls, Bunds, and fully government guaranteed, exchange-traded debt securities of the Treuhandanstalt with a remaining term upon delivery of 1¾ to 2¼ years.	2 exchange trading days before the delivery day of the contract month	Delivery	The 10th calendar day of the respective delivery month
10-year Japanese Government Bond	Tokyo Stock Exchange	¥100,000,000	6%	Japanese government bonds with a remaining term of 7 to 11 years	7th business day before the delivery date	Delivery	20th of each contract month
Korean Treasury Bond	Korean Futures Exchange	KRW 100,000,000	8%	3-year Korean Treasury bonds designated by the Exchange before the first day of trading	1st trading day before the 3rd Wednesday of the contract month	Cash	Third Wednesday of the contract month
10-Year Canadian Government Bond	Bourse de Montreal	C$100,000	6%	Canadian government bonds with a remaining term of 8 to 10½ years as of the first delivery day of the contract month	7th business day preceding the last business day of the contract month	Delivery	Any business day in the delivery month (at seller's choice)
Long UK Gilt	Euronext Liffe	£100,000	7%	Gilts with a remaining term of 8¾ to 13 years as of the first delivery day of the contract month	2nd business day before the last business day of the contract month	Delivery	Any business day in the delivery month (at seller's choice)

MATURITIES, SETTLEMENT WINDOWS, AND LAST TRADING DAYS

The contracts differ mainly in the maturities that define the underlying deliverable bonds, last trading day, and delivery or settlement window. For example, the 10-year government market is liquid almost everywhere, but the contracts that target this segment of the yield curve differ quite a lot in the breadth of eligible maturities. For example, the Eurobund basket includes maturities from 8-1/2 to 10-1/2 years, while the long Gilt basket includes maturities from 8-3/4 to 13 years. As with U.S. Treasury futures, Gilt and Canada futures allow for delivery on any business day in the contract month. All other contracts provide for a single delivery or settlement day.

Cash Settlement of SFE's CGB Contracts

Although most of the world's government bond futures contracts are delivery contracts patterned after the Chicago Board of Trade's Treasury futures, some contracts—most notably Australia's CGB contracts—are cash-settled. The method that the Sydney Futures Exchange (SFE) has chosen to cash-settle its 3-year and 10-year contracts produces an interesting linkage between the way the contract is quoted (i.e., 100 minus a yield) and the way the contract is valued. Consider the way the Sydney Futures Exchange values the 10-year CGB contract. By definition, the value of the 10-year contract for marking to market purposes is

$$\text{Value} = 1,000 \left\{ \frac{\dfrac{C}{2}\left(1 - \left(1 + \dfrac{R}{200}\right)^{-20}\right)}{\dfrac{R}{200}} + 100\left(1 + \dfrac{R}{200}\right)^{-20} \right\}$$

where C is the hypothetical coupon rate of 6% and R is the futures rate. Before expiration, the value of R is 100 less the futures price. At expiration, R is the average yield on bonds in the deliverable set as determined by a survey of dealers in Australian Government Bonds. For the 3-year contract, you would substitute –6 for –20 as the exponents to reflect the six semiannual compounding periods in the life of a 3-year bond.

Suppose, for example, that the futures contract price is 95.00, which implies a futures rate of 5.00% [= 100.00 – 95.00]. Substituting

EXHIBIT 9.5

Change in Australian 10-Year CGB
Contract Value for a 1-Basis-Point
Change in the Futures Rate

Rate level	Rate change		Average
	0.01	−0.01	
4.00	−89.60	89.69	89.65
5.00	−81.59	81.67	81.63
6.00	−74.35	74.42	74.39
7.00	−67.82	67.88	67.85
8.00	−61.91	61.96	61.93

this rate for R in the preceding expression produces a futures value of A$107,795.58. If the futures price were to increase to 95.01, implying a futures rate of 4.99%, the futures value would increase to A$107,876.25, which would be an increase of A$81.67. If the futures price were to decrease to 94.99, implying a futures rate of 5.01, the futures value would decrease to A$107,712.99, which would be a decrease of $81.59. The average of these two changes is A$81.63, which is what you would use as the futures contract's value of a basis point, at least with respect to a change in the forward yield on bonds in the deliverable set.

One consequence of this approach to valuing the contract is that the value of a tick varies with the level of rates and the direction of rates. In this simple example, the long would make A$81.67 if the futures price increases by 0.01 and would lose $81.59 if the futures price falls by 0.01. On the other hand, if the initial futures rate were 6.00%, the long would make $74.42 if the futures price increased by 0.01 and would lose A$74.35 if the futures price were to fall by 0.01. Exhibit 9.5 shows the value of a basis point change in the underlying futures rate for five different rate levels.

Up-to-Date Information

Exchanges revise their contract specifications from time to time as a way of keeping up with changing market conditions. The most common changes have been in the choice of hypothetical coupon. Other changes may affect the eligibility of deliverable issues or delivery

EXHIBIT 9.6

Exchange Web Addresses for Contract Specifications

Sydney Futures Exchange	www.sfe.com.au/site/html/trading/products/con_specs/con_specs.pdf
Eurex (Germany)	www.eurexchange.com/index2.html?mp&1&6&marketplace/products_specifications_en.html
Tokyo Stock Exchange	www.tse.or.jp/english/option/jgbf/jgbf4.html
KOFEX	www.kofex.com/english/pro/pro_ktb.asp?sm=1_0
Bourse de Montreal	www.me.org/produits_en/produits_d_inter_long_en.php
MEFF	www.meff.com/ing/productos/bonoe10.html
Eurex (Switzerland)	www.gammafutures.com/news/eurex/conf.html
Euronext/Liffe	www.liffe.com/products/bonds/specs/longgilt.htm

procedures and timing. The best way to stay on top of these changes is to ask your futures account executive. Failing this, the exchanges post useful information on their Web sites, whose addresses are shown in Exhibit 9.6.

CASH/FUTURES RELATIONSHIPS

Although the principles that govern the pricing of bond futures are much the same abroad as they are in the United States, many of the important particulars are different. These differences can have important effects on carry and arbitrage relationships, as well as on the richness and diversity of the deliverable sets. To supplement the brief discussion that follows, we have included five appendices for those who want to know more:

- Conventions in Major Government Bond Markets (Appendix C)
- German Government Bond Market Characteristics (Appendix D)
- Japanese Government Bond Market Characteristics (Appendix E)
- U.K. Government Bond Market Characteristics (Appendix F)
- Glossary of Government Bond Market Terms (Appendix G)

Key Cash Market Features

A complete understanding of the relationship between bond futures prices and the prices of underlying cash bonds requires a thorough appreciation of cash market conventions. These include

- Price and yield quotes
- Settlement lags

- Accrued interest and day count conventions
- Dividend payment practices
- Repo liquidity and day count conventions
- Taxes
- Fail penalties

Exhibit 9.7 illustrates some of the key differences in these practices for Germany, Japan, and the United Kingdom. For example, coupons are paid annually in Germany, but semiannually in Japan and the United Kingdom. Because the coupon on Gilts is paid seven days before its coupon date, Gilts can trade ex-dividend. As a result, accrued interest during these seven days can be negative. Germany and the United Kingdom use actual/actual for reckoning fractions of the year (or half years), while Japan uses actual/365. Settlement practices differ somewhat as well. Settlement occurs

EXHIBIT 9.7

Bond Market Characteristics

	Germany	Japan	UK
Accrued interest			
Coupon (date)	annual	semi (20th)	semi
Ex-dividend (days)	no	no	yes (7)
Accrual basis	actual	actual	actual
Year basis	actual	365	actual
Settlement time frame			
Domestic	T+2	T+3	T+3
Internatinoal	T+3	na	na
Trading basis			
Quotation	price	simple yield	price
Tick	decimal	bp	decimal
Tax (non-resident)	0	0	0
Price/yield method	ISMA	Simple	DMO
Repo			
Accrual basis	actual	actual	actual
Year basis	360		365

Source: *JPMorgan*

two business days after the trade in Germany (three if done outside of Germany) and three business days after trades in Japanese and U.K. bonds.

In most cases, paying attention to this kind of detail is simply a matter of being careful when calculating carry. On occasion, though, a cash market practice can have a huge effect on the pricing of a contract. A case in point was the result of a deliverable Gilt that went special ex-dividend during the delivery month. Exchange rules prohibit delivery of a bond during this special period. In this particular instance, however, it was cheapest to deliver right up until the day it went special ex-dividend. As a result, the contract was priced to this bond until the last day it was deliverable and was then priced to the next cheapest to deliver the following day. In a case like this, the only rational thing for shorts to do was to cover or deliver the original cheapest to deliver on the last possible day it was deliverable. In principle, all open positions should have been closed out on that day. The discontinuity in deliverable bonds produced a discrete jump in the futures price, a temporary squeeze on the original cheapest to deliver, and windfall gains and losses for the longs and shorts that happened, through the inattention of the shorts, to remain open.

Auction Cycles and Deliverable Sets

As with the U.S. Treasury market, the funding practices of the governments that supply the deliverable bonds determine the size and complexity of the deliverable sets of bonds. They also influence the problem of correctly valuing futures contracts, especially in those cases where new issues may enter the deliverable set. Issuance practices vary over time, but some idea of differences in funding practices can be gained from a look at the ways Germany, Japan, and the U.K. issue bonds.

Germany publishes an issuance calendar during the last 10 days of each quarter. The calendar includes planned issues (including coupons, maturities, and whether the issues are to be reopened) and target auction sizes, but no specific dates. Schätze typically are issued in a March, June, September, and December quarterly cycle. Bobls are auctioned in a February, May, August, and November quarterly cycle. And Bunds, although the calendar is somewhat variable, tend to be issued in a January, April, July, and October cycle.

Japan tends to issue JGBs monthly. The size of the issue is announced one week before it is auctioned. The coupon is announced the day of the auction. Because coupons are paid in a standard March/September or June/December semiannual cycle, the practice of issuing bonds monthly produces odd first coupons.

The United Kingdom announces a schedule of auctions for each fiscal year in March. Thereafter, at the end of each quarter, it issues a calendar that provides precise dates and the bonds to be issued. Auctions usually fall on the last Wednesday of the month.

Basis Reference Sheets for Germany, Japan, and the United Kingdom

The basis reference sheets in Exhibits 9.8 through 9.10 provide examples of the kinds of deliverable sets that these issuance practices produce when combined with the respective futures contract specifications for each market. For example, the deliverable set tends to be quite large for JGBs, while it is not uncommon for only one, two, or three issues to be deliverable into the Bund contract.

E X H I B I T   9.8

Basis Reference Sheet; Eurobund, Bobi, and Schätz Futures
(Pricing: January 3, 2003; Settlement: January 9, 2003)

MAR (LTD: 3/6, 59 days; Deliv: 3/10, 63 days)

Futures	Price	Fair	R/C	OA Duration II	OA Duration B-adj	OA BPV II	OA BPV B-adj	Basis IVol	Opt. IVol
Bund	112.54	112.55	-1	7.28	7.33	81.94	82.48	9.29	5.45
Bobl	110.59	110.6	-1	4.42	4.26	48.83	47.08	N/A	3.63
Schatz	105.54	105.54	0	1.85	1.85	19.54	19.54	N/A	1.39

Issue	Coupon	Maturity	March Basis	Factor	June Basis	Factor	Price	Yield	BPV	Mdur
Bund Futures										
DBR	5	Jul12	49	0.929856	105	0.931516	105.14	4.324	790	7.33
DBR	5	Jan12	35	0.9328	95	0.93413	105.33	4.273	758	7.19
Bobl Futures										
DBR	4 1/8	Jul08	78	0.916472	121	0.920051	102.13	3.685	495	4.75
DBR	4 3/4	Jul08	83	0.944188	141	0.946664	105.25	3.671	505	4.69
DBR	5 1/4	Jan08	42	0.969159	116	0.970404	107.6	3.559	471	4.38
Schatz Futures										
OB136	5	Aug05	181	0.979791	105.05	2.953	257	2.4		
OB135	5	May05	142	0.979765	134	0.982085	104.82	2.851	233	2.16
DBR	6 7/8	May05	151	1.017053	187	1.015297	108.85	2.894	238	2.1
WI-BKO	2 3/4	Mar05				0.946764		-3.0*		
OB134	4 1/4	Feb05	75	0.968682			102.98	2.773	207	1.94
DBR	7 3/8	Jan05	83	1.022733			108.77	2.769	203	1.87
BKO	3	Dec04		0.951276			100.45	2.754	185	1.84

* WI issue; yield refers to the assumed aset swap spread to the current benchmark on last delivery day.

Source: *JPMorgan*

Optionality and Futures Mispricings

Hedgers, speculators, and basis traders all want to know something about the value of embedded delivery options and possibilities for mispricings. A history of embedded delivery option value for the Eurobund, Bobl, and Schätz contracts is provided in the upper panel of Exhibit 9.11, while a similar history for the delivery option value in long Gilt futures is shown in the lower panel. In both cases, it is apparent that the value of optionality can vary significantly over time. In the German complex, delivery optionality was fairly valuable in 1997 and again at the end of 1999 and the beginning of 2000. At other times, delivery option value has been close to zero. In the long Gilt contract, delivery option value was fairly high early in 2000, but for the most part has been close to zero.

Exhibit 9.12 provides a history of contract pricing for the German and U.K. contracts. On average, the German contracts have been fairly priced. The average mispricing, measured as the difference between market price and fair value, has been less than one tick (1 cent). The standard deviation of the contracts' mispricings

JUN (LTD: 6/5, 150 days; Deliv: 6/10, 155 days)

Price	Fair	R/C	OA Duration		OA BPV	
			II	B-adj	II	B-adj
111.74	111.72	2	7.39	7.44	82.55	83.14
109.69	109.77	-8	4.49	4.32	49.24	47.34
105.37	105.43	-6	2.11	2.11	22.28	22.28

March						June					
ImpRP	Carr	BNOC	OABNOC	Repo	FwdYld	ImpRP	Carr	BNOC	OABNOC	Repo	FwdYld
1.83	33	16	1	2.73	4.358	2.26	89	17	-2	2.63	4.419
2.67	34	1	1	2.74	4.306	2.54	97	-1	-2	2.51	4.375
-0.57	19	58	1	2.79	3.714	1.15	52	68	8	2.71	3.77
-0.29	29	54	1	2.74	3.701	1.25	75	66	8	2.71	3.756
2.46	41	1	1	2.52	3.597	2.27	108	7	7	2.43	3.669
						0.6	86	95	7	2.71	2.99
-3.3	32	110	1	2.79	2.85	1.64	85	49	6	2.71	2.869
-2.01	60	91	1	2.79	2.897	2.1	158	29	6	2.71	2.923
								5			2.856
-0.27	23	52	1	2.67	2.776						
2.1	75	8	0	2.56	2.782						
2.63	5	0	0	2.64	2.759						

EXHIBIT 9.9

Basis Reference Sheet; JGB Futures
(Pricing: January 6, 2003; Settlement: January 10, 2003)

MAR (LTD: 3/6, 59 days; Deliv: 3/10, 63 days)

				OA Duration		OA BPV		Basis
Futures	Price	Fair	R/C	//	B-adj	//	B-adj	IVol
JGB	142.06	142.043	2	6.8	5.93	96648	84250	N/A

Issue	Coupon	Maturity	March Basis	Factor	June Basis	Factor	Price	Yield	BPV
#244	1	Dec12	1067	0.634914	1017	0.641905	100.867	0.909	9.53
#243	1.1	Sep12	980	0.649066	933	0.65598	102.011	0.883	9.37
#242	1.2	Sep12	973	0.656228	928	0.662999	102.951	0.882	9.41
#241	1.3	Sep12	965	0.66339	922	0.670018	103.891	0.881	9.46
#240	1.3	Jun12	884	0.670018	840	0.676792	104.025	0.856	9.25
#239	1.4	Jun12	877	0.677036	835	0.683669	104.946	0.854	9.29
#238	1.4	Mar12	797	0.683669	755	0.690348	105.092	0.824	9.08
#237	1.5	Mar12	789	0.690545	750	0.697077	105.994	0.822	9.12
#236	1.5	Dec11	708	0.697077	667	0.703762	106.109	0.791	8.9
#235	1.4	Dec11	716	0.690348	672	0.697179	105.228	0.793	8.86
#234	1.4	Sep11	631	0.697179	587	0.704059	105.349	0.763	8.63
#233	1.4	Jun11	544	0.704059	498	0.711094	105.455	0.733	8.41
#232	1.2	Jun11	559	0.691197	508	0.698533	103.779	0.738	8.34
#231	1.3	Jun11	551	0.697628	503	0.704814	104.617	0.735	8.37
#230	1.1	Mar11	480	0.692253	426	0.69981	103.14	0.705	8.08
#229	1.4	Mar11	453	0.711094	408	0.718182	105.548	0.703	8.19
#228	1.5	Mar11	445	0.717375	403	0.724306	106.365	0.7	8.22
#227	1.6	Mar11	438	0.723655	398	0.73043	107.183	0.697	8.26
#226	1.8	Dec10	327	0.742678	290	0.749303	108.77	0.665	8.09
#225	1.9	Dec10	319	0.748802	286	0.755272	109.568	0.662	8.12
#224	1.8	Sep10	230	0.749303	194	0.755959	108.747	0.634	7.85
#223	1.7	Sep10	237	0.743334	198	0.750152	107.973	0.637	7.82
#222	1.8	Jun10	132	0.755959	94	0.762782	108.709	0.602	7.61
#221	1.9	Jun10	124	0.761767	89	0.76843	109.462	0.599	7.64
#220	1.7	Mar10	40	0.757134			107.962	0.57	7.34
#219	1.8	Mar10	33	0.762782			108.692	0.566	7.37

Source: *JPMorgan*

EXHIBIT 9.10

Basis Reference Sheet; U.K. Gilt Futures
(Pricing: January 3, 2003; Settlement: January 9, 2003)

MAR (LTD: 3/27, 80 days; Deliv: 3/31, 84 days)

				OA Duration		OA BPV		Basis	Opt.	
Futures	Price	Fair	R/C	//	B-adj	//	B-adj	IVol	IVol	Price
Gilt	119.38	119.4	-2	7.42	7.42	88.6	88.61	13.75	6.61	118.6

Issue	Coupon	Maturity	March Basis	Factor	June Basis	Factor	Price	Yield	BPV	Mdur	March ImpRP
UKT	8	Dec15	418	1.0833461	512	1.0824994	133.51	4.542	1169	8.71	-7.71
UKT	5	Sep14	362	0.8436629	403	0.8457881	104.34	4.517	923	8.7	-10.41
UKT	8	Sep13	150	1.0737468	248	1.0724706	129.68	4.481	995	7.54	1.12
UKT	5	Mar12	26	0.8679425	64	0.8704894	103.88	4.479	762	7.22	3.69

Source: *JPMorgan*

has been about seven ticks for the Bund and Bobl contracts and only three ticks for the Schätz contract.

In slight contrast, the long Gilt contract has tended, on average, to trade somewhat cheap relative to fair value. On average, the market price was between 3 and 4 cents below fair value, and the standard deviation of the contracts mispricing has been about 6 cents.

JUN (LTD: 6/5, 150 days; Deliv: 6/10, 155 days)

Price	Fair	R/C	OA Duration //	B-adj	OA BPV //	B-adj
141.29	141.393	-10	7.04	6.06	99478	85567

March ImpRP	Carr	BNOC	OABNOC	Repo	June ImpRP	Carr	BNOC	OABNOC	Repo
-54.19	19	1049	12	0.02	-21.56	42	976	29	0.06
-48.9	21	960	11	0.02	-19.8	46	887	27	0.06
-47.95	23	950	10	0.02	-19.39	51	877	27	0.06
-47.02	25	940	10	0.02	-19	55	867	27	0.06
-43.08	24	860	9	0.02	-16.81	55	785	25	0.06
-42.23	26	851	9	0.02	-16.46	59	776	25	0.06
-38.07	27	770	8	0.02	-14.99	60	696	23	0.06
-37.27	29	761	8	0.02	-14.65	64	686	22	0.06
-33.4	28	680	7	0.02	-12.66	64	604	21	0.06
-34.15	26	690	7	0.02	-12.96	59	613	21	0.06
-29.78	27	604	6	0.02	-11.28	59	528	19	0.06
-25.57	26	518	5	0.02	-9.25	59	439	18	0.06
-26.93	22	537	5	0.02	-9.8	50	458	18	0.06
-26.24	24	527	5	0.02	-9.52	55	449	17	0.06
-23.12	21	459	4	0.02	-8.26	46	380	16	0.06
-20.97	27	426	4	0.02	-7.37	59	348	16	0.06
-20.34	29	417	4	0.02	-7.12	64	339	16	0.06
-19.73	30	408	4	0.02	-6.87	68	330	16	0.06
-14.02	34	293	2	0.02	-4.32	77	213	13	0.06
-13.48	35	284	2	0.02	-4.11	81	204	13	0.06
-9.33	34	196	1	0.02	-2.34	77	117	10	0.06
-9.84	32	205	1	0.02	-2.55	73	126	10	0.06
-4.68	34	98	-1	0.02	-0.29	77	17	8	0.06
-4.22	35	89	-1	0.02	-0.1	81	8	8	0.06
-0.36	32	8	-1	0.02					
0.08	34	-1	-1	0.02					

JUN (LTD: 6/26, 171 days; Deliv: 6/30, 175 days)

Fair	R/C	OA Duration //	B-adj	OA BPV //	B-adj	Basis IVol	Opt. IVol
118.7	-10	7.54	7.53	89.44	89.33	14.14	6.51

Carr	BNOC	OABNOC	Repo	FwdYld	June ImpRP	Carr	BNOC	OABNOC	Repo	FwdYld
67	351	2	3.79	4.561	-2.04	138	375	11	3.83	4.582
22	340	3	3.83	4.534	-3.33	46	356	10	3.83	4.553
71	79	2	3.75	4.504	2.14	148	100	11	3.75	4.527
24	2	2	3.78	4.501	3.5	54	10	9	3.7	4.53

TRADING THEMES IN EUROPEAN BOND BASES

Although basis trading in Europe has many similarities to the United States, key differences between the Treasury and German government bond markets create different opportunities for trading

E X H I B I T   9.11

Delivery Options Values for German
and U.K. Bond Contracts
(1997 through June 2003)

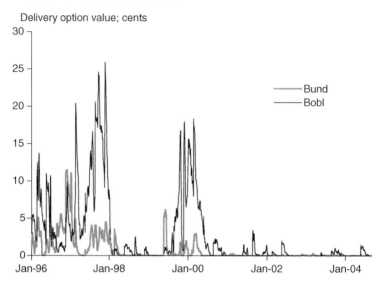

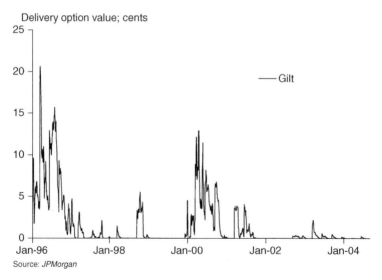

Source: *JPMorgan*

the basis in Europe than in the United States. Three classes of basis
trades are more common in Europe than in the United States,
including

- Profiting from potential squeezes in the cheapest to deliver
  (CTD) bond

EXHIBIT 9.12

History of Mispricings in
German and U.K. Bond Contracts
(June 15, 1999 to June 13, 2003; Units Are Cents)

	Germany			UK
	Bund	Bobl	Schätz	Long gilt
Average	0.85	-0.31	0.52	-3.65
Std Dev	6.59	7.94	3.08	5.95
Min	-21.97	-28.16	-15.93	-34.19
Max	23.63	21.51	17.31	11.18

Source: *JPMorgan*

- Positioning for bonds exiting from the basket
- New issuance trades

We consider each of these in turn.

Squeezes of CTD Bonds

Compared to the U.S. markets, government bond bases in Europe are more often influenced by a shortage of deliverable supply and the risk of a short squeeze of the cheapest to deliver bond. This is partly the result of large open interest relative to the supply of deliverable bonds, as well as structural factors that make fails in the repo market more common for German government bonds than in the United States.

A recent and now infamous example of a short squeeze that produced severe price dislocations in both the futures contract and the CTD bond was the March 2001 Bobl contract. A number of factors contributed to the dislocation:

- The CTD bond—DBR 6.5% of 10/05—was an old illiquid Bund with relatively small traded float.
- There was a large differential in the net basis of the first and second (DBR 6% of 1/06) cheapest to deliver issues. This contributed to the lack of effective deliverable supply.
- Open interest in the March 2001 Bobl futures stayed at very high levels as expiration approached, peaking at €57 billion two weeks before expiration.

The lack of supply in the CTD caused extreme price dislocations in both the cash and futures market as expiration approached. For example, the basis net of carry of the CTD traded below zero,

Effect of a CTD Squeeze on the Eurobund Calendar Spread

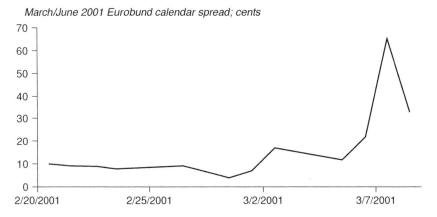

March/June 2001 Eurobund calendar spread; cents

reaching the extreme level of –70 cents in early March of 2001. This apparent violation of an arbitrage condition reflected the risk of a delivery failure into March futures. An arbitrageur that bought the CTD bond and sold futures at a negative net basis is exposed to the risk of a fail in the cash market. If this cash market fail meant that the arbitrageur was unable to obtain the CTD in time to deliver into the futures contract, any potential profit from basis convergence would be offset by exchange penalties for late delivery. Since these penalties can be substantial (and much larger than the penalties for failing in the cash market), CTD issues that are in short supply can, and regularly do, trade at a negative net basis.

The short squeeze in the DBR 6.5% of 10/05 also caused the March–June calendar spread to widen dramatically during the March delivery month as shorts rolled their positions from March to June (see Exhibit 9.13). This reflected the unwillingness of shorts to risk going to delivery in March even though March futures and the March–June calendar spread were expensive.

Bonds Exiting the Basket Trades

As is sometimes the case with Treasury note futures, the Bund, Bobl, and Schätz contracts occasionally offer opportunities to profit in cases where the CTD issue is preparing to exit the deliverable basket. This occurs whenever the CTD in the front-month futures contract is the shortest maturity issue in the basket and is not eligible

EXHIBIT 9.14

Moving Out of the Basket Trade

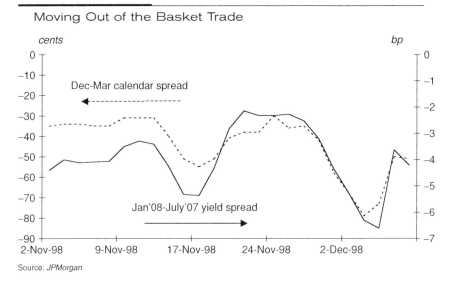

Source: *JPMorgan*

for delivery into the back-month contract. Typically, when the CTD issue exits the deliverable basket, it tends to lose the liquidity premium associated with being CTD and cheapen to levels of nondeliverable bonds. Traders can profit from the anticipated loss of CTD status either by buying the basis on the second cheapest to deliver bond or by selling the calendar spread as the expiration of the front-month contract approaches.

Exhibit 9.14 illustrates the impact of the CTD exiting the basket for the December 1998 Bund futures contract. The 6% of July 2007 was CTD into December futures but not eligible for delivery into March 1999 futures. The CTD for March 1999 futures was the 5.25% of January 2008. As December expiration approached, the liquidity premium associated with the status of front-month CTD began to transition from the July 2007 issue to the January 2008. This caused the yield spread between the January 2008 and July 2007 issues to narrow and the front-month futures to underperform back-month futures.

New Issuance

A third class of basis trades commonly done in European markets relates to new issuance. This is a regular opportunity on the Schätz contract and was a frequent trade on the MATIF Notionel futures when the contract was actively traded in the 1990s.

New issues create especially interesting opportunities in basis markets whenever they are expected to be cheapest to deliver in a contract. Determining the fair value of futures is more difficult in these cases, because, before the issue begins trading, the futures price depends on a bond whose price and yield are not yet observable. If the new CTD ends up trading cheaper on the yield curve than the market originally expected, the futures price should decline after the CTD is issued, causing the basis of non-cheap bonds to widen. Similarly, if the new CTD trades richer on the yield curve than the market originally expected, the futures price should rise after the CTD is issued, causing the basis of non-cheap bonds to decline.

Accounting for the effects of new issues on futures prices is important when trading Schätz calendar spreads. Since the CTD in the back contract is often a security that has not yet been issued, valuing back-month futures and the calendar spread requires an estimate of the likely yield spread between the new issue and existing deliverables. Traders that expect the new issue to be large and trade cheap on the curve (causing the back-month futures to decline after the new CTD is issued) can profit by buying the calendar spread. Traders that expect the new CTD to be in short supply and trade rich on the curve can profit by selling the calendar spread.

A WORD OF CAUTION

Using bond and note futures contracts correctly requires a healthy respect for detail. And, although most of the government bond futures contracts traded outside of the United States look very much like the Treasury futures traded at the Chicago Board of Trade, there are a number of important differences in both the futures and the cash markets. Delivery and settlement procedures, for example, are not only different across countries but also can be different for domestic and foreign participants. The RP markets differ a great deal in their levels of sophistication and ease of use. Yield quote conventions are different, as are day-count conventions. Accrued interest practices are very different in some countries. The chances for short squeezes vary. The tax consequences for domestic and foreign market participants are different.

In short, any successful foray into these markets requires that a great deal of homework be done ahead of time.

CHAPTER 10

Applications for Portfolio Managers

Because bond and note futures can be used to construct positions that behave very much like the bonds and notes themselves, futures provide a powerful tool with a wide range of applications for portfolio managers. Day in and day out, the most widely used applications will employ futures in hedges and in portfolio construction. In this chapter, we show practical examples of both kinds. In particular, we show how futures can be used to

- Manage duration and yield curve exposure
- Enhance returns on bond portfolios

The first focuses on questions of hedging and asset allocation that can be handled with futures in lieu of other kinds of spot and forward bond transactions. The second looks at the possibilities of increasing returns on bond portfolios by creating synthetic assets with futures.

HEDGING AND ASSET ALLOCATION

We have already shown how to hedge with Treasury futures (see Chapter 5). In this section, we take a closer look at just why a portfolio manager would want to use futures as a portfolio management tool. We also look at how futures can be used to manage the duration of a portfolio and, in some cases, to manage yield curve exposure in a portfolio.

Advantages of Using Futures for Hedging and Asset Allocation

Because the most effective way to eliminate the risk of a bond in your portfolio is to sell it to someone else, there must be good reasons for using futures, which are imperfect substitutes for actual bonds and notes. These reasons include lower transactions costs, increased efficiency of the actual bond portfolio, ease of financing, better credit risk than forwards, and efficiencies in hedging foreign exchange risk (when dealing with foreign bonds). Also, if futures are used to create synthetic assets, there are no custodial costs, which can be large for foreign investments.

Low Transactions Costs   Except for the on-the-run and fairly recently issued Treasury bonds and notes, the costs of trading futures are lower than the costs of trading actual bonds. Exhibit 10.1 shows typical bid/asked spreads for cash government bonds and 10-year government bond futures for various markets. In all four of the major markets, the bid/asked spreads for futures contracts are 0.02% or smaller, and in all cases are smaller than typical spreads in the cash market.

In addition, there are no hidden costs of repo in a futures trade. What you see in the bid/asked spread is what you get. In a cash market trade, on the other hand, the bid/asked spread between repo and reverse repo rates can easily be 20 basis points. For a three-month period, a 20-basis-point repo spread could amount to another 1.6/32nds [= ($100,000 × 0.0030 × 90)/360 / $31.25] or so for someone buying and then selling cash bonds.

EXHIBIT 10.1

Bid/Asked Spreads in Government Bond Markets

Market	Cash		Futures
	OTR	Other	
		(in %)	
US Treasuries	0.031	0.047	0.016
US Agencies	0.150	na	
UK Gilts	0.130	0.130	0.020
German bunds	0.060	0.060	0.010
Japanese Government Bonds	0.160	na	0.010

10-year maturies for all markets except UK, which is 12-year
Source: Calyon Financial, October 2003

Leaving the Core Portfolio Intact   You may have reasons for not wanting to sell a bond immediately. You may be an underwriter managing the distribution of a new issue. You may have tax reasons for not wanting to sell an issue. The underlying market may be illiquid (when compared with futures). You may have devoted a considerable amount of research to the task of finding the bonds and notes in your portfolio. In these cases, being able to sell futures allows you to keep your portfolio intact, or to manage more carefully the pace of liquidation, and it gives you a useful tool for increasing the efficiency of your operation.

Built-In Financing   Because futures are like forwards with an allowance for the value of delivery options, financing is not an issue. You can increase or decrease exposure to changes in bond and note prices without having to worry about repo and reverse repo and the transaction costs associated with having to unwind positions in those markets.

Better Credit Risk   Some sectors of the bond market enjoy well-developed forward markets, but even here, futures provide superior credit risk. The complex set of financial guarantees provided by the clearinghouse is better than what the over-the-counter market can provide under the best of circumstances.

Built-In Foreign Currency Hedges   This applies only to foreign portfolios, but the fact that futures come with a built-in foreign currency hedge can be useful. If you sell Eurobunds or long Gilt futures to hedge a European or British bond portfolio, or JGB futures to hedge a Japanese bond portfolio, the futures themselves represent no currency exposure. A change in the dollar prices of the Euro, pound, or yen does not, by itself, produce any gain or loss on a foreign bond futures position. Thus, one can use foreign government bond futures to create synthetic bond portfolios whose dollar returns depend only on local bond returns rather than on foreign currency returns. By the same token, if you use foreign bond futures to hedge price exposure in a foreign bond portfolio, you will have no effect on your overall foreign currency exposure.

Managing a Portfolio's Duration with Futures

As we showed in Chapter 5, a bond or note futures contract can be assigned a duration even though it has no coupons, no principal, and hence no yield or asset value. The chain of reasoning that allows us to do this is that yield changes cause changes in the prices of cash bonds and notes, which in turn cause changes in bond and note futures prices. For our purposes, then, the effective duration of a futures contract is simply the percentage change in its price for a 100-basis-point increase in the yield of its underlying cash issue. Defined this way, the effective duration of a futures contract would be like the modified duration of a cash bond—measuring the relative sensitivity of its price to a change in an underlying yield.

Calculating the Duration of a Portfolio That Contains Futures

Once we are comfortable with the notion that a futures contract can be assigned an effective duration, the task of reckoning the duration of a portfolio that contains futures is simple enough. The main thing to remember is that futures represent pure price exposure but neither add to nor detract from the net liquidating value of the portfolio.

Consider, for example, the standard definition of modified duration for a portfolio that contains bonds, notes, and cash.

$$MD(\text{Portfolio, Raw}) = \frac{MD(\text{Bonds}) \times MV(\text{Bonds}) + MD(\text{Notes}) \times MV(\text{Notes}) + MD(\text{Cash}) \times MV(\text{Cash})}{MV(\text{Portfolio, Raw}) = MV(\text{Bonds}) + MV(\text{Notes}) + MV(\text{Cash})}$$

The numerator is the sum of the modified durations (MDs) of the various items in the portfolio weighted by the amount invested in each. The market values (represented by MV) are full market values, including all accrued interest, and can be either positive or negative. The denominator of this expression is the net liquidating value of the portfolio. The resulting modified duration for the portfolio is simply a market value weighted average of the modified durations of the components of the portfolio.

If we now add futures to the portfolio, we add pure price exposure to the numerator but do not change the portfolio's net liquidating value in the denominator. Our new duration calculation would be

$$MD(\text{Portfolio, Augmented}) = \frac{MD(\text{Portfolio, Raw}) \times MV(\text{Portfolio, Raw}) + MD(\text{Futures}) \times PEV(\text{Futures})}{MV(\text{Portfolio, Raw})}$$

where PEV represents the portfolio equivalent value of the futures position. For the purposes of reckoning the portfolio equivalent value of bond, 10-year, and 5-year note futures, we treat each futures contract as if it is worth the futures price multiplied by $1,000 (per price point). Given this hypothetical portfolio equivalent value per futures contract, the portfolio equivalent value of an entire futures position would be calculated as

$$PEV(Futures) = Number(Futures) \times \$1,000 \times Price(Futures)$$

If you are working with 2-year note futures, you would multiply the futures price by \$2,000 to capture the larger notional size of this contract.

Example of Targeting Portfolio Duration When Futures Are in the Mix

Suppose you have a \$1 billion market value portfolio with a modified duration of 10.00% and that you are long 1,000 June 2001 Treasury bond contracts. As shown in Exhibit 10.2, these contracts have a theoretical price of 103-25/32nds, which would give them a portfolio equivalent value of \$103,781.25 [= \$1,000 × 103.78125]. They also have an option-adjusted DV01 of \$122.42 (with respect to a change in the cheapest to deliver bond's yield), which corresponds to an option-adjusted effective duration of 11.80% = [100 × (100bps × \$122.42)/\$103,781.25]. This position would have a modified duration of

$$MD(Portfolio, Augmented) = \frac{10.00\% \times \$1,000,000,000 + 11.80\% \times \$103,781,250}{\$1,000,000,000} = 11.22\%$$

which illustrates something about the potency of using futures. If you had added cash bonds worth \$103,781,250 and with a duration of 11.80% to a \$1 billion portfolio with an original duration of 10.00%, the value of the bonds would have been added to the denominator as well and the final weighted average duration of the portfolio would have been only 10.17%.

Example of Solving for Hedge Ratios Using Target Durations

You can use this approach to achieve any target duration you like. Suppose you have a \$1 billion market value portfolio with a modified duration of 3.0%. Suppose, too, that you want to reduce the modified duration of the portfolio to 2.00% without changing your actual holdings of bonds and notes. On April 5, 2001, the June 2001 5-year note contract was trading at a price of 105-22/32nds, which would correspond to a portfolio equivalent value of \$105,687.50 [= \$1,000 ×

E X H I B I T   10.2

Futures Risk Measures
(Close 4/4/01, Trade 4/5/01, Settle 4/6/01)

(Contract June 2001)

	2-year	5-year	10-year	Bond
Market Price	103-04+	105-22	106-08	103-30
Theoretical Price	103-05+	105-21	106-09+	103-25
Rule-of-Thumb DV01	38.63	42.84	60.76	121.86
Option-Adjusted DV01 wrt				
CTD yield	39.06	43.20	66.13	122.42
OTR yield	39.07	43.20	69.75	132.92
Option-Adjusted Duration wrt				
CTD yield	1.89	4.09	6.22	11.80
OTR yield	1.89	4.09	6.56	12.81
Repo DV01	−5.06	−2.50	−2.53	−2.46

(Contract September 2001)

	2-year	5-year	10-year	Bond
Market Price	103-06+	105-08	105-25+	103-14
Theoretical Price	103-06+	105-06+	105-28+	103-08+
Rule-of-Thumb DV01	43.57	42.82	62.31	121.96
Option-Adjusted DV01 wrt				
CTD yield	45.25	44.23	69.06	124.20
OTR yield	44.99	44.23	72.71	134.85
Option-Adjusted Duration wrt				
CTD yield	2.19	4.20	6.52	12.03
OTR yield	2.18	4.20	6.87	13.06
Repo DV01	−10.43	−5.24	−5.27	−5.10

105.6875]. As shown in Exhibit 10.2, this contract had an option-adjusted DV01 of $43.20, which corresponds to an option-adjusted effective duration of 4.09% [= $100 \times (100\text{bps} \times \$43.20)/\$105,687.50$].

Given these particulars, and given the definition of the duration of a portfolio that contains futures, we could solve for the number of 5-year note futures, which would give you a target duration of

$$2.00\% = \frac{[(3.00\% \times \$1\ \text{Billion}) + 4.09\% \times \text{Number(Futures)} \times \$105,687.50]}{\$1\ \text{Billion}}$$

which would be

$$\text{Number(Futures)} = \frac{-1.00\% \times \$1\ \text{Billion}}{4.09\% \times \$105,687.50} = -2,313$$

or a short position of 2,313 5-year note contracts.

Controlling Yield Curve Exposure   A portfolio manager may also be concerned with exposure to changes in the slope or shape of the yield curve. The values of a wide class of callable bonds, including mortgage backed securities, are highly sensitive to the slope of the curve. Or a portfolio might simply be more heavily concentrated at one part of the curve than at another. If so, the portfolio manager can choose between futures that are positioned at four places (actually regions) along the yield curve.[1]

Consider the problem faced by a manager whose portfolio contains a high proportion of long bonds, who is generally bullish on interest rates, but who is worried about a steepening of the yield curve. Any drop in the yield curve will increase the value of the portfolio, but a steepening of the yield curve would cause the bond portfolio to underperform a note portfolio with the same duration.

The portfolio manager's problem, then, may be to reduce exposure at the long end of the yield curve and increase exposure to the middle or short end of the yield curve without changing materially the portfolio's overall duration. Such an objective can be achieved by selling bond futures and buying the appropriate note futures in numbers that leave the overall duration of the portfolio unchanged.

For example, given the futures risk measures shown in Exhibit 10.2, the manager could sell bond futures, which have an option-adjusted DV01 of $122.42 per contract and, for each bond contract sold, buy 1.85 10-year note futures (which have an option-adjusted DV01 of $66.13) or 2.83 5-year note futures (which have an option-adjusted DV01 of $43.20). Either combination would leave the overall duration of the portfolio unchanged, but would protect against a steepening of the curve.

Asset Allocation   Much of a portfolio manager's stock in trade is the business of asset allocation. In addition to conventional diversification, portfolio managers undertake what has come to be called *tactical asset allocation*. This strategy requires changes in the distribution of holdings across broad asset classes in anticipation of changes in market prices. How much of a portfolio should be in stocks, bonds, and cash, for example, is a perennial problem for many managers. We also find dynamic asset allocation strategies, which are designed

---

1 The choice is actually richer if we include the three-month Eurodollar time deposit contracts traded at the Chicago Mercantile Exchange. For example, with expirations extended out a full 10 years, Eurodollar futures can be used to hedge nearly any segment of the private credit yield curve out to 10 years. How this is done is shown in Burghardt, *The Eurodollar Futures and Options Handbook* (McGraw-Hill, 2003).

to increase exposure to assets whose prices are rising and to reduce exposure to assets whose prices are falling. Asset allocation may also entail the problem of distribution holdings across the bonds of two or more countries.

All of these efforts lend themselves to the use of futures. Instead of selling bonds and buying stocks, for example, a portfolio manager can sell bond futures and buy stock index futures. Instead of selling notes as a way of moving into cash, the portfolio manager can simply sell note futures. Instead of selling Treasury notes and investing the proceeds in German Bunds and Japanese government bonds, the portfolio manager can sell Treasury note futures and buy Bund and JGB futures.

The financial arithmetic needed to do asset allocation with futures is really the same as that used to solve hedging problems. The only difference is that you may need to understand a broader range of futures.

SYNTHETIC ASSETS

In addition to managing duration and yield curve exposure, asset managers also use futures to create synthetic assets that can enhance returns on bond portfolios. Anyone who is naturally long bonds, unless constrained by charters or regulation, has two choices:

- Hold the bonds
- Sell the bonds, go long futures, invest the proceeds short term (and possibly buy back the bonds at a later date)

Creating synthetic assets, then, is a strategy in which a natural long position in bonds is replaced with an appropriate long position in futures, together with an investment in short-term money market instruments.

One of the driving forces behind the strategy of synthetic assets is the potential for enhancing the yield on a bond portfolio. The potential for yield enhancement reflects, in part, the premium in the basis. Exhibit 10.3 illustrates the typical relationship, for a positive yield curve setting, between the current spot price of the cheapest to deliver, carry to expiration of the futures contract, and the market futures price. For this illustration, we have assumed that the bond carries a 6% coupon and has a conversion factor of 1.000.

The bond's basis is the distance between A and C. Carry to expiration, however, is only the distance between A and B. The rest of the basis, or the premium, is the distance between B and C. From

EXHIBIT 10.3

Basis, Carry, and Premium of Cheapest to Deliver
(6% Coupon Bond)

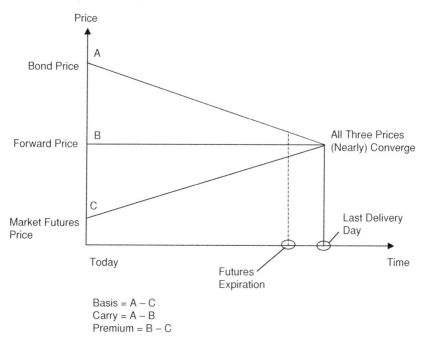

Basis = A − C
Carry = A − B
Premium = B − C

a strict carry standpoint, the futures price is too low. One could sell the bond at A, finance the short position at a cost of A − B, and buy the futures contract at C. At expiration, when the spot and futures prices come together, and if there has been no change in the cheapest to deliver, the short basis trader will make B − C, which was the original basis net of carry. That is, the short basis trader will pocket the entire premium paid for the embedded options.

Trade Construction

There are two steps in creating a synthetic bond or note using futures. The first step is to sell the underlying bond or note and to invest the proceeds in a short-term money market instrument. The investment can be either an overnight investment that is rolled every day, in which case the portfolio manager incurs reinvestment risk, or a term investment with a maturity date that matches the last delivery day of the futures contract. Strictly speaking, cash should be invested in short term repo or Treasury bills if the credit risk of the synthetic asset is intended to match the credit risk of a government security. In practice, however, money managers often invest in non-government short-duration assets in order to enhance yield when using futures to create synthetic assets. A common investment choice is AAA-rated floating-rate credit card asset-backed securities. These typically earn LIBOR plus returns, have relatively low credit risk, and are reasonably liquid because of the large size of the asset-backed market.

The second step in creating a synthetic bond is to establish a long position in futures that provides the same price exposure as the exposure in the original cash bond being sold. The hedge ratio that accomplishes this is simply the dollar value of a basis point for the cash security that has been sold divided by the option-adjusted dollar value of a basis point for the futures contract. (See Chapter 5 for an explanation of this hedge ratio.)

Example   Consider, for example, how a portfolio manager could enhance the yield on a 10-year Treasury portfolio on September 20, 2001. The portfolio manager owns

$100 million par value of the 6-1/2% of 2/15/10

which was the cheapest to deliver note at the time, and

$100 million par value of the 5% of 8/15/11

which was the current on-the-run 10-year note. The cheapest to deliver was trading at 10.1/32nds over carry, and the chances of a switch in the cheapest to deliver appeared to be extremely small. The relevant market data on September 20 were as follows:

6-1/2% of 2/15/10
Price	112-12.5/32nds
Full price	113.0441
DV01/$100,000 face	$73.80

5% of 8/15/11
Price	102-1.5/32nds
Full price	102.5374
DV01/$100,000 face	$79.20

December 2001 10-Year Treasury Note Futures
Price	107-17.5/32nds
Option-adjusted DV01	$73.84
Term repo rate	2%

Given these data, the opening trades in the yield enhancement exercise would have been to sell both the 6-1/2% of 2/10 and the 5% of 8/11 and collect a total of $215,581,500 (the market values of the two bonds valued at their full prices, including accrued interest). All of this would then be invested at the term repo rate of 2%.

At the same time, the portfolio manager would have to buy the appropriate number of note futures. To replace the 6-1/2% of 2/10, the portfolio manager would have to buy 999 note futures [= $73,800/$73.84]. To replace the 5% of 8/11, the portfolio manager would have to buy 1,073 note futures [= $79,200/$73.84]. Thus, the portfolio manager would go long a total of 2,072 of the December 2001 note futures contracts at a price of 107-17+/32nds.

Now suppose that three months (89 days) later, on December 18, 2001, cash and futures prices are

6-1/2% of 2/10	109-8.5/32nds
5% of 8/11	99-1.5/32nds
December futures	105-25.5/32nds

How Well Has the Synthetic Asset Strategy Worked?

To see how well the synthetic note strategy worked, compare the investment results summarized in Exhibit 10.4. The results of continuing to own the actual notes are reported on the left-hand side. For example, by continuing to hold the 6-1/2% of 2/10, the portfolio manager would have earned an additional $1,572,011 in accrued interest over the 89 days and would have incurred a capital loss of $3,125,000. Taken together, the portfolio manager would have lost $1,552,989 on the issue for a raw return of −1.37%, or an annualized return of −5.63%.

In contrast, the synthetic version of the 6-1/2% of 2/10 earned $558,940 [= 0.02 × (89/360) × $113,044,100] in RP interest over the 89 days. The fall in 10-year Treasury note futures prices produced a capital loss on the long position of 999 note futures contracts equal to −$1,748,250 [= 999 contracts × (−56 ticks) × $31.25 per tick]. Taken together, the total earned on the synthetic note position was −$1,189,310 [= $558,940 − $1,748,250] for a raw return of −1.05%, or an annualized return of −4.31%.

By losing less money in a falling market, the synthetic version of the 6-1/2% of 2/10 outperformed the real 6-1/2% issue by 1.32%

EXHIBIT 10.4

Examples of Yield Enhancement

	Actual Notes			Synthetic Notes					
				6-1/2% of 2/10		5% of 8/11		Portfolio	
	6-1/2% of 2/10	5% of 8/11	Portfolio	999 Futures	Cash	1073 Futures	Cash	2072 Futures	Cash
9/20/01									
Market Value	113,044,100	102,537,400	215,581,500	0	113,044,100	0	102,537,400	0	215,581,500
12/18/01									
Accrued Interest Earned	1,572,011	1,209,239	2,781,250						
RP Interest Earned					558,940		506,990		1,065,931
Capital Gain	-3,125,000	-3,000,000	-6,125,000	-1,748,250		-1,877,750		-3,626,000	
Total Gain	-1,552,989	-1,790,761	-3,343,750	-1,189,310		-1,370,760		-2,560,069	
Raw Return	-1.37%	-1.75%	-1.55%	-1.05%		-1.34%		-1.19%	
Annualized Return	-5.63%	-7.16%	-6.36%	-4.31%		-5.48%		-4.87%	

[= –4.31% – (–5.63%)], or 132 annualized basis points. The synthetic version of the 5% of 8/11 outperformed the real 5% issue by 168 basis points, and the synthetic portfolio outperformed the real portfolio by 149 basis points.

As with a successful basis trade, the performance gain is the combined effect of the difference between coupon income, RP interest, and the capital gains or losses on the cash instruments and the futures contracts. In these instances, the RP interest earned was less than the coupon income that would have been earned, but the capital losses on the futures used to replicate the price exposure in the notes were much smaller than the capital losses on the notes themselves. The results for both the 6-1/2% of 2/10 and the 5% of 8/11 were net losses that were smaller than they otherwise would have been if the portfolio manager had kept the two notes in portfolio.

Historical Record on Yield Enhancement

Over the past several years, the best opportunities for yield enhancement in the United States have centered on 10-year note futures. Because many participants in the mortgage market actively short 10-year note futures to hedge their risks, these have tended to trade cheap relative to cash Treasuries, thereby creating yield enhancement opportunities for investors in intermediate Treasuries. Exhibit 10.5 provides a summary of how a regular program of selling the CTD note three months before expiration and replacing it with a synthetic note constructed with 10-year futures would have improved the return on a note portfolio. The calculation assumes short-term cash is invested at Treasury general collateral repo rates. In 19 of the last 21 quarters, the synthetic asset constructed with 10-year futures outperformed owning the CTD note. The average total return pickup equaled 61 bp, which is respectable given the comparatively low risks involved. Note that the outperformance would have been larger still if the investment manager had invested cash in AAA-rated floating-rate asset-backed securities or other low-risk short-duration assets that provide a higher return than repo.

Variations on a Theme

Although our discussion thus far has centered on using Treasury futures to create a synthetic position in Treasury securities, futures can also be used to synthetically create exposure to other fixed-income

E X H I B I T   10.5

Yield Enhancement on Cheapest to Deliver 10-Year
(June 1998 to June 2004)

Cheapest to Deliver			BNOC	Synthetic Outperformance	
Contract	Coupon	Maturity	3m to Expiry	32nds	Ann Return (bp)
Jun-98	7.5	Feb-05	2.1	2.1	24.8
Sep-98	6.5	May-05	6.9	7.8	94.7
Dec-98	6.5	Aug-05	3.2	1.8	21.7
Mar-99	5.875	Nov-05	-0.1	-1.6	-19.6
Jun-99	6.875	May-06	5.3	4.3	51.1
Sep-99	6.875	May-06	4.2	4.9	59.3
Dec-99	7	Jul-06	1.0	1.6	19.2
Mar-00	4.75	Nov-08	7.4	7.3	104.0
Jun-00	4.75	Nov-08	9.3	5.5	77.7
Sep-00	4.75	Nov-08	11.0	10.6	149.8
Dec-00	5.5	Feb-08	9.0	0.3	3.7
Mar-01	5.5	Feb-08	4.1	4.8	57.9
Jun-01	5.5	Feb-08	3.8	-3.2	-38.9
Sep-01	6	Aug-09	11.9	8.5	100.8
Dec-01	6.5	Feb-10	10.1	10.4	118.0
Mar-02	6.5	Feb-10	12.7	12.3	142.8
Jun-02	5.75	Aug-10	11.7	9.0	110.9
Sep-02	6.5	Feb-10	9.7	5.2	57.5
Dec-02	6	Aug-09	3.5	1.5	16.0
Mar-03	6.5	Feb-10	4.7	5.0	52.9
Jun-03	6.5	Feb-10	5.3	6.1	66.6
Sep-03	5.75	Aug-10	2.2	2.2	23.0
Dec-03	5.75	Aug-10	13.4	13.9	161.2
Mar-04	5	Feb-11	6.4	6.6	78.1
Jun-04	5	Feb-11	3.7	2.1	24.5
Average				5.2	62.3

assets, including corporate bonds. Synthetic corporates usually involve combining swap futures or swaps with credit derivatives to match the credit exposure in a portfolio of corporates. In a typical transaction used to create a synthetic corporate bond, the investor

- Sells the bond and invests the proceeds in short-duration floating-rate assets
- Goes long swap futures, or receive fixed in a plain-vanilla interest rate swap, to match the duration of the initial bond position
- Sells protection in a credit default swap to match the credit exposure in the bond being sold

The long futures or swaps position matches the duration of the corporate bond being replicated. The credit default swap matches the credit spread exposure in the portfolio of corporates. The accompanying box describes the mechanics of credit default swaps, which have increasingly become an important portfolio management tool for spread product investors.

Credit Default Swaps   A credit default swap is a bilateral contract by which the protection buyer pays a periodic fee in return for a contingent payment by the protection seller. The contingent payment is made if a credit event occurs with respect to a designated reference entity. The definition of a credit event is based on guidelines set by the International Swap Dealers Association (ISDA) and usually includes bankruptcy, failure to pay, and restructuring. The standard settlement method for credit default swaps is physical settlement. Following a credit event, the protection buyer will deliver obligations from a predefined set of obligations in return for a payment of par. Credit default swap maturities usually range between 1-year and 10-years, with 5-years as the most liquid maturity.

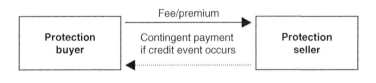

The use of swap futures and credit default swaps to create synthetic exposure to corporate bonds has two main advantages over investing in corporate bonds. First, it allows investors to more easily unbundle their decision on interest rate duration from their decision on spread duration. An investor in a 5-year fixed rate corporate bond, by necessity, is simultaneously making a decision to own an asset that has both 5-year interest rate duration and 5-year spread duration. The use of derivatives makes it possible for investors to unbundle those decisions. For example, an investor in a 5-year corporate bond that was expecting interest rates to decline but credit spreads to widen could easily use futures to lengthen its interest rate duration and credit derivatives to reduce its spread duration.

Second, the pricing of credit default swaps regularly provides bond investors the opportunity to add yield without increasing credit risk. Banks and other financial institutions that have exposure to particular credits through the loan market have strong demand to buy protection in the credit default swap market. This causes spreads on credit default swaps to trade wide relative to the bond market, creating opportunities for investors to add yield without increasing risk.

CAVEATS

A few words of caution are in order. First, gains and losses on a long bond position are unrealized as long as the portfolio manager holds the bonds. Gains and losses on a long futures position are marked to market daily. That is, gains produce cash inflows that must be invested short-term, while losses require cash to be paid out. As a result, yield enhancement entails active cash management, while a straight, long bond portfolio does not.

Second, opportunities for yield enhancement come and go. Moreover, taking advantage of them requires a solid framework for valuing bond and note futures contracts correctly.

Third, gains and losses on futures are treated differently for tax purposes than gains and losses on actual bonds. Whether the incremental yield from pursuing yield enhancement strategies really represents an increase in after-tax yields depends on the tax status of the institution and the care with which it handles its taxes.

Even so, opportunities for yield enhancement appear from time to time and deserve the attention of active portfolio managers who are interested in beating their bogeys.

Calculating Conversion Factors

A bond's conversion factor is defined as

$$\text{Factor} = a\left[\frac{\text{Coupon}}{2}+c+d\right]-b$$

where the Factor is rounded to four decimal places and Coupon is the bond's annual coupon in decimals. For the purpose of this calculation, given the Chicago Board of Trade's current 6% yield assumption:

$$a = \frac{1}{1.03^{\frac{v}{6}}}$$

$$b = \frac{\text{Coupon}}{2} \times \frac{6-v}{6}$$

$$c = \begin{cases} \dfrac{1}{1.03^{2n}} & \text{if } z < 7 \\[3mm] \dfrac{1}{1.03^{2n+1}} & \text{otherwise} \end{cases}$$

$$d = \frac{\text{Coupon}}{0.06} \times (1-c)$$

where:

$$v = \begin{cases} z & \text{if } z < 7 \\ 3 & \text{if } z > 7 \text{ (bonds and 10-year note futures)} \\ (z-6) & \text{if } z > 7 \text{ (5-year and 2-year note futures)} \end{cases}$$

and where z is

the number of months between n and the maturity (or call) date rounded down to the nearest quarter for bond and 10-year note futures (so z can take on the values 0, 3, 6, or 9) and to the nearest month for 5-year and 2-year futures (so z can be any integer between 0 and 11).

As an example, consider the conversion factor for the 4-7/8% of 2/15/12 for the June 2004 contract. On the first day of the delivery month, which was June 1, 2004, this note had 7 years, 8 months, and 15 days to maturity. Hence:

$$n = 7$$
$$z = 6$$
$$v = 6$$
$$\text{Coupon} = 0.04875$$
$$a = 1/1.03 = 0.970874$$
$$b = (0.04875/2) \times [(6 - 6)/6] = 0$$
$$c = 1/1.03^{14} = 0.661118$$
$$d = (0.04875/2) \times (1 - 0.661118) = 0.275342$$
$$\text{Factor} = 0.970874 \times [(0.04875/2) + 0.661118 + 0.275342] - 0$$
$$= 0.932849$$

which is rounded to 0.9328.

Or consider the conversion factor for the 3-5/8% of 5/15/13. On the first delivery day of the contract month, this note had 8 years, 11 months, and 15 days to maturity. Hence:

$$n = 8$$
$$z = 9$$
$$v = 3$$
$$\text{Coupon} = 0.03625$$
$$a = 1/1.03^{3/6} = 0.985329$$
$$b = (0.03625/2) \times [(6 - 3)/6] = 0.009063$$
$$c = 1/1.03^{17} = 0.605016$$
$$d = (0.03625/0.06) \times (1 - 0.605016) = 0.238636$$
$$\text{Factor} = 0.985329 \times [(0.03625/2) + 0.605016 + 0.238636]$$
$$- 0.840072$$
$$= 0.840072$$

which is rounded to 0.8401.

Calculating Carry

Carry is defined as

$$\text{Carry} = \text{Coupon Income} - \text{Financing Cost}$$

If there is no intervening coupon, total carry in dollars, per $100 face value of the bond, is based on

$$\text{Coupon Income} = \left(\frac{C}{2}\right) \times \left(\frac{D}{\text{DCOUP}}\right)$$

$$\text{Financing Cost} = (P + \text{AI}) \times \left(\frac{\text{RP}}{100}\right) \times \left(\frac{D}{360}\right)$$

where:

C	is the annual coupon on the bond.
D	is the actual number of days for which carry is calculated. If it is calculated to delivery, for example, D is the actual number of days from the settlement date of the bond to the delivery day.
DCOUP	is the actual number of days between the most recent coupon payment date and the next coupon date.
P	is the clean price of the bond.
AI	is accrued interest on the bond.
RP	is the term RP rate.

If there is one intervening coupon:

$$\text{Coupon Income} = \left(\frac{C}{2}\right) \times \left[\left(\frac{D1}{\text{DCOUP1}}\right) + \left(\frac{D2}{\text{DCOUP2}}\right)\right]$$

$$\text{Financing Cost} = \left[(P + \text{AI}) \times \left(\frac{\text{RP}}{100}\right) \times \left(\frac{D1}{360}\right)\right] + \left[P \times \left(\frac{\text{RP}}{100}\right) \times \left(\frac{D2}{360}\right)\right]$$

where:

D1	is the number of days from settlement to the coupon payment date.
D2	equals $D - D1$.
DCOUP1	is the actual number of days in the current coupon period.
DCOUP2	is the number of days in the next coupon period.

The financing costs in these calculations are only estimates, even if one uses a term repo rate. The repo market has a lot of rules, and a thorough understanding of these rules will go a long way in helping you be a better trader.

Conventions in Major Government Bond Markets[1]

---

1 Excerpted from JPMorgan Government Bond Outlines, October 2001. Reprinted with
   permission of JPMorgan.

	Australia	Austria	Belgium	Canada	Czech Republic	Denmark	Finland
Instrument	CGBs	Bunds	OLOs	Canadas	T-Bonds	DGBs	Serial Bonds
Market Characteristics							
Current Outstanding							
Local (billions)	62.5	89	173	323	102	663	37
USD (billions)	32.6	81	151	211	2.6	76	32
Longest Maturity Issued (years)	12	30	30	30	10	30	10
Typical Denomination (local)	1,000	1,000	1 (mln)	1,000	10,000	1,000	100,000
Typical Outstanding per Issue (local, millions)	2,600 to 6,100	2,000 to 9,000	5,000 to 14,000	7,000 to 12,000	12,000 to 15,000	15,000 to 75,000	200 to 9,000
Accrued Interest Characteristics							
Coupon (date)	Semi (15th)	Ann	Ann	Ann	Ann	Ann	Ann
Ex-Dividend (days)	Yes (7)	Yes (1)	No	No	Yes (30)	No	No
Accrual Basis	Actual	Actual	Actual	Actual	30	Actual	Actual
Year Basis	Actual	Actual	Actual	365	360	Actual	Actual
Settlement Characteristics							
Time Frame							
Domestic	T+3M	T+3M	T+3M	T+2T+3M	T+3M	T+3M	T+3M
International	T+3M	T+3M	T+3M	T+3M	T+3M	T+3M	T+3M
International	Yes	Yes	Yes	Yes	Yes	Yes	Yes
Trading Basis							
Quotation	Yield	Price	Price	Price	Price	Price	Yield
Tick	bp	Decimal	Decimal	Decimal	Decimal	Decimal	bp
Bid/Offer Spread	2–5 bp	0.1	0.1	0.02–0.10	0.30–0.35	0.1	2 bp
Commission (%)	0	0.75	0	0	0	0	0
Tax (nonresident, %)	10	0	0	0	15%	0	0
Typical Transaction Size (local, millions)	10	10	10 to 50	10 to 25	20 to 50	25 to 50	5 to 10
Price/Yield Method	U.S. (s.a.)	ISMA	ISMA	U.S. (s.a.)	ISMA	ISMA	ISMA

* Typical outstanding is defined as average outstanding amount after initial tender and subsequent reopenings.

Instrument	France		Germany			Greece	Hungary
	BTAN	OATs	Schätze	Bobls	Bunds	GGBs	T-Bonds
Market Characteristics							
Current Outstanding							
Local (billions)	148	415	44	125	411	19,000	2,000
USD (billions)	129	361	38	109	358	58	7
Longest Maturity Issued (years)	5	30	2	5	30	20	10
Typical Denomination (local)	1 (mln)	1 (mln)	1,000 (mln)	100 (mln)	1,000 (mln)	100,000 (mln)	10,000
Typical Outstanding per Issue (local, millions)*	10,000 to 40,000	>20,000 20,000	5,000 to	5,000 to 7,000	10,000 to 10,000	1,000,000 to 20,000	10,000 to 2,000,000
Accrued Interest Characteristics							
Coupon (date)	Semi (12th)	Ann	Ann	Ann	Ann	Ann	Semi
Ex-Dividend (days)	No	No	No	No	No	No	No
Accrual Basis	Actual	Actual	Actual	Actual	Actual	Actual	Actual
Year Basis	Actual	Actual	Actual	Actual	Actual	Actual	365
Settlement Characteristics							
Time Frame							
Domestic	T+1M	T+3M	T+2M	T+2M	T+2M	T+3M	T+2M
International	T+3M	T+3M	T+3M	T+3M	T+3M	T+3M	T+2M
International	Yes	Yes	Yes	Yes	Yes	Yes	Yes
Trading Basis							
Quotation	Yield	Price	Price	Price	Price	Price	Price
Tick	bp	Decimal	Decimal	Decimal	Decimal	Decimal	Decimal
Bid/Offer Spread	2 bp	0.04 to 0.08	0.05 to 0.08	0.05 to 0.08	0.06 to 0.10	0.10 to 0.20	0.30 to 0.35
Commission (%)	0	0	0	0	0	0	0
Tax (nonresident, %)	0	0	0	0	0	0	0
Typical Transaction Size (local, millions)	20 to 50	10 to 100	10 to 50	10 to 50	10 to 100	2,000	300
Price/Yield Method	ISMA	ISMA	ISMA	ISMA	ISMA	ISMA	ISMA

* Typical outstanding is defined as average outstanding amount after initial tender and subsequent reopenings.

Instrument	India	Ireland	Italy		Japan	Korea	Netherlands	New Zealand	Poland
	G-Secs	IGBs	BTPs	CCTs	JGBs	TBs, FXSBs, MSBs	DSLs	NZGB	T-Bonds
Market Characteristics									
Current Outstanding									
local (billions)	4358	21.9	601	240	295,000	23,600	170	23.8	36.5
USD (billions)	93	25.2	523	209	2,800	18,030	148	9.6	8.3
Longest Maturity Issued (years)	20	16	30	7	30	10	30	10	10
Typical Denomination (local)	10,000 (mln)	1,000	1,000	varies	10,000	1	10,000 (mln)	1,000	
Typical Outstanding per Issue (local, millions)	50,000 to 100,000	3,000 to 6,500	10,000 to 23,000	10,000	200,000 to 3,200,000	800, 000 to 2,000,000	10,000 to 20,000	2,600 to 3,000	500 to 1,500
Accrued Interest Characteristics									
Coupon (date)	semi	ann	semi	semi	semi (20)	Qtrly.	ann	semi (15)	ann
Ex-dividend (days)	yes (3)	no	no	no	no	yes (3)	no	yes (10)	yes (6)
Accrual basis	30E	actual	actual	actual	actual	actual	actual	actual	actual
Year basis	360	actual	actual	actual	365	actual	actual	actual	actual
Settlement Characteristics									
Timeframe									
domestic	T+1M	T+3M	T+3M	T+3M	T+3M	T (same day)	T+3M	T+2M	T+2M
international	T+1M	T+3M	T+3M	T+3M	T+3M	T (same day)	T+3M	T+2M	T+2M
International	yes	yes	yes	yes	no	yes	yes	yes	yes
Trading Basis									
Quotation	price	price	price	price	simple yield	yield	price	semi yield	price
Tick	decimal	decimal	decimal	decimal	bp	decimal	dedmal	bp	decimal
Bid/Offer spread	.01 to .04	.05 to .20	.04 to .08	.04 to .08	1 to 3 bp	1 to 2 bp	.08 to .15	2 to 5 bp	.10 to .15
Commission (%)	0	negotiated	0	0	0	flat 0.01%	0	0	0
Tax (non resident, %)	varies	0	0	0	0	varies	0	0	yes
Typical Transaction size (local, millions)	50	5 to 10	10 to 50	2.5 mln	500 to 5000	10	10 to 50	5	10 to 20
Price/Yield method	U.S. (s.a.) South	ISMA	ISMA	ISMA	simple	U.S. (qtrly)	ISMA	U.S. (s.a.)	ISMA

* Typical outstanding is defined as average outstanding amount after initial tender and subsequent reopenings.

Instrument	Portugal	Singapore	Africa	Spain	Sweden	Switzerland	UK	US
	Ofs	SGSs	Gilts Semi-gilts	Bonos Obligaciones	Stats	CONFs	Gilts	Treasurys
Market Characteristics								
Current Outstanding								
local (billions)	34	307	334	220	687	538	216	2,240
USD (billions)	30	178	44	191	91	29.8	309	2.24
Longest Maturity Issued (years)	15	10	26	30	15	30	32	30
Typical Denomination (local)	0.01	1,000	1,000,000	1,000	100,000 mln	1,000	0	1,000 mln
Typical Outstanding per Issue (local, millions)	2,000 to 5,000	1,000 to 2,000	250 to 10,000	3,000 to 18,000	35,000 to 60,000	500 to 5,000	4,000 to 12,000	6,000 to 12,000
Accrued Interest Characteristics								
Coupon (date)	ann	semi (1 or 15)	semi	ann	ann	ann	semi	semi
Ex-dividend (days)	no	yes (3)	yes (30)	no	yes (5)	no	yes (7)	no
Accrual basis	actual	actual	actual	actual	3OE	30E	actual	actual
Year basis	actual	actual	actual	actual	360	360	actual	actual
Settlement Characteristics								
Timeframe								
domestic	T+3M	T+1M	T+3M	T+3M	T+3M	T+3M	T+3M	T+1M
international	T+3M	T+1M	T+3M	T+3M	T+3M	T+3M		
International	yes	yes	yes	yes	yes	yes	no	no
Trading Basis								
Quotation	price	price	yield	price	ann yield	price	price	price
Tick	decimal	decimal	bp	decimal	bp	decimal	decimal	1/256-1/32
Bid/Offer spread	.05 to .10	.05 to .20	2 to 4 bp	.05 to .10	2 bp	.10 to .50	.05 to .10	1/128-4/32
Commission (%)	0	0	0	0	0	negotiated via treaty	0	0
Tax (non resident, %)	0	0	0	0	0		0	0
Typical Transaction Size (local, millions)	2.5 to 5.0	2 to 5	5 to 100	5 to 50	50 to 100	5 to 20	5 to 100	25 to 100
Price/Yield method	ISMA	U.S. (s.a.)	U.S. (s.a.)	ISMA	ISMA	ISMA	DMO	U.S. (s.a.)

* Typical outstanding is defined as average outstanding amount after initial tender and subsequent reopenings.

German Federal Bonds and Notes (Bubills, Schätze, Bobls, and Bunds)[1]

CHARACTERISTICS

Brief Description

Treasury Discount Bills (Bubills)

Germany introduced six-month treasury discount bills (Unverzinsliche Schatzanweisungen, or Bubills) in 1997. They are issued quarterly with a standardized issue size of €4 to €6 billion. Bubills have a maturity of six months, so that, at any one point, there are only two Bubills outstanding for about €10 billion. Bubills are discount securities that trade on a yield basis and are not listed on any exchanges.

German Federal Government Notes (Schätze)

In September 1996, the federal government began issuing new 2-year Bundesschatzanweisungen (Schätze), which have since been launched quarterly with a size of about €5 to €7 billion. Other old short- and medium-term issues also exist, but are very illiquid and directed primarily at retail investors.

German Special Federal Notes (Bobls)

Bundesobligationen (Bobls) are 5-year special federal notes that have been issued since 1979. These notes were originally intended to promote the formation of financial capital by different social groups in Germany. Only since 1988 have foreign investors been permitted to purchase these securities. Bobls are issued quarterly, with a size of about €5 billion. New Bobls are now issued twice a year, and reopened once in the following quarter. Each auction is around €5 billion, to bring the final size to approximately €10 billion.

The Treuhand agency has also issued Bobls, but they have now all reached maturity.

---

1 Excerpted from JPMorgan Government Bond Outlines, April 2005. Reprinted with permission of JPMorgan.

German Federal Government Bonds (Bunds)

Bonds (Anleihen) are issued by the federal government (Bund) and previously were also issued by the German Unity Fund (Unities), the Treuhandanstalt (Treuhand), the Federal Railway (Bundesbahn), the Federal Post Office (Bundespost), and the Economic Recovery Program (ERP). The privatization of the Federal Railway (Bahn AG), the telecommunication part of the Federal Post Office (Telekom), and the inclusion of Treuhand debt and German Unity Fund debt into the so-called Debt Inheritance Fund has led to an explicit debt service of outstanding issues through the federal government. Currently, only the federal government is issuing Bunds, with maturities of either 10 or 30 years, on (generally) a quarterly basis. 10-year Bunds have a typical size of €20 billion, although older issues are much smaller. New Bunds have been strippable since 1997.

Issuer.   Federal Republic of Germany.

Typical Issue Size and Maturity

Bubills issues are typically about €5 billion.

Schätze issues are typically in the €5 to €7 billion range.

Bobls issues have until recently been around €5 billion, often followed by taps, raising the total size by €1 to €3 billion.

New Bobls will now be issued twice a year, and reopened once, bringing the total size to around €10 billion.

Bund issues currently range €10 to €20 billion, including taps.

Original maturities are typically 10 years and 30 years.

Form

A collective debt-book entry system is maintained by the Kassen-verein (Central Depository Banks for securities). There are no physical bond certificates.

Typical Denomination

For new debt issued after March 10, 1999, €1,000 is the minimum lot for Bunds and Schätze, €100 for Bobls, and €1 million for Bubills.

Listing

Two days after issuance, German bonds are traded on one or more of the eight domestic stock exchanges (Frankfurt is the most important exchange). Prices are fixed once during stock exchange hours.

The Bundesbank makes a market in these bonds on the stock exchange (buys a variable amount) to provide a liquid market during the fixing. Most of the trading, however, takes place OTC.

Structure

Schätze, Bobls, and Bunds carry a fixed coupon and are bullet maturities.

TRANSACTIONS

Trading Basis

Schätze, Bobls, and Bunds trade on a (clean) price basis.

Typical Transaction Size

€10 to €50 million for Schätze and Bobls, €10 to €100 million for Bunds.

Bid/Offer Spread

For Schätze and Bobls, the price spread is normally 5 ticks for liquid issues and up to 8 ticks for others. For Bunds, it is normally 6 ticks for liquid issues and up to 10 ticks for others.

Commission, Transaction Costs

No commission is charged for OTC trades. Commissions for stock exchange transactions are usually negotiated.

Tax

Since January 1, 1993, there has been a withholding tax on coupons. Since January 1, 1994, a withholding tax has also been charged on accrued interest. A solidarity surcharge tax on withholding tax amounts went into effect on January 1, 1995. Banks and non-German taxpayers are exempt from this tax.

Settlement Date Conventions

Stock-exchange settlement takes place two market days after the trade date. International settlement takes place three market days after the trade date.

Clearing System

Bonds are cleared via the Kassenverein, Euroclear, and Cedel. Settlement is usually delivery versus payment.

Liquidity

The most recent Schätze, Bobls, and Bunds are the most liquid, as well as those issues deliverable into futures contracts traded on EUREX.

The most liquid German bonds are also being traded on MTS and EuroMTS, two electronic trading markets.

As with many types of German short-term paper, activity in Bubills is quite cyclical. The limited market size hampers liquidity.

Benchmarks

The most recently issued bonds serve as the benchmark for 2- (Schätze), 5- (Bobls), 10-, and 30-year (Bunds) bonds. However, provided the bond has good liquidity, old Bunds are sometimes used as benchmarks for shorter maturities as well (i.e., older Bunds with a remaining maturity of 3.5 to 5 years are deliverable into the Bobl future contract).

System of Issue

The Bundesbank publishes an issuance calendar in the last 10 days prior to the beginning of each quarter. This calendar shows which issues are planned, along with target auction sizes. The exact auction dates are not given. Rather, the Bundesbank indicates in which 10-day period of the month the auctions will take place. Note that recently there have been important changes to previously issued calendars. Schätze are issued every March, June, September, and December. Bobls are issued in February, May, August, and November. The frequency is more variable for Bunds, but they are typically issued in January, April, July, and October.

Bubills

Auctions take place on Wednesdays, with the listing and settlement on the following Friday. The bids must be expressed in terms of full 0.005 yield points. Noncompetitive bids (no price attached) are allowed. Bids must be submitted by 11:00 a.m. local time. The Bundesbank publishes the results one hour later on Reuters.

Schätze and Bunds

Both Schätze and Bunds are issued via auctions, with the allocation at individual bid prices. The Bundesbank typically retains a proportion of the auction for price management operations via the fixings.

The issuance procedure of Bunds has changed since the beginning of 1998. The old system, under which consortium members were allocated part of an issue before it was auctioned, has been abolished. Bunds are now fully issued via auctions.

A Bund Issues Auction Group has been formed comprising 80 member institutions. These members are entitled to bid in all auctions. Applicants for group membership are limited to security houses, brokers, and banks located in Germany. They must hold an account with a Land Central Bank and the Kassenverein. They must also verify the ability to bid during a year a minimum of 0.05% for all federal government auctions.

Generally, auctions are held on Wednesdays, with the listing and settlement occurring on the following Friday. Noncompetitive bids (no price attached) are allowed. Bids must be submitted by 11:00 a.m. local time. The Bundesbank publishes the results half an hour later on Reuters.

Every year the Bundesbank publishes a ranking of the bidding volumes of all group members. The ranking shows an aggregate number for all issues over the year, with no separation by types or maturities of bonds issued.

Bobls

Bundesobligationen (BOBLs) are issued first via a tap system to non-professional investors for three months, and thereafter auctioned to professional investors. During the initial three-month selling period, Bobls are issued in tap form with a stated coupon and price. Purchasers can place orders through domestic banks. The price is periodically adjusted by the Ministry of Finance to reflect changes in market conditions.

When this selling period is over, the issue is auctioned to the Bond Issues Auction Group (using the same mechanism as for Schätze and Bunds described previously).

Trading Hours

Local time, GMT + 1
OTC: 8:30 a.m. to 5:30 p.m.
Stock Exchange Fixing: 11:00 a.m. to 1:30 p.m.

INTEREST AND YIELD CALCULATIONS

Coupon Payment

Interest on Schätze, Bobls, and Bunds is paid annually. The redemption dates for Schätze issues generally fall between the 18th and 22nd of the month. For Bobls issued during the past few years, redemption dates have been between the 20th and 22nd of the month. For new Bunds, issued after 1997, the coupon dates are either January 4 or July 4.

Bubills are discount securities that do not pay coupons.

Coupon Accrual

Interest on Schätze, Bobls, and Bunds accrues from the previous coupon date (inclusive) to the settlement date (exclusive). The value date is always the same as the settlement date.

Ex-Dividend Date Rule

As of January 1, 1994, German federal bonds and notes no longer trade ex-dividend.

Year Basis

Act/act (see Appendix G) for Bunds, Bobls, and Schatze; Act/360 for Bubills.

Yield Calculation Method

In Germany, the ISMA yield method is now used for Bunds, Bobls, and Schätze. The yield on Bubills is calculated using the money market convention.

SPECIAL OR UNUSUAL FEATURES

- Very liquid 2-, 5-, and 10-year futures contracts on EUREX. There is also a now illiquid Bund futures contract on LIFFE.
- Daily fixing at the stock exchange.

SCREENS

Reuters

JPMEURO	Government benchmarks
JPMDE01-05	Government bonds
JPMSTRIPDE	Strips
ESZB/BBK	Bundesbank menu page

Web Sites

News, statistics, and auction results published by the Bundesbank can be found on www.bundesbank.de/en/presse/pressenotizen/presseindex00.htm.

The German Finance Ministry's Web site is located at www.bundesfinanzministerium.de.

Japanese Government Bonds (JGBs)[1]

CHARACTERISTICS

Brief Description

Construction bonds, deficit financing bonds, and refunding bonds are the three types of JGB issues; however, from an investment perspective, there is no difference among these bonds. The most common maturity is 10 years, and these issues are frequently referred to by their issue number (e.g., #225). The total outstanding amount for all government debt issues is approximately ¥332 trillion (US$3.2 trillion) as of the end of March 2000. Current term JGBs market outstanding total approximately ¥295 trillion (US$2.8 trillion), and the outstandings with maturities of 2-, 4-, 5-, 6-, 10-, 20-, and 30-year JGBs is approximately ¥11, ¥15, ¥1.6, ¥21, ¥218, ¥27, and ¥0.5 trillion, respectively.

Issuer. Government of Japan.

Typical Issue Size and Maturity

Issue sizes range from ¥200 to ¥3,200 billion. Coupon bonds are issued with original maturities of 2, 4, 5, 6, 10, 20, and 30 years; A very small amount of 3-year discount bonds are also issued. A 15-year floating-rate note was reintroduced in FY2000.

Form

JGBs are typically issued in registered form (about 99 percent), but they may be converted into bearer form (or vice versa) within two market days of issue. Over half of the registered JGBs are entrusted to BoJNet; most resident investors use BoJNet, while nonresidents mainly use the name registration system (NRF). Withholding tax changes are, however, likely to decrease the usage of NRFs.

---

1 Excerpted from JPMorgan Government Bond Outlines, October 2001. Reprinted with permission of JPMorgan.

Typical Denomination

While there is no typical denomination, issue denomination ranges from ¥50,000 to ¥1 billion.

Listing

Although most coupon JGBs (except 4- and 6-year JGBs) are listed on the Tokyo Stock Exchange (TSE), their trading volume is small. The majority of trading occurs on the Broker's Broker (BB) and in the OTC market. Upon the abolishment of compulsory centralization of trading small lot JGBs in TSE on December 1, 1998, the TSE ended its role of providing "official" closes for JGBs as a public pricing source. Now market participants can choose among a variety of closings such as leading dealers', BB's, Japan Dealers Association's, and so on.

Structure

JGBs have bullet maturities. From January 1999, call provisions have been eliminated from the bonds; in addition, the MoF announced that it will not allow bonds issued before this period to be exercised. 10- and 20-year JGBs pay interest on the standard March/September or June/December semiannual coupon cycle. As new issues may appear monthly, the practice of using quarterly coupon payment dates leads to odd-first coupons for both 10- and 20-year JGBs. Successive issues with the same coupon and maturity date are fungible if under the same budget year.

However, they trade separately until the first coupon payment. These successive tranches are labeled by the month of issue. From the bond to be issued March 2001, the immediate reopen method will be adopted.

TRANSACTIONS

Trading Basis

Bonds are traded on a simple-yield basis (see "Interest and Yield Calculations").

Typical Transaction Size

¥500–5,000 million.

Bid/Offer Spread

The yield spread is typically 1/2 bps for the benchmark; for issues deliverable into the JGB 10-year bond futures contract (7- to 11-year maturities), the spread runs 1 to 2 bps, while for up to 7-year maturities and superlongs, the spread can be as large as 2 to 3 bps.

Transfer Tax

The transfer tax was repealed at the end of March 1999. JGBs are not subject to it.

Withholding Tax

The withholding tax on capital gains by discount short-term bills was rescinded in April 1999.

Furthermore, withholding tax on interest income of coupon bonds was repealed for qualified international investors starting with bonds whose accrual period occurs after September 1, 1999. Although global custodians are not yet approved as agents for tax-exempt holdings, this is expected to change in April 2001. NRF transactions are, however, becoming tax-liable: once any bond has paid a coupon in 2001, it must be held instead in book-entry form to be able to qualify for tax exemption. An additional requirement is that the end investor must be a nonresident foreign corporate entity; this means that mutual and leverages funds would be required to disclose their end investors to take advantage of potential tax exemption. This requirement is currently proving problematic.

Settlement Date Conventions

Effective April 21, 1997, JGBs generally settle three business days after trade date (T+3); however, longer settlements can be arranged according to investors' needs.

Clearing System

JGBs are not delivered abroad and are not cleared through Euroclear. Foreign investors need to appoint a custodian in Japan to handle settlement.

Effective from January 2001, JGBs will mostly settle on an real-time gross basis (RTGS) rather than under the current designated-time net system. There are exceptions that will remain on the old net basis, e.g., transactions with the BoJ such as new issuance, or trades with central banks who use the BoJ as a custodian. Yucho (postal savings) and Kampo (postal insurance) will use the RTGS system, but they are imposing additional timing restrictions.

Liquidity

Although the benchmark bond still accounts for the majority of trading volume, liquidity for other issues has increased dramatically in recent years, particularly in the deliverable 7- to 10-year sectors. Former benchmarks (#203, #182, #174, #164, #157, #145, and #129) tend to define the most liquid points of the JGB yield curve.

Benchmarks

The most recently issued 10-year JGB is used as the key benchmark.

System of Issue

A syndicate comprising banks, life insurance companies, and securities firms underwrites 40 percent of each 10-year issue. The remaining 60 percent is issued via a competitive auction. The size of the issue is announced one week prior to the auction, and the coupon is announced on the day of the auction after consultation with the syndicate. The average auction price determines the price of the syndicated portion. No firm may bid for more than 30 percent of the tranche issued via competitive auction. All 2-, 4-, 5-, 6-, and 20-year bonds are issued via a fully competitive price auction (no syndicated tranche), while 30-year bonds are issued via competitive yield auction. Reintroduced 15-year floating-rate JGB are issued at par and participants can bid by the spread "alpha" to base rate, which is calculated from the successful average price, deducting a handling fee (63 sen), of the 10-year JGB auction immediately prior to the 15-year coupon setting date.

Trading Hours

Local time, GMT + 9 Weekdays
(BB – Broker's Broker): 8:40 a.m. to 11:05 a.m. and 12:25 p.m. to 5:00 p.m.

INTEREST AND YIELD CALCULATIONS

Coupon Payment

Interest is paid semiannually, usually on the 20th of the month. The final redemption date always falls on a market day. In cases where the bond matures on the 21st or 22nd and the coupon date the 20th, the final coupon payment is increased by an additional one or two days' accrued interest.

Coupon Accrual

Interest accrues from the previous coupon date (inclusive) to the settlement date (exclusive). Thus, the value date is the same as the settlement date. The dated date always falls on the day prior to the issue date. This means that accrued interest during the first coupon period is one day greater than usual.

Ex-Dividend Date Rule

JGBs do not trade ex-dividend; however, registered bonds cannot settle within seven business days of the nominal payment date.

Year Basis

Actual/365; the 366th day in a leap year is counted.

Yield Calculation Method

Simple yield-to-maturity is given by the following formula:

$$\text{Yield (\%)} = \frac{\text{Coupon Rate (\%)} + [(100\text{-Price})/\text{Remaining Life}]}{\text{Price}/100}$$

Special Rules Concerning Interest Calculations

Remaining life is the number of days from the settlement date (inclusive) to the maturity date (exclusive) divided by 365. For a bond with more than one year until maturity, the numerator of this ratio must be reduced for each February 29 that falls between the settlement and maturity dates. The price used in the yield calculation is net of accrued interest.

SCREENS

Reuters

JPMJGB JPMorgan closings
JPMA Hourly indications

Telerate

3024 Auction information (Kyodo News)
3036 JGB quotation

Bloomberg

JPMJ JPMorgan JGB/non-JGB spread, etc.
BBJC Bloomberg closing prices for JGBs
JGBB BB's closing prices for JGBs
JPEX Executable prices

Government Bonds of the United Kingdom of Great Britain and Northern Ireland (Gilts)[1]

CHARACTERISTICS

Brief Description

Gilt-edged stocks, or gilts, are tradable securities issued and guaranteed by the U.K. government. They are identified by coupon, maturity, and name, and are referred to as "stocks." The most common name is Treasury, followed by Conversion and Exchequer. Other names relate to old issues include War Loan, Funding, Consolidated, and Annuities, but the names are ignored by the market, as they all have identical credit.

Typical Issue Size and Maturity

The initial issue size of a conventional gilt is usually £2 billion to £3 billion but is increased with repeated reopenings. Almost all conventional issuance is by auction, although rarely there are small taps.

Recently, the U.K. Debt Management Office has also introduced switch auctions, which are designed to increase liquidity in newly issued gilts by organizing exchanges out of old gilts.

Form

Gilts are generally held in registered form in the domestic settlements system, the Central Gilt Office (CGO), although they can also be held via Euroclear and Cedel. The National Stock Savings Register is available for small investors, and some gilts can be held in bearer form, but this is rare. Gilts may be purchased in increments of one penny, £0.01.

---

1 Excerpted from JPMorgan Government Bond Outlines, April 2005. Reprinted with permission of JPMorgan.

Listing

Gilts trade on the London Stock Exchange.

Structure

For partly historical reasons, there are several different types of gilts:

- *Strippable gilts* are conventional semiannual bullet bonds, paying coupons on the 7th of June and December. The strip market was launched in December 1997. Liquidity is increasingly dominated by the strippables, of which there are currently 11. The net worth of the strippables totals about £120 billion (US$170 billion). Note that gilt strips are direct obligations of the government, and thus have the same credit as coupon-paying gilts.

- *Nonstrippable conventional gilts* are bullet bonds with a variety of maturity dates. Because of the mixed maturity dates, the coupons do not align; accordingly, none of these gilts will be made strippable.

- *Index-linked gilts* are fixed-maturity bonds with principal and coupon payments linked to the Retail Price Index (RPI). Coupons paid by index-linked gilts are determined by multiplying the notional coupon amount by the ratio of the RPI eight months before the month in which payment is due to the RPI eight months before the month in which the gilt was issued. For new bonds issued from April 2005 onwards the RPI lag will be three months. The principal is adjusted in a similar way. This method of coupon payment provides a real return, rather than a nominal return. There are £64 billion in issue (inflation-adjusted nominal).

- *Double-dated gilts* are increasingly illiquid old callable gilts—no new double dates have been created since 1980. They can be called by the government at any time between two quoted redemption dates (which are two and five years apart), after at least three months' notice.

- *Perpetuals* are very old gilts with no final redemption date and with only limited liquidity.

There are also six foreign currency bonds, denominated in USD and EUR, including a dollar-denominated FRN.

TRANSACTIONS

Trading Basis

Gilts prices are quoted in decimal form (with two decimals), on a price basis (clean).

Typical Transaction Size

£5–100 million.

Bid/Offer Spread

For liquid issues with a maturity of up to seven years, the price spread is normally 5 ticks or less; for liquid issues in longer maturities, it is 5 to 10 ticks; and for illiquid issues and index-linked dealing, spreads can be wider.

Commission, Transaction Costs

There is no stamp duty or clearinghouse fee. While market makers do not a charge commission, agency brokers do.

Repo

Gilts have an open repo market, which uses the PSA/ISMA documentation, with a separate annex applicable to gilts. Generic repo documentation will not suffice; the annex is necessary.

Tax

Since April 1998, all gilt interest is payable gross, with no withholding tax. This applies to all categories of investors, including individuals and corporates, residents and nonresidents.

Settlement Date Conventions

Settlement usually takes place on the business day following the trade date. Three-and seven-day settlement are also common.

Clearing System

Gilts are usually cleared though the Bank of England's Central Gilt Office, and settlement is now possible through Euroclear or Cedel.

Liquidity

Liquidity is increasingly concentrating on strippable paper. Strippable gilts at the very long end of the curve have been quite illiquid lately, because of the imbalances between supply and demand in the ultra long end. A number of older issues, or those held largely overseas, are tightly held and it may be difficult to deal in these issues.

System of Issue

The Debt Management Office (DMO) primarily issues stock at auction, with bidders paying the price bid. The dates of the auctions during the fiscal year are announced in March. At the end of each quarter, a calendar is issued that gives precisely the dates of the auctions and the bonds to be issued. Auctions normally occur on the last Wednesday of the month. The DMO can also tap the market in extreme circumstances—these are sales at a fixed price of a fixed amount of stock. Almost all funding is by auction.

Trading Hours

There are no official hours for the cash market. However, bid/ask spreads tend to be much tighter when the futures contract is open from 8:00 a.m. to 4:15 p.m. and from 4:30 p.m. to 6:00 p.m.

INTEREST AND YIELD CALCULATIONS

Coupon Payment

Interest is paid semiannually, except on the FRN, three of the illiquid perpetuals that pay quarterly, and on the nonsterling bonds that pay annually.

Coupon Accrual

Interest accrues from the previous coupon (inclusive) to the settlement date (exclusive). This means that the value date is the same as the settlement date.

Ex-Dividend Date Rule

Gilts go ex-dividend seven business days before the coupon date, except the perpetual 3 1/2 percent War Loan, for which the rule is

10 business days. Accrued interest is negative if the date is ex-dividend. Floating-rate gilts have no ex-dividend rules.

Year Basis

Act/Act.

Yield Calculation Method

Yields are calculated according to the DMO yield convention, using semiannual compounding, with certain rules applying to the movement of the next coupon past weekends.

SPECIAL OR UNUSUAL FEATURES

- Strip market
- Ex-dividend convention
- Index-linked gilts

SCREENS

Reuters

JPMGB01 to 03	Bond prices and yields
JPMSTRIPUK	Strip prices
DMO/INDEX	Menu page for the U.K. Debt Management Office

Web Sites

The U.K. Debt Management Office Web site is accessible at www.dmo.gov.uk/.

More information on gilts may be found in *Gilt: An Investor's Guide*, published by the DMO in September 1999.

Glossary[1]

This glossary defines important terms used in government bond markets worldwide. The following definitions may differ from those found in other sources.

Accrued interest: Interest that has been earned on a bond but not yet paid. Typically, interest accrues on a daily basis from the previous coupon date (inclusive) to the value date (exclusive). An investor buying a bond must pay accrued interest to the seller.

ADRs: American Depository Receipts. A depository receipt issued against foreign securities by an American bank that holds those securities. Currently only French OATs are listed on the New York Stock Exchange through ADRs.

Allotment letter: *See* Form.

Announcement date: *See* Dates.

Auction: *See* Method or system of issue.

Average life: The arithmetic-weighted average life of a bond where the weights are the proportion of the principal amount being redeemed *(see* Equivalent life).

$$\text{Average life } (t) = \frac{\Sigma \, w(i) \, D(i)}{\Sigma \, w(i)}$$

where $i = 1$ to N; N is the number of redemptions.

      $w(i) =$ The amount redeemed at the ith redemption price on the ith redemption date.

      $D(i) =$ The time measured in years from t to the ith redemption date.

Bad days: *See* Dates.

Bearer form: *See* Form.

Benchmark: A bond, frequently the most recent, sizable issue, whose terms set a standard for the market. The benchmark bond usually has the greatest liquidity and the highest turnover, and is the most frequently quoted. In certain markets (e.g., Japan), there is a seasoning period during which the bond is not the benchmark.

Blind broker system: A mechanism for interdealer transactions that maintains the anonymity of both parties to the trade. The broker serves as the agent to the principals' transactions.

Book-entry form: *See* Form.

Bps: Basis points.

Bullet maturity: A bond whose principal is paid only on the final maturity date.

Callable bond: A bond that provides the borrower with an option to redeem the issue before the original maturity date. Usually, certain terms are set before the issue, such as the date after which the bond is callable and the price at which the issuer may

---

1 Excerpted from JPMorgan Government Bond Outlines, April 2005. Reprinted with permission of JPMorgan.

retire the bond. The holder of the bond is usually paid a premium for early termination of the investment.

Call date: *See* Dates.

Cash settlement: *See* Settlement.

Cedel: Centrale de Livraison de Valeurs Mobilières; a clearing system for Eurocurrency and international bonds. Cedel is located in Luxembourg and is jointly owned by a large number of European banks.

Clean price: A bond that does not include accrued interest (*see* Dirty price).

Clearing system: A system established to facilitate the transfer of ownership for securities (*see* Securities depository).

Closed-book period: A period of time, usually two or three weeks, before each coupon due date. The coupon is paid to the person holding the bond prior to the closed-book period. If this person sells the bond during this period, he or she must compensate the buyer for any accrued interest.

Competitive auction: *See* Method or system of issue.

Convertible bond: A bond that offers the holder the option to convert into another issue, possibly with different terms, at a specified coupon date(s).

Corporate settlement: *See* Settlement.

Coupon dates: *See* Nominal payment dates under Dates.

Coupon due dates: *See* Nominal payment dates under Dates.

Current yield: *See* Interest calculations.

Cutting date: *See* Dates.

Dated date: *See* Dates.

Dates: There are some important dates that one must keep in mind when describing bond markets. It is important to note that date terms are not used consistently across markets. The following definitions allow for a consistent comparison and are used in the government bond outlines.

Announcement date (or launch date): The day when most of the terms of the bond are made public, such as the issue size and maturity date.

Bad days: Refers to days delayed in the receipt of redemption proceeds because the maturity date falls on a weekend or a holiday.

Call date: The date on which a call option may be exercised (*see* Callable bond).

Cutting date: The day on which the coupon is physically cut from the bond (*see* Record date under Dates).

Dated date (or coupon start date): The day interest starts accruing on a new issue or tap, frequently the issue date.

Ex-dividend date: The ex-dividend date determines who, from a trading perspective, receives the next coupon payment. Transactions settled on or after the ex-dividend date are deemed to be ex-coupon and, therefore, the buyer does not receive the next coupon. The seller must compensate the buyer with negative accrued interest. In some markets such as Germany, the trade date rather than the settlement date determines custody.

Issue date (or payment date or primary date): The day the issuer receives payment for a new issue or tap.

Market day: A day when the domestic bond market is open.

Nominal day: Any calendar day without regard to whether the bond market is open or not.

Nominal payment dates (or coupon dates or coupon due dates): The dates on which coupons are scheduled to be paid. This day is used to calculate the accrued interest due to the holder. If the nominal payment date falls on a nonmarket day, the actual coupon payment is usually on the next market day.

Nonmarket day: A day when the domestic bond market is closed.

Record date (or cutting date): The record date determines, from a custodial perspective, who actually receives the next coupon payment. This is usually the market day preceding the coupon due date (or ex-dividend date). Ownership of the next coupon payment is determined by who holds the securities after close of business on the record date.

Secondary date: The first day that the bond is available for trading in the secondary market.

Settlement date: The day on which settlement is scheduled to take place. In the Eurobond market, this is referred to as "value date."

Subscription period: The period during which investors place their bids for a new issue with a syndicate.

Value date: The day the buyer begins to earn interest on his or her investment, often referred to as the interest bought/sold date. In many markets this is the same as the settlement date. Value dates may fall on nonmarket days.

Day-count basis: Following is a list of conventions used to count the appropriate number of days between two dates in order to calculate accrued interest, yields, and odd coupon amounts. For each rule, the numerator indicates the number of days between the dates and determines what happens if one of the dates falls on the 31st of a month. The denominator indicates how many days are considered in a year.

Actual/Actual: Numerator—The actual number of days between two dates. Denominator—The actual number of days in the coupon period times the coupon frequency resulting in values ranging from 362 to 368 for semiannual bonds.

Actual/360: Numerator—The actual number of days between two dates. Denominator—360.

Actual/365: Numerator—The actual number of days between two dates. Denominator—365.

Actual/365L: This rule is used for some Sterling floating rate notes (FRNs). Numerator—The actual number of days between two dates. Denominator—If the next coupon payment date falls within a leap year, use 366; otherwise, use 365.

30/360 rules: Numerator—The basic 30/360 method for calculating the numerator is illustrated by the following expression:

$$D \text{ days} = D2 - D1 + 30 (M2 - M1) + 360 (Y2 - Y1)$$

Where:

    M1/D1/Y1 is the first date

    M2/D2/Y2 is the second date.

Denominator — 360.

The following three variants of this basic rule differ by making certain adjustments to D1, D2, and M2:

30/360

1. If D1 falls on the 31st, then change it to the 30th.
2. If D2 falls on the 31st, then change it to the 30th only if D1 falls either on the 30th or 31st.

30E/360

1. If D1 falls on the 31st, then change it to the 30th.
2. If D2 falls on the 31st, then change it to the 30th.

30E+/360

1. If D1 falls on the 31st, then change it to the 30th.
2. If D2 falls on the 31st, then change it to 1 and increase M2 by 1.

Deep discount bond: A bond issued at a very low issue price. Deep discounts have low coupons offering an investor high-principal return and low-interest income. An extreme example is a zero-coupon bond that pays all of its return in principal on the redemption date.

Delivery versus payment basis: *See* Settlement.

Dirty price: The price of a bond that includes accrued interest (*see* Clean price).

Dutch auction: *See* Competitive auction under Method or system of issue.

English auction: *See* Competitive auction under Method or system of issue.

Equivalent life: The arithmetic weighted average maturity of a bond where the weights are the present value of the redemption payments discounted by the internal rate of return.

$$\text{Equivalent life } (t) = \frac{\Sigma \, PV[w(i)] \, D(i)}{\Sigma \, PV[w(i)]}$$

Where:

$i = 1$ to N; N is the number of redemptions.

$w(i) = $ The amount redeemed at the ith redemption price on the ith redemption date.

$D(i) = $ The time measured in years from t to the ith redemption date.

$PV = $ The present value function.

Euroclear: An international clearing system for Eurocurrency and foreign securities. Euroclear is based in Brussels (*see* Cedel).

Euroclear settlement: *See* Settlement.

Ex-dividend date: *See* Dates.

Extendible (or retractable) bond: A bond with a call provision that gives the issuer the option to extend the maturity date (if the call is not exercised) and reset the coupon at any rate. The investor then may choose to put the bond at the call price or accept the new coupon.

Form

Allotment letter: The issuer sends the buyer a letter representing ownership of the bond.

Bearer form: The holder of the bond is the owner. Physical certificates exist.

Book-entry form (or inscribed form): The issuer or agent records the ownership of the bond, usually in computerized records. There are no bond certificates.

Registered form: The issuer or agent records bond ownership. Occasionally bond certificates are allotted.

Free-payment basis: *See* Settlement.

Index-linked bond: A bond whose coupon payments are a function of an index. For example, coupons on index-linked gilts are linked to the Retail Price Index.

Inscribed form: *See* Book-entry form under Forms.

Interest calculations

Current yield: The annual coupon rate divided by the clean price of the bond.

DMO yield: The standard yield to maturity calculation recommended by the U.K. Debt Management Office for gilt instruments. Yield is compounded on quasi-coupon dates. Quasi-coupon dates are the dates on the semiannual or quarterly cycle (dependent on instrument) defined by the maturity date, irrespective of whether cash flows occur on those dates.

ISMA yield: A standard yield-to-maturity calculation recommended by the ISMA (formerly AIBD). Yield is compounded annually, regardless of the coupon frequency.

SABE: Semi-Annual Bond Equivalent yield; a method of converting yields and other measures of value in order to place them on a comparable basis. This method assumes interest is reinvested semiannually. SABE is often applied to discount securities in order to compare their rate of return to the yield to maturity on coupon bonds.

Simple yield: A modified version of the current yield that accounts for a deviation in a bond's clean price from par. Any capital gain or loss is assumed to occur uniformly over the life of the bond.

U.S. Street method: The standard yield-to-maturity calculation used in the United States by market participants other than the U.S. Treasury. Yield is compounded semiannually regardless of the coupon frequency. If the value date does not fall on a coupon date, the present value of the bond on the next coupon date is discounted over the fractional period with compound interest (*see* U.S. Treasury method, which follows).

U.S. Treasury method: The yield to maturity used by the U.S. Treasury to price bonds at auction. Partial periods are discounted using simple rather than compound interest (*see* U.S. Street method, previously).

Yield-to-average life: A yield that assumes the entire issue amount matures on the average life date rather than the maturity date. This is a quick-and-dirty method for comparing bonds with sinking funds with straight issues (*see* Average life).

Yield-to-equivalent life: The discount rate that equates the present value of the future cash flows to the dirty price, where the cash flows take into account the bond's amortization schedule. This calculation is appropriate for sinking funds; however, it is rarely used because of its complexity (*see* Equivalent life).

Yield to maturity: The yield if the bond is held to maturity. This is the most frequently used measure of value for a bond. Generally, the calculation is a function of coupon payments, dirty price, and the method for discounting coupons and the redemption value. However, the exact functional form is determined by market or dealer conventions.

ISMA: International Securities Market Association (formerly the Association of International Bond Dealers).

ISMA yield: *See* Interest calculations.

Issue date: *See* Dates.

Launch date: *See* Announcement date under Dates.

Market day: *See* Dates.

Method or system of issue

Auction: A method of issue where brokers or dealers submit bids to the issuer on either a price or yield basis. Auction rules vary considerably across markets.

Competitive auction: There are two types of competitive auctions: English and Dutch. In an English auction, bidders buy bonds at their bid price if they bid above the stop price.

In a Dutch auction, bidders buy bonds at the stop price as long as their bid prices are above the stop price. For an oversubscribed auction, bids at the stop price are scaled proportionately.

Noncompetitive auction: An auction at which bidders receive bonds at the average price.

Subscription offering: Practice of issuing a security(s) by allotment to distributors or a syndicate who agree to distribute the issue(s) by procuring subscribers. The terms of the issue(s) are widely publicized in advance.

Syndicate: A group consisting of managers, underwriters, and selling groups that is responsible for distributing new issues or taps.

Tap (or reopening): A method of reissuing an already existing bond; also, the term used to describe such an issue.

Nominal day: *See* Dates.

Nominal payment date: *See* Dates.

Noncompetitive auction: *See* Method or system of issue.

Odd coupons: Sometimes, the first or last coupon period is either longer or shorter than a normal coupon period. Therefore, the coupon payment is more or less than a normal coupon payment. Calculating the odd coupon payment is roughly the same as calculating accrued interest for the number of days in the odd coupon period.

Odd-lot: Refers to a trading unit of a bond that is some fraction of a round lot. A premium is usually charged for odd-lot transactions.

Partly paid: In the United Kingdom, the full issue price of a gilt is often paid in either two or three installments. The initial payment is made upon application and the remaining payment(s) is made within a couple of months. For example, £50 of the 8.5 percent February 1994 "B" tranche was paid on March 16, 1988, while the remaining £47 of the £97 issue price was paid on April 25, 1988.

Payment date: *See* Issue date under Dates.

Primary date: *See* Issue date under Dates.

Purchase fund: A type of bond whose issuer may retire up to specified amounts of the issue in the open market if the price remains below a certain level.

Record date: *See* Dates.

Registered form: *See* Form.

Regular-way settlement: *See* Regular-way settlement under Settlement.

Reopening: *See* Tap under Method or system of issue.

Retractable bond: *See* Extendible bond.

Round lot: The minimum amount of a bond acceptable for dealing. Round lots vary according to the type of security, liquidity, and currency of denomination.

SABE: Semi-Annual Bond Equivalent. *See* Interest calculations.

Secondary date: *See* Dates.

Securities depository: A company, usually a domestic bank, whose responsibility includes the custody of securities, the administration of fungible securities, and the settlement of securities transactions, including payment.

Selling period: *See* Subscription period under Dates.

Settlement

Cash settlement: Same-day settlement.

Corporate settlement: Settlement five market days after the trade date (term used in the U.S. market).

Delivery versus (or against) payment basis: Under this settlement rule, the delivery of and payment for bonds are simultaneous.

Domestic settlement: Settlement according to the accepted market convention.

Euroclear settlement: Settlement is seven calendar days after the trade day. Since June 1995, settlement is three market days after the trade day.

Free-payment basis: The delivery of a bond and the payment for it are not necessarily simultaneous.

International settlement: The settlement of securities is effected through an international clearing agency such as Euroclear or Cedel. International settlement usually assumes no local or generally recognized holidays.

Regular-way settlement: In the United States, settlement is on the next market day after the trade date. *See also* Domestic settlement.

Skip-day settlement: Settlement on the day after the next market day.

Settlement date: *See* Dates.

Simple yield: *See* Interest calculations.

Sinking-fund bond: A bond with gradual retirement of the original issue at specified dates (usually coupon dates). For certain serial issues, a drawing (or lottery) determines which bonds of the original issue are retired early.

Skip-day settlement: *See* Settlement.

Stop price: The lowest price the issuer accepts in an auction for a new issue.

Street method: *See* Interest calculations.

STRIP: Separate Trading of Registered Interest and Principal of Securities. Process by which a bond is separated into its corpus and coupons, which are then sold separately as zero-coupon securities.

Subscription offering: *See* Method or system of issue.

Subscription period: *See* Dates.

Syndicate: *See* Method or system of issue.

Tap: *See* Method or system of issue.

Tick size: The increments used for expressing bond prices. For example, the tick size for United Kingdom Gilt stocks is 1/32nd.

Trade date: *See* Dates.

Tranche: There are two type of tranches:

1. One of a series of two or more issues with the same coupon rate and maturity date, but with different dated dates. The tranches become fungible at a future date, usually the first coupon date.

2. A bond that shares documentation with another issue but has different terms.

U.S. Street method: *See* Interest calculations.

U.S. Treasury method: *See* Interest calculations.

Value date: *See* Dates.

Warrant: A provision that gives the bondholder the option to purchase a certain number of shares of the borrower's stock or more bonds at a specified price.

"When-issued" trading: Trading a bond before the issue date; no interest accrues during this period.

Yield-to-average life: *See* Interest calculations.

Yield-to-equivalent life: *See* Interest calculations.

Yield to maturity: *See* Interest calculations.

INDEX

Page numbers followed by *t* indicates table(s).

Galen Burghardt, Ph.D., is senior vice president and director of research for Calyon Financial . An adjunct professor of finance at the University of Chicago Graduate School of Business, Dr. Burghardt is the former vice president of financial research for the Chicago Mercantile Exchange. He is the author of *The Eurodollar Futures and Options Handbook*.

Terry Belton, Ph.D., is managing director, global head of derivatives strategy, and co-head of North America for J.P. Morgan's futures and options business. An adjunct professor of finance at the University of Chicago Graduate School of Business, Dr. Belton was formerly director of research for Discount Corporation of New York Futures and a senior economist at Freddie Mac.

Morton Lane is currently president of Lane Financial.

John Papa was Vice President of Discount Corporation of New York Futures and is currently retired.

Printed in Dunstable, United Kingdom